Just some of the rave reviews for RELEASE ME and CLAIM ME, the first two books in J. Kenner's powerfully sensual and erotic Stark Trilogy:

'J. Kenner's evocative writing thrillingly captures the power of physical attraction, the pull of longing, the universe-altering effect one person can have on another. She masterfully draws out the eroticism between Nikki and Damien ... *Claim Me* has the emotional depth to back up the sex ... Every scene is infused with both erotic tension, and the tension of wondering what lies beneath Damien's veneer – and how and when it will be revealed' *Heroes and Heartbreakers*

'*Claim Me* by J. Kenner is an erotic, sexy and exciting ride. The story between Damien and Nikki is amazing and written beautifully. The intimate and detailed sex scenes will leave you fanning yourself to cool down. With the writing style of Ms Kenner you almost feel like you are there in the story riding along the emotional rollercoaster with Damien and Nikki' *Fresh Fiction*

'PERFECT for fans of *Fifty Shades of Grey* and *Bared to You*. *Release Me* is a powerful and erotic romance novel that is sure to make adult romance readers sweat, sigh and swoon' *Reading, Eating & Dreaming Blog*

'*Release Me* sucked me in from the very beginning. I started cheering for the heroine, Nikki Fairchild, on the first page ... An emotional roller coaster, full of tenderness, love, mystery and ... hot sex – *Release Me* is definitely one you'll want to add to your TBR list' *Scandalicious Book Reviews Blog*

'*Release Me* ... just made the top of my list with Damien and Nikki ... the way in which J. Kenner tells the story, how vulnerable and real Damien and Nikki feel, makes this story so good, and re-readable many times over' *In Love With Romance Blog*

'This is deeply sensual and the story packs an emotional punch that I really hadn't expected ... If you enjoyed *Fifty Shades* [and] the Crossfire books, you're definitely going to enjoy this one. It's compelling, engaging and I was thoroughly engrossed' *Sinfully Sexy Blog*

D0281906

'I will admit, I am in the "I loved *Fifty Shades*" camp, but after reading *Release Me*, Mr Grey only scratches the surface compared to Damien Stark' *Cocktails and Books Blog*

'I couldn't put this book down. I HAD to know what happened next . . . If you liked *Fifty* and the Crossfire series, you will love *Release Me*' *Bungalow Books Blog*

'Damien Stark . . . belongs with some of the greatest fictional characters . . . what makes *Release Me* stands out from the crowd is the fact it has such memorable characters . . . it was good, very good' *Book Passion For Life Blog*

'It is not often when a book is so amazingly well-written that I find it hard to even begin to accurately describe it . . . I recommend this book to everyone who is interested in a passionate love story' *Romancebookworm's Reviews*

'I really wasn't expecting it to be as mind-blowing as this was. *Release Me* was SO MUCH MORE EMOTIONAL and DEEP and COMPLEX than I was expecting, I loved it . . . simply amazing' *Romance Books Forum*

'The story is one that will rank up with the *Fifty Shades* and Crossfire books. I am impatiently awaiting book two! A definite read for those who enjoyed *Fifty Shades* and *Bared to You*' *Incubus Publishing Blog*

'*Release Me* by J. Kenner will undress you and leave you breathless! Kenner's erotic story brings two souls together, where a love that has been elusive is suddenly craved. The attraction between Damien and Nikki is palpable, they are two strong personalities with past demons to contend with. *Release Me* gives readers tantalizing pages of sensual delight, leaving us reeling as we journey with this couple and their passions are released. *Release Me* is a must read . . . !' *Readaholics Anonymous*

'J. Kenner has written a sensually seductive storyline that catches your imagination and pulls you in' *The Reading Café*

J. **Kenner** loves wine, dark chocolate, and books. She lives in Texas with her husband and daughters. Visit her online at **www.jkenner.com** to learn more about her and her other pen names, to get a peek at what she's working on, and to connect through social media.

By J. Kenner

The Stark Trilogy
Release Me
Claim Me
Complete Me

COMPLETE ME

J. Kenner

headline
ETERNAL

Published by arrangement with Bantam Books,
an imprint of The Random House Publishing Group,
a division of Random House, Inc.

First published in Great Britain in 2013
by HEADLINE ETERNAL
An imprint of HEADLINE PUBLISHING GROUP

12

Cataloguing in Publication Data is available from the British Library

ISBN 978 1 4722 0609 1

Offset in Sabon by Avon DataSet Ltd, Bidford-on-Avon, Warwickshire

Printed and bound by CPI Group (UK) Ltd, Croydon, CR0 4YY

Headline's policy is to use papers that are natural, renewable and
recyclable products and made from wood grown in sustainable forests.
The logging and manufacturing processes are expected to conform to the
environmental regulations of the country of origin.

HEADLINE PUBLISHING GROUP
An Hachette UK Company
338 Euston Road
London NW1 3BH

www.eternalromancebooks.co.uk
www.headline.co.uk
www.hachette.co.uk

Acknowledgments

For all the wonderful readers who have taken the time to contact me through my website, email, or social media to tell me how much they've loved spending time with Nikki and Damien. Your words, support, and enthusiasm mean the world to me!

Special thanks to the folks at the German Consulate General in Houston and to Jacqueline Jugenheimer for the help with German legal procedure. Any errors or oversights are my own.

An extra hug to Kathleen O'Reilly for texting and phoning beyond the call of duty, K. J. Stone and Jessica Scott for their early reads and comments on the manuscript, and Jean Brashear for the early read, brainstorming, and lunch and coffee sessions!

Finally, a huge, never-ending thank you to the folks at Trident Media Group, especially Kimberly Whalen, and everyone at Bantam who has made this adventure with the Stark Trilogy such a wonderful experience, especially Maggie Oberrender, Gina Wachtel, and the amazing Shauna Summers.

COMPLETE ME

1

Fear yanks me from a deep sleep, and I sit bolt upright in a room shrouded with gray, the muted green light from a digital alarm clock announcing that it is just after midnight. My breath comes in gasps, and my eyes are wide but unseeing. The last remnant of an already forgotten nightmare brushes against me like the tattered hem of a specter's cloak, powerful enough to fill me with terror, and yet so insubstantial that it evaporates like mist when I try to grasp it.

I do not know what frightened me. I only know that I am alone, and that I am scared.

Alone?

I turn swiftly in bed, shifting my body as I reach out to my right. But even before my fingers brush the cool, expensive sheets, I know that he is not there.

I may have fallen asleep in Damien's arms, but once again, I have awakened alone.

At least now I know the source of the nightmare. It is the same fear I have faced every day and every night for weeks. The fear I try to hide beneath a plastic smile as I sit beside Damien day in and day out as his attorneys go over his defense in meticulous detail. As they explain the procedural ins-and-outs of a murder trial under German law. As they practically beg him to shine a light into the dark corners of his childhood because they know, as I do, that those secrets are his salvation.

But Damien remains stubbornly mute, and I am left huddled against this pervasive fear that I will lose him. That he will be taken from me.

And not just fear. I'm also fighting the damnable, overwhelming, panic-inducing knowledge that there isn't a goddamn thing in the world I can do. Nothing except wait and watch and hope.

But I do not like waiting, and I have never put my faith in hope. It is a cousin of fate, and both are too mercurial for my taste. What I crave is action, but the only one who can act is Damien, and he has steadfastly refused.

And that, I think, is the worst cut of all. Because while I understand the reason for his silence, I can't quell the selfish spark of anger. Because at the core of it all, it's not just himself that Damien is sacrificing. It's me. Hell, it's *us*.

We are running out of time. His trial will begin only a few hours from now, and unless he changes his mind about his defense, it is very likely that I will lose this man.

I squeeze my eyes shut, forcing the tears to remain at bay. I can push the fear back, but my anger is like a living thing, and I am afraid that it will explode no matter how hard I try to quell it. For that matter, I'm afraid that suppressing it will make the ultimate explosion all the more brutal.

When the indictment came through, Damien had tried to push me away, believing that he was protecting me. But he'd been wrong—and I'd flown all the way to Germany to tell him so. I've been here for over three weeks now, and there has not been a day when I have regretted coming, and I do not doubt that what he said when I arrived on his doorstep is true—he loves me.

But that knowledge doesn't diminish the sense of foreboding that has been rising within me. A trepidation that is especially potent at night when I wake alone and know that he has turned to solitude and Scotch when I want him in my arms. He loves me, yes. But at the same time I'm afraid that he is pushing me away again. Not in big steps, but in little ones.

Well, screw that.

I peel myself away from the cool comfort of our bed and stand up. I'm naked, and I bend to retrieve the white, lush robe provided by the Hotel Kempinski. Damien brushed it back off my shoulders after our shower last night, and I left it where it fell, a soft pile of cotton beside the bed.

The sash is a different story, and I have to dig in the rumpled sheets to find it. Sex with Damien is always intense, but as the trial comes closer, it has been wilder, more potent, as if by controlling me Damien can control the outcome.

Idly, I rub my wrists. They bear no marks, but that is only because Damien is careful. I can't say the same about my ass, which still tingles from the feel of his palm against my skin. I like it—both this lingering sting and the knowledge that he needs my submission as much as I need to give myself to him.

I find the sash shoved down near the foot of the bed. Last night, it had bound my wrists behind my back. Now, I tie it around my waist and tug it tight, relishing the luxurious comfort after waking so violently. The room itself is equally soothing, every detail done to perfection. Every piece of wood polished, every tiny knickknack and artistic addition thoughtfully arranged. Right now, however, I am oblivious to the room's charms. I only want to find Damien.

The bedroom connects to an oversized dressing area and a stunning bathroom. I check briefly in both, though I do not expect to find him, then continue through to the living area. The space is large and also well-appointed with comfortable seating and a round worktable that is now covered with sheafs of papers and folders representing both the business that Damien continues to run despite the world collapsing around our ears, and the various legal documents that his attorney, Charles Maynard, has ordered Damien to study.

I let the robe drop where I stand and pull on the stunning trompe l'oeil patterned sheath that Damien cavalierly tossed over the arm of a chair after peeling it off me last night. We've spent a few hours escaping reality by shopping on Munich's famous Maximilianstrasse, and I have acquired so many shoes and dresses I could open my own boutique.

I run my fingers through my hair as I cross the room to the phone by the bar. I force myself not to go into the bathroom to primp and freshen the makeup that has surely rubbed off. It's more challenging than it sounds; the mantra that a lady doesn't go out unfinished has been beaten into my head since birth. But with Damien at my side I have thumbed my nose at many of the tribulations of my youth, and right now I am more concerned with finding him than with applying fresh lipstick.

I pick up the receiver and dial zero. Almost immediately there is an accented voice on the other end. "Good evening, Ms. Fairchild."

"He's in the bar?" I do not need to explain who "he" is.

"He is. Shall I have a phone brought to his table?"

"No, that's all right. I'll come down."

"*Sehr gut.* Is there anything else I can do for you?"

"No, thank you." I'm about to hang up when I realize there is something. "Wait!" I catch him before he clicks off, then enlist his help with my plan to distract Damien from his demons.

Despite the age of the building and the elegance of the interior, the hotel boasts a modern ambiance, and I have come to feel at home within these walls. I wait impatiently for the elevator, and then even more impatiently once I'm in the car. The descent seems to take forever, and when the doors finally open to reveal the opulent lobby, I aim myself straight for the Old English–style bar.

Though it's late on a Sunday, the Jahreszeiten Bar is bustling. A woman stands by the piano softly singing to the gathered crowd. I barely pay her any heed. I don't expect to find Damien among the listeners.

Instead, I wander through the wood and red leather interior, shaking off the help of a waiter who wants to seat me. I pause for a moment, standing idly beside a blond woman about my age who is sipping champagne and laughing with a man who might be her father, but I'm betting is not.

I turn slowly, taking in the room around me. Damien is not with the group at the piano, nor is he sitting at the bar. And he does not occupy any of the red leather chairs that are evenly spaced around the tables.

I'm starting to worry that perhaps he was leaving as I was coming. Then I take a step to the left and realize that what I thought was a solid wall is actually an optical illusion created by a pillar. Now I can see the rest of the room, including the flames leaping in the fireplace set into the opposite wall. There is a small love seat and two chairs surrounding the hearth. And, yes, there is Damien.

I immediately exhale, my relief so intense I almost use the blonde's shoulder to steady myself. Damien is seated in one of the chairs, his back to the room as he faces the flames. His shoulders are broad and straight, and more than capable of bearing the weight of the world upon them. I wish, however, that they didn't have to.

I move toward him, the sound of my approach muffled by both the thick carpet and the din of conversation. I pause a few feet behind him, already feeling the familiar pull I experience whenever I am near Damien. The singer is now crooning "Since I

Fell for You," her voice cutting sharp and clear across the room. Her voice is so mournful that I'm afraid it is going to unleash a flood of tears along with all of the stress of the last few weeks.

No. I'm here to comfort Damien, not the other way around, and I continue toward him with renewed resolve. When I finally reach him, I press my hand to his shoulder and bend down, my lips brushing his ear. "Is this a private party, or can anyone join in?"

I hear rather than see his answering smile. "That depends on who's asking." He doesn't turn to face me, but he lifts his arm so that his hand is held up in a silent invitation. I close my hand in his, and he guides me gently around the chair until I am standing in front of him. I know every line of this man's face. Every angle, every curve. I know his lips, his expressions. I can close my own eyes and picture his, dark with desire, bright with laughter. I have only to look at his midnight-colored hair to imagine the soft, thick locks between my fingers. There is nothing about him that is not intimately familiar to me, and yet every glance at him hits me like a shock, reverberating through me with enough power to knock me to my knees.

Empirically, he is gorgeous. But it is not simply his looks that overwhelm. It is the whole package. The power, the confidence, the bone-deep sensuality that he couldn't shake even if he tried.

"Damien," I whisper, because I can't wait any longer to feel his name on my lips.

That wide, spectacular mouth curves into a slow smile. He tugs my hand, pulling me onto his lap. His thighs are firm and athletic, and I settle there eagerly, but I don't lean against him. I want to sit back enough that I can see his face.

"Do you want to talk about it?" I know what his answer will be, and yet I hold my breath, praying that I am wrong.

"No," he says. "I just want to hold you."

I smile as if his words are sweetly romantic, refusing to let him see how much they chill me. I need his touch, yes. But I need the man more.

I stroke his cheek. He hasn't shaved since yesterday, and the stubble of his beard is rough against my palm. The shock of our connection rumbles through me, and my chest feels tight, my breath uneven. Will there ever come a time when I can be near him without yearning for him? Without craving the touch of his skin against my own?

It's not even a sexual longing—not entirely, anyway. Instead, it's a craving. As if my very survival depends on him. As if we are two halves of a whole and neither can survive without the other.

With Damien, I am happier than I have ever been. But at the same time, I'm more miserable, too. Because now I truly understand fear.

I force a smile, because the one thing I will not do is let Damien see how terrified I am of losing him. It doesn't matter; Damien knows me too well.

"You're scared," he says, and the sadness that colors his voice is enough to melt me. "You're the one person in all the world I cannot bear to hurt, and yet I'm the one who put fear in your eyes."

"No," I say. "I'm not scared at all."

"Liar," he says gently.

"You forget that I've seen you in action, Damien Stark. You're a goddamn force of nature. They can't possibly hold you. Maybe they don't know it yet, but I do. You're going to walk away from this. You're going home a free man. There's no other way that this can end." I say the words because I need to believe them. But he is right. I am desperately afraid.

Damien, of course, sees through my bullshit. Gently, he tucks a strand of hair behind my ear. "You should be scared. This is the kind of case that has prosecutors salivating."

"But you were only fourteen," I say.

"Which is why they're not trying me as an adult."

I frown because even though he was only fourteen, he's looking at a decade in prison.

"But you didn't kill Merle Richter." That, after all, is the most important point.

His expression darkens. "Truth is a malleable thing, and once I walk into that courtroom, the truth is what the court says it is."

"Then you need to make sure the judges know the real truth. Dammit, Damien, you didn't kill him. But even if you had, there were mitigating circumstances." Only recently had Damien told me what happened. He and Richter fought, and when Richter fell, Damien held back, refusing to step forward to help the coach who'd abused him for so many years.

"Oh, Nikki." He pulls me against him, his arm swooping around my waist and shifting me on his lap so quickly that I gasp. "You know I can't do what you're asking."

"I'm not asking anything," I say, but the words sound brittle, because of course I'm asking. Hell, I'm begging. Damien damn well knows it, too. And yet he is denying me.

Anger flares within me, but before it explodes, his mouth crushes against mine. The kiss is deep and raw and all-consuming, and warm desire blooms within me. It doesn't erase my anger or my fear, but it does soothe it, and I shift closer to him, wishing I never had to leave the safety of his arms.

His body tightens beneath mine, the bulge of his erection under his jeans teasing my rear as I shift my weight and lean closer, deepening this kiss and wishing like hell we were in our suite instead of in a very public bar.

After a moment, I pull back, breathless. "I love you," I say.

"I know," he says, and though I wait for the reciprocal words to come, he doesn't say them back to me.

My heart twists a little, and I force a smile. A pageant-quality

All I Want Is World Peace kind of smile. The kind of smile I show the public, but not Damien.

I tell myself that he's just tired, but I don't believe it. Damien Stark does nothing without a purpose. And though it is impossible to truly get inside that head of his, I know him well enough to guess at his motivations, and I want to jump to my feet and scream at him. I want to beg him not to push me away. I want to shout that I get it, that he's trying to protect me because he knows that he might lose the trial. That he might be ripped from me. But goddammit, doesn't he know that all he's doing is hurting me?

I believe with all my heart that Damien loves me. What I fear is that love isn't enough. Not when he's determined to push me away in some misguided attempt to protect me.

So I don't lash out. That's not a fight I can win, but I can play the game my own way.

With renewed resolve, I kick the wattage up on my smile and slide off his lap, my hand extended to him. "You have to be in court at ten, Mr. Stark. I think you'd better come with me."

He stands, his expression wary. "Are you going to tell me I have to get some sleep?"

"No."

His gaze slides over me, and my body quivers in response as if he had physically touched me. "Good," he says, and that one simple word not only conveys a world of promises but takes the edge off the chilly fear that has filled me.

I allow the corner of my mouth to quirk up into a hint of a smile. "Not that, either. Not yet, anyway."

The confusion on his face brings a genuine smile to my lips, but he doesn't have the chance to ask, as the concierge has approached. "Everything is ready, Ms. Fairchild."

My smile broadens. "Thank you. Your timing is perfect."

I take the hand of the very confused man that I love and lead him through the lobby, following the concierge to the front of the hotel. There, parked on the street beside a very giddy valet, is a cherry red Lamborghini.

Damien turns to look at me. "What's this?"

"A rental. I thought you could use a little fun tonight, and the A9's just a few miles away. Fast car. German autobahn. It seemed like a no-brainer to me."

"Boys and their toys?"

I lower my voice so that the concierge can't overhear. "Since we already have some interesting toys in the room, I thought you might enjoy a change of pace." I lead him closer to where the valet stands by the open passenger door. "I understand she's very responsive, and I know you'll enjoy having all that power at your command."

"Is she?" He looks me up and down, and this time the inspection is tinged with fire. "As a matter of fact, that's exactly what I like. Responsiveness. Power. Control."

"I know," I say, and then slide into the passenger seat, letting more than a little thigh show as I do.

An instant later, Damien is behind the wheel and he's fired the powerful engine.

"Drive fast enough, and it's almost like sex," I tease. And then, because I can't resist, I add, "At the very least, it makes for exceptional foreplay."

"In that case, Ms. Fairchild," he says, with a boyish grin that makes this all worthwhile, "I suggest you hold on tight."

2

Even at almost midnight on a Sunday, traffic seems to spill out over the narrow Munich streets. The Lamborghini's engine revs and purrs, the power pent-up and antsy, as if it is as frustrated by its inability to break free and fly as I am by my inability to make things right for Damien.

I am nestled in the red-leather bucket seat, my body turned slightly to the left so that I can watch him. Despite the snarl of traffic that I would find exasperating, Damien is calm and in complete control. His right hand rests loosely on the gear stick, his fingers curved slightly. I draw a slow breath, imagining his touch against my bare knee. Since I've met Damien, I've done a lot of fantasizing. Honestly, I can't say that I mind.

His left hand grips the steering wheel, and despite the shit-storm in which we now live, he looks relaxed and confident. From my perspective, I am looking at his profile—that sculpted jaw, his deep-set eyes, his glorious mouth now curved into just the hint of a smile.

His unshaved jaw and finger-mussed hair combine with the low-interior light of the car to give him the look of a dangerous rebel. It's true, I think. Damien is as rebellious as they come. He lives his life by nobody's rules but his own. It is one of the qualities that I most love about him, which is why it makes it that much harder knowing that if he simply played the game like a good little defendant, everything could turn around.

We are standing still at an intersection, and now the light in front of us changes to green. He accelerates, then switches lanes so sharply I reach up to grab the handhold so that I don't list to one side. He turns to look at me, and I see nothing but pure pleasure in his eyes. I meet his smile eagerly, and for that moment, there is nothing in the world that can harm us. There is only freedom and joy, and I wish that it could continue like this. That we could drive on and on and never stop, just the two of us soaring off into eternity.

I may be lost in the fantasy of getting lost, but Damien exists entirely in the moment. I can see the tenseness in his muscles, the power and the control as he puts the car through her paces, testing her limits as he lets the power of that incredible engine build and build before we hit the autobahn, where he will finally let her explode onto the open road.

I swallow and shift a little in the seat. I thought I'd been teasing when I'd said this drive would be like sex. Apparently, I was wrong.

"You're smiling," he says, without turning to look at me.

"I am," I admit. "Because you're happy."

"I'm with you," he replies. "Why wouldn't I be happy?"

"Keep talking," I say. "Flattery will get you everywhere."

"I certainly hope so." His voice is barely a murmur, but it is more than sufficient to make my body respond. My skin heats and beads of perspiration rise on the back of my neck at my hairline. My breasts feel heavy, as if I need the support of Damien's hands upon them, and my now-hard nipples press enticingly against the silk of my sheath dress.

His comment may be simple and straightforward, but it holds a world of meaning. After all, he and I both know that there's nowhere Damien can take me that I won't be willing to go.

"We're here," Damien says, and I jump a little at the odd juxtaposition of his words to my thought. I gather myself, quickly realizing that he means that we've reached the A9. He accelerates onto the entrance ramp, the force pushing me back against the seat. I suck in air, invigorated by the speed and by the man beside me. "Do you have a plan?" he asks as he shifts gears.

I glance over and see that the speedometer is already approaching 175 kilometers per hour. "A plan?"

His brow quirks up with amusement. "This was your idea, remember? I thought you might have had something specific in mind."

"No plan," I admit as I toe off my shoes and put my feet up on the seat. "Nothing more than just cutting loose with you."

"I like that plan," he says. "And I know exactly where I want to get off." He glances at me as he says the last, the deliciously devious gleam in his eyes so exaggerated that I can't help but laugh.

"Perv," I say.

"Only for you," he retorts. I am hugging my knees, and he reaches over and traces his fingertip over the platinum and emerald ankle bracelet that was a gift from him, a physical reminder that I am his. As if I could ever forget.

His hand moves from the bracelet to the back of my thigh, the touch light and sensual. It's nothing more than a simple caress, but my reaction to it is all sorts of complicated. Taut ribbons of heat shoot through me to pool between my legs, to tug at my nipples. How simple it is to fall into a pattern of touch and pleasure, of need and desire. It is as if I am in a constant state of starvation, and he is the sweetest ambrosia.

All too soon, though, the pressure is gone as he moves his

hand to the radio, rolling through the stations until he settles on something with a heavy techno beat that fills the car. He shifts again and the engine hums as Damien weaves in and out of the minimal traffic. I settle back and let the rhythm pound through me as I watch this man who loves me. This man who I love, too. Who belongs entirely to me.

The thought comes unbidden, and I find myself frowning because it isn't true. If he were truly my private property—mine, and mine alone—I could take him away from here. I could save him. I could make all of this legal horribleness go away.

But I can't, and that inescapable truth creeps back under my skin, turning my previously light and giddy mood into something dark and foreboding.

I shift so that I am looking out of the passenger window at the line of trees passing in the night, odd shadows dancing across them, cast from the illumination of our headlights. I shiver, feeling unwound from such an ominous sight, as if we're driving into a netherworld, but even that won't save us from the desolate pull of reality.

I want to keep driving—I want to head east to where the sun will rise in five or so hours. I want to push this car to its limit and never stop. We're in a bubble right now, safe from those dark grasping shadows. But the moment we stop . . . the moment we go back . . .

No. I draw a deep breath. I have to be strong. Not for me, but for Damien. "We should head back," I say, but my voice is so low that I am certain he cannot hear me over the music that now fills the car. I reach for the radio and press the power button, throwing us into silence.

Damien glances at me, and I see the joy on his face shift to concern as his eyes meet mine. "What is it?"

"We should go back." I try to speak up, but my voice is still unnaturally soft, as if my will is fighting me, silently begging me to urge him to run. "You need rest." I force the words out, pitching my voice to sound natural. "Tomorrow's going to put us both through the wringer."

"All the more reason to keep going as long as we can."

I swallow a throat full of tears. "Damien."

I expect him to say soothing words. To reassure me that everything will be okay. Instead, he simply brushes my cheek, the gesture sending shock waves through me and once again making tears well in my eyes. I clench my hands into fists and fight against the crying jag that is about to explode out of me. I can't lose it. Not now. Hell, not ever. If I lose Damien, I'll cry then. And until I know one way or the other, I want to spend every second doing nothing but simply being with him.

I manage a smile that is almost genuine and turn to him.

"Soon." He hits the accelerator, and the car speeds up.

"Where are we going?"

"Someplace I want you to see."

My expression must be more confused than I realize, because he laughs softly. "Don't worry. We're not running away."

I grimace. I almost wish we were.

He keeps his left hand on the steering wheel, but he rests his right hand on my knee. The touch is more possessive than sexual, as if he simply needs to know that I am there. I lean my head back, torn between wanting to relish the feel of his fingers against my flesh, and the need to rail on him. To scream and yell. To beg and plead for him to fucking *defend* himself. Because Damien Stark is not a man who stands back and gets whipped. He is not a man who puts up with losing.

He is not a man who hurts the woman he loves.

And yet he is doing all of these things.

My thoughts, violent and dangerous, swirl inside me as the last of the city lights fade, leaving nothing but the forested acres that line the highway. The engine is smooth, remarkably quiet, and I am tired. Not simply because of the late hour, but because of everything that has been resting upon me. I close my eyes and relax, only to sit up again with a jolt seconds later when I realize the car is stopped, the engine turned off.

"What?" I feel groggy, my mind full of cobwebs. "What happened?"

"You had a nice nap," Damien says.

A nap?

I frown. "How long?"

"Almost half an hour."

That startles me to wakefulness, and I sit up and look around. We appear to be in the parking lot of a rustic restaurant with plenty of outdoor seating. It's closed now, the empty picnic tables seeming eerie rather than welcoming. "Where are we?"

"Seehaus Kranzberger," he says. I must look as confused as I feel, because he grins. "This used to be one of my favorite places near Munich. Alaine and Sofia and I used to come here once Alaine was old enough to drive. Later, I would come by myself. There are a lot of memories here," he adds, an odd catch in his voice.

"But it's closed," I say stupidly.

"We didn't come for the food," he says. He gets out, then comes around the car and opens my door before I have a chance. He reaches a hand down to help me out, and I stand gracefully.

"Why did we come?"

"Walk with me."

I study his face, unable to read his mood. He takes my hand and leads me down a narrow path that meanders through tall, leafy trees, their green leaves now black and gray in the moonlight. I cannot imagine where we are going, but then we turn, and I gasp. A lake is spread open in front of us, a wilderness surrounding it, the moonlight sparkling on the surface, and the giant orb of the moon itself reflected in such a way that it appears that we could dive in and capture it for ourselves. "It's beautiful," I say.

"Welcome to Kranzberger See. I used to spend hours here," he says. "I would sit on the bank and listen to the water and the birds and the wind in the trees. I would close my eyes and get lost." He has been looking at the lake, but now he turns to look at me. "I wanted to show you," he says. What I hear is, *I'm sorry.*

I swallow and nod, feeling overwhelmed. "Thank you."

He lifts our joined hands and gently kisses my palm. The gesture is soft and sweet and achingly romantic, and I can't help but wish that we could stay here, lost in the dappled light, hidden away by the fantasy of being all alone in the world.

A tremor ripples through my body, and I turn away. I've fallen so fast for this man, and I am terrified of losing him. Terrified that whatever good we've discovered together despite our shitty pasts will be ripped away. I press my lips together to hold back an anguished scream, because that is all I want to do right now—scream and yell and cry until Damien does whatever he has to do to fix this and make all the horror go away.

But I don't. Instead I stand firm like a rock, knowing that the slightest motion could set me off. I feel wild and volatile and dangerous. And right now, the last thing either of us needs is an explosion.

"Nikki." My name is soft upon his lips, and he lets go of my hand as he moves to stand behind me. His palms press down on my shoulders, the pressure warm and sweet. I feel the gentle touch of his lips upon the top of my head, and the soft squeeze of his fingers as he strokes my arms, bare in the sleeveless dress. "I pissed you off that first night at Evelyn's, remember? I should have let you stay pissed. I should have walked away from you and never looked back."

My mouth is dry, and my chest feels tight. I do not want to hear these words. I don't want to believe that there is even some tiny part of him that would prefer to have never been with me, not even if that fantasy springs from a desire to protect me. "No," I say. It's the only word I can manage, and it sounds strangled and raw.

He turns me gently, then presses his palm to my cheek. "It rips me apart to see the fear in your eyes."

His words are soft and gentle, but they hit me with as much force as a kick in the chest, and I respond in kind, surprising both of us when I lash out and slap him across the face.

"Stop it!" I shout, all of my self-control exploding out in a maelstrom of wild emotions. "Just fucking stop it! You think that's a solution? Wishing that we'd never gotten together? God-dammit, Damien, I'm so in love with you it hurts, but you're going to fucking *coddle* me? I don't need you to soothe me, I need you to *do* something." I smack him in the chest with both palms, then gasp when he grabs my wrists and holds me still, his hands painfully tight against my skin.

"Nikki." His voice isn't soothing now. It's raw and dangerous and I know that I've pushed him too far, but I don't care. As far as I'm concerned, I can't push him far enough, because right then, all I want is to break him. To break through that goddamned stubbornness and somehow get it through his head that the only way to save himself—to save us—is to put forward a defense.

"They're going to put you in a cage." My voice is clipped and precise. "Christ, Damien, how can you not be scared shitless? I'm so scared I can barely get out of bed every day!"

He stares at me as if I'm speaking Greek. "Not afraid?" His words are heavy with barely contained fury. I don't know if it's directed at me or not, but it is strong enough that it makes him tremble. "Is that what you think?"

I take an involuntary step back, but he stops me, his hands clutching my arms, his fingers digging into my flesh and holding me firmly in place. "Is that really what you think? Jesus Christ,

Nikki, I'm terrified of being ripped away from you. Of not being able to touch you. To kiss you. To hear you laugh, to look at you. To be with you."

I am so lost in his words that I do not realize that he has been easing me backward and now I am pressed up against a tree, the bark rough through the thin material of my dress. His hands slide possessively down my arms, then back up my torso to roughly cup my breasts. I gasp as desire, hot and demanding, cuts through me.

He leans in closer, his lips brushing my cheek. "I can handle anything except the thought of losing you." His mouth burns against my ear. His hand slides down, then slowly up my thigh, taking the thin material of the skirt with him.

"Not scared?" he whispers as his palm cups my sex. I'm not wearing underwear, and he slips easily inside me. I bite my lower lip, grateful that he is there to hold me up because my entire body feels like liquid fire.

"I'm more terrified than I've ever been in my life," he says, and then his mouth closes over mine and his fingers inside me move slowly in time with the deepening rhythm of his kiss. For one beautiful, blissful moment I am lost in his kiss, in his arms. I've forgotten where we are and why we are here. There is only Damien and the sensual, comforting warmth of his body pressed against mine.

Then something snaps inside me, bursting past the desire and this desperate need that has my pulse pounding and my sex drawing tight around his fingers. I press my palms up hard against his chest and push him back again.

"How dare you be afraid. Goddammit, Damien, how *dare* you say that you're afraid of losing me when you could make it all go away. You could make this be over. You could end it and we could go home."

He's staring at me, and there is infinite sadness in his eyes. "Oh, baby. If I could take away your fear, I would."

"*If* you could?" I repeat. "You can, and you damn well know it, and I'm fucking pissed off that you won't do anything about it."

I'm screaming at him. I'm like a shrewish harpy and I hate it. Hate myself. But dammit, right now I hate Damien, too.

Tears stream down my face, and my legs seem to fall out from under me. I start to collapse and Damien catches me, easing me down to my knees. The irony isn't lost on me; Damien will always be there to catch me. At least I thought he would. Now I don't know, and for the first time, I feel alone in Damien's arms.

"I've thought about it." His voice is low and as serious as I've ever heard.

I freeze. I never knew that hope could feel so cold and lifeless, but it does. "Thought about what?" I ask cautiously.

He hesitates so long that I begin to think he's not going to answer. When he speaks, the words come slowly. "I've wanted you for so long," he says. "And now that I have you, I'm risking everything there is between us."

Yes, I want to shout. *Yes!* I realize that I'm digging my fingernails into the soft, damp earth, and I force myself to relax as I try not to anticipate his next words. As I try not to get my hopes up.

"I'm not convinced that revealing what Richter did to me is the panacea you and Maynard and the rest of them think it is. But maybe I should try. If it means that the charges will go away, then maybe I should sacrifice the privacy that I've spent my whole life fighting to maintain."

I hear the bitterness in his voice, and I want to reach for him and hold his hand tight in mine. I don't, though. I stay absolutely, perfectly still.

"There is no shame in being a victim, right? So why should I care if the world knows the vile things he did to me? Why should it matter if the press writes about the dark nights in my dorm room. The debasing things he made me do. Things I haven't even told you. Things that I wish I could forget."

He meets my eyes, but I see only the hard lines and angles of his face. "If it means that I can walk to you as a free man, shouldn't I want to shout that story from the rooftops? Shouldn't I want it plastered everywhere? On television, on talk shows, on the front page of newspapers? Shouldn't I want to make my personal hell fodder for the whole damn world?"

Something cool brushes my cheek, and I realize that I am crying.

"No," I whisper, hating the truth even as I say it. But this is the heart of who Damien is. A man who lives by his own code, and it is that core of him that I fell in love with. "Not even for me," I say. "Not even to stay out of prison."

I squeeze my eyes shut, and fresh tears spill out over my lashes.

The pad of his thumb brushes my cheek.

"You understand?"

"No," I say, but I mean yes, and when I open my eyes I can see that he knows it. He moves closer to me, and my breath hitches. I hiccup a little, tasting tears as his mouth closes over mine. The kiss is soft at first, gentle and sweet. Then his hand cups the back of my head even as his other arm snakes around my waist and tugs me onto his lap.

I gasp with surprise at the movement, and he takes advantage, his mouth hardening, his tongue finding mine, his kiss becoming deeper and more demanding. I twine my fingers through his silky hair and lose myself in the sensual firmness of his mouth. In the wildness of this kiss. Our tongues meeting, our teeth clashing. My mouth will be bruised in the morning, but I cannot resist this kiss that is setting us both on fire.

I am breathing hard when he finally pulls away. My lips feel swollen and used and spectacular. I wonder if I've ever truly been kissed before, even by Damien. And right then, all I want is more.

I lean toward him in silent demand, but he catches me with a firm hand under my chin. I stay there, my position awkward, my eyes lifted to his.

"You are my everything, Nikki. You have to know that. You have to believe it."

"I do," I whisper. I see the tremor run through his body, then the way his muscles tighten as he pulls me against him and holds me close. I melt into his arms, so in love with this man that it almost hurts.

"You are my everything," he repeats. "But I can't be true to you if I'm not true to myself."

"I know," I say, my lips against the cotton of his shirt. "I get it." I tilt my head back and look up into his eyes. "That doesn't mean it hurts any less."

"Then let me try to make it better." He eases me away from his body, then bends down to kiss the corner of my mouth. "Is that where it hurts?"

I shake my head as tears tease my eyes and a small smile tugs at the corner of my mouth.

"No? Then how about here?" His lips brush my jawline, and I suck in a breath, undone by the sweetness of his touch.

"No," I say, and my smile is no longer tremulous.

This time, his lips find the indentation at the base of my throat. I tilt my head back, giving him better access, and feel my pulse beat wildly against his lips. "That's not it, either," I whisper.

"Tricky," he says. "How can I kiss it and make it better if I can't even find it?"

"Keep looking," I say.

"I'll never stop," he promises. His lips drift down, pausing over my heart that is pounding in my chest. "Not here, surely," he says, then moves on as I laugh, the sound cut off by a raw, sensual cry when his mouth closes suddenly over my breast.

"Damien!"

His arms around my back support me as he suckles me

through the silky material of this insanely expensive dress. His teeth graze my sensitive nipple, and I arch back, lost in a desperate haze of pleasure.

"Here?" he murmurs, his lips never fully releasing me.

"Yes," I say. "Oh, God, yes."

"I'm not so sure," he says when he takes his mouth off me. "I'd better keep looking."

He shifts me gently off his lap and lays me down on the soft grass, his legs straddling my waist.

"Damien," I murmur. "What are you—"

He hushes me with a finger, then leans over me, his mouth on my breast again. I groan with pleasure. "I told you," he says. "I'm going to kiss it and make it better."

His mouth closes this time over my left breast as his hand cups my right. It is as if his body is a live wire, sending current through me at every point of contact. Sparks shoot from his fingertips through my breasts, curling through me and making my body arch up with an insatiable desire for more.

All too soon he shifts, his mouth leaving my breast to trail gently down my body, nothing between his lips and my skin but this thin layer of silk.

His mouth is on my belly, his teeth nipping at my navel. His hands have slid down over the dress, and he is easing it up. The soft material glides over my skin even as Damien's lips ease down. His kisses are feather soft across my skin, along the rise of my hip bone and then gently, sweetly, over my pubis before he continues lower, and then lower still. My back arches involuntarily, and I gasp as his tongue flicks playfully over my clit before his mouth closes, hot and demanding, over my sex.

His hands move to my thighs, his thumbs grazing my scars before stroking the soft inner skin at the apex of my thighs. He pushes my legs apart, opening me wider for him. I want to shift my hips, to writhe from the pleasure of his oh-so-intimate kiss, but he holds me fast, keeping me exactly as he wants me. I raise my hand to my mouth, then bite down on the soft pad at the base of my thumb as I turn my head from side to side in time with the pleasure that grows inside me as Damien's expert mouth and tongue increase the sweet pleasure, slowly, slowly, so painfully slowly.

And then it all explodes, and I arch up, my mouth open, but my cry silenced by Damien who has slid up my body and now holds me down with the weight of his. His mouth closes over mine, and I taste my own arousal. I kiss him deeply, hungrily, then moan in protest when he pulls away. He presses his hands against the soft earth at either side of me as he lifts himself and looks into my eyes. There is heat there, but it is fast fading to playfulness.

"Better?" he asks with a cocky grin.

"Oh, yes," I say, then ease up onto my elbows so that I can sit up.

"No," he says. "Lay back."

I arch a brow, amused. "So demanding, Mr. Stark. What exactly do you want from me?"

"I want you naked," he says, and now the playfulness is gone as fast as it came, replaced by lust and heat so potent it makes me wet all over again.

"Oh."

Slowly, he lifts the hem of my dress. I don't protest. I simply shift my body so that he can pull the garment up and over my head. He tosses it aside, then pulls his white T-shirt off before his fingers go to the buttons of his jeans.

"I'm going to fuck you, Nikki. Right here, on the warm earth with the sky open above us. I'm going to claim you with the entire universe looking on, because you are mine, and you always will be, no matter where we go from here."

"Yes," I say, though his words were not a question but a demand. "Oh, yes."

His hands skim over me, his eyes full of adoration. I have always known that I am pretty, but when Damien looks at me, I feel more than beautiful. I feel special.

I reach up and stroke his cheek and watch as the passion builds in his eyes. I twine my fingers in his hair, grasp the back of his head, and pull his lips down to mine. Our kiss is hungry and wild, like the trees and vines around us. I pull him closer, unable to get enough of him. His hands stroke me, caressing my sides, stroking my breasts, sliding between my legs. His moan when he finds me wet and ready seems to reverberate through me.

He breaks the kiss, using one hand to prop himself above me. "Now." He doesn't wait for my reply, but my legs are already spread in demand, and I lift my hips to meet him as he thrusts inside me. I cry out, not in pain, but in the rightness of it all. This is how it is supposed to be, Damien and I joined together. Damien and I standing fast against the whole of the world.

We move together, wild and frenzied, and when the orgasm explodes through me, I realize that my face is streaked with tears.

"Baby," he whispers, pulling me close.

"No, no," I say. "It's just that it's too big to hold inside."

"I know," he says, and holds me tighter. "Sweetheart, I know."

I do not know how long we stay like that. I only know that I never want to move again. All too soon, though, Damien rubs his hand along my bare arm, then kisses the lobe of my ear. "Are you ready to go back?"

I'm not, of course. I never will be. But I know that Damien needs my strength as much as I need his. And so I only nod and grab my dress before standing up. I reach my hand down for him. "I'm ready," I say. "Let's go."

3

Again and again in my dreams I go tumbling over the side of the building, falling down, down, down. Damien reaches for me, his face frantic as he thrusts his arm out, trying to grab me. But it's no use. He is trapped above me and I am drawn unrelentingly toward the hard, cold earth where I will shatter, broken into a million pieces, praying that Damien will come and put me together again, but knowing that he won't. That he can't. Because he is the one who pushed me over that edge in the first place.

I wake screaming, clinging to Damien, my arms wrapped around him. Even the steady beat of his heart and his soft words cannot soothe me, because I can no longer tell what is the nightmare and what is reality.

All I want is for this to be over, but as we exit the Kempinski lobby two hours later—as the cameras flash and the reporters scream questions about the trial that is beginning today—I take it all back. I'm afraid that in wishing for it to end that I have been wishing for my own destruction. Instead, I want all this pre-trial nonsense to continue. I want to stay cocooned in the safety of the hotel if that's what it takes to avoid reality.

From the moment we met, it was as if a magical bubble surrounded us. But the real world has begun to intrude. My mother, who flew into Los Angeles like a storm and ripped apart the fragile life I was finally building for myself. The paparazzi who almost broke me after they learned that I posed nude in exchange for a million dollars. And now this trial that is poised to rip away everything that Damien and I have managed to build together.

I have no intention of leaving Damien, and I believe that he has no intention of leaving me. But I can't shake the fear that despite what we want, fate has other plans. Damien might be the strongest man I know, but can he fight the whole world?

The ride is all too short, and soon we arrive at the Criminal Justice Center, which houses the Munich District Court where Damien's trial will take place. The building is modern, boxy in white stone and glass. It reminds me of both the federal courthouse in Los Angeles and the Dorothy Chandler Pavilion. Considering the show that is about to be put on, I suppose that's appropriate.

Over the last few days, I've been here a number of times for meetings between the attorneys. Those times, though, I hadn't trembled. Today, I can't stop shaking. A bone-deep quivering as if I am too cold. As if I will never be warm again.

I take a deep breath and ease toward the door that the driver is now holding open. I am stopped, however, by Damien's hand upon mine.

"Wait," he says, his voice low. "Here." He shrugs out of his jacket and puts it around my shoulders.

I close my eyes—just for a moment. Just long enough to curse myself. Because, dammit, Damien shouldn't be looking out for me. I should be the one supporting him, and I turn in the limo and pull him close and press a quick, firm kiss to his lips. "I love you," I whisper, and hope those simple words say everything that I'm not saying.

His eyes lock on mine. "I know," he says. "Now put the jacket on."

I nod, understanding the unspoken message: No matter what, he will never stop looking out for me. I can't argue with him about that; after all, I feel the same way.

I climb out of the car and stand up, my Public Nikki smile plastered across my face because reporters surround us, representing all of Europe and the States and even Asia. I'm practiced enough at hiding my emotions that I'm certain I look cool and confident. I'm not. I'm terrified. And from the way Damien grips my hand, I know that he realizes it. I wish I could be stronger, but it's impossible, and I'm simply going to have to accept that. Until this is over—one way or the other—I'm going to be walking on a knife edge. I only hope that in the end, I can tumble into Damien's arms, and not fall in the other direction where I am left to plummet into the abyss alone.

"Herr Stark! Fräulein Fairchild! Nikki! Damien!"

The voices surround us, some English, some German, some French. Other languages, too, that I do not recognize.

Ever since I arrived in Munich, the press has been all over us. And not just about the trial. No, the tabloids are just as eager to analyze Damien's love life. They are not—thank God—harping on endlessly about my portrait or the money Damien paid me. But they are gleefully digging through their morgues and running photos of Damien with the steady stream of other women who have been on his arm. Runway models. Actresses. Heiresses. Damien told me himself that he used to fuck a lot of women. And he told me that none of them were special. For him, there is only me.

I believe him, but I still don't like seeing those pictures on newsstands and all over the television and Internet.

Right now, though, I'd be happy if the press's only interest in us was who Damien was sleeping with. But that is not the focus

of their attention today. Today, they're out for blood, and murder
is on the agenda.

It isn't until we cross the threshold and enter the building that
I realize that I have forgotten to breathe. I glance at Damien and
manage a wan smile. He shakes his head. "If I could have left you
in the hotel today, I would have."

"I'd rather die than not be here with you." Unfortunately, I
think, being here may come close to killing me.

The halls are bustling with attorneys and court personnel, all
moving efficiently to wherever it is they are going. I barely notice
them. Honestly, I barely notice anything, and it's with a bit of
surprise that a uniformed guard hands me my purse and I realize
that we've stepped through security.

A polished man in his midfifties with salt-and-pepper hair is
hurrying toward us. This is Charles Maynard, the attorney who
has represented Damien since he burst onto the tennis scene as a
nine-year-old prodigy. He holds out his hand for Damien even as
his eyes go to me. "Hello, Nikki. My staff will be in the row of
seats immediately behind the witness stand. You'll sit there too,
of course."

I nod, grateful. If I can't be beside Damien, at least I'll be
nearby.

"We should talk before this begins," he continues, his words
directed to Damien. He glances at me. "You'll excuse us?"

I want to scream in protest, but instead I nod. I don't try to
speak, too afraid that my voice will shake and betray me.

Damien reaches out and squeezes my hand. "Go on in," he
says. "I'll see you shortly."

Once again, I nod assent, but I don't move. Instead I stand
dully in the hallway as Maynard leads Damien a few yards away
and then through the doors of the small conference room that I
know has been assigned to his team for use during the trial. I
stand a moment longer, unwilling to go through the heavy

wooden doors that lead to the courtroom. Maybe if I never go in, the proceedings can never start.

I'm still there, cursing my own foolishness, when I think I hear my name from somewhere behind me, muddled by the sound of the crowd bustling in this wide, echoing hall. At first, I think it's one of the reporters trying to get my attention. But there's something familiar about it. I frown, because surely it's not—

But it is. *Ollie.*

I see him the instant I turn around. Orlando McKee, the boy I grew up with, who has been one of my best friends since forever. The man who has repeatedly said that Damien is a danger to me.

The man who Damien believes is in love with me.

There was a time when I would have run to him, thrown my arms around him, and spilled out all my fears. Now, I'm not even certain how I feel about seeing him here.

I stand frozen as he hurries toward me. He arrives out of breath, his hand outstretched for mine. Slowly, he drops his when he realizes that I am not reaching out in return.

"I didn't know you were going to be here," I say blandly.

"I tried to reach you at the Kempinski this morning," he says, "but you'd already left."

"I have a cell phone," I say.

He nods. "I know. I should have called. This was last minute. Maynard learned that I went to school with one of the junior attorneys on the prosecutor's staff, and he wanted me here."

"Law school?" I can't figure out why a German prosecutor would go to a United States law school.

He shakes his head. "Undergrad. Small world, huh?"

"Does Damien know you're here?" My voice is cold and clipped, and I'm certain that Ollie knows why. If Damien were selecting the legal team, Ollie would not be included.

Ollie has the good grace to look embarrassed. "No," he says, then runs his hand through his hair. His usually unruly waves are combed back, and his fingers loosen a few strands that now fall in his face, brushing over his John Lennon–style glasses. "What was I supposed to tell Maynard?" he asks. "That Stark doesn't want me around? I say that and I have to say why. And if Stark hasn't told Maynard that I told you attorney-client privileged information, then I don't see any reason to tell him myself."

"You could have thought of something," I say.

He nods slowly. "Maybe. But I've been working on Stark's defense from Los Angeles. It's been my full-time gig for over three weeks. I'm not here just because I have a personal connection, I'm here because I understand the law. I can be an asset, Nikki. And you know as well as I do that Damien needs all the help he can get."

I force myself not to ask him what he means. Maynard is aware of the abuse in Damien's past, that much I know for certain. But it was my understanding that not everyone on the team knows. Does Ollie? The thought makes me queasy, because I know how much Damien wants that aspect of his past to stay private. I can't ask without revealing the facts, though. All I can do is hope that the reason Ollie isn't in the current meeting is because he isn't in that inner circle.

"Are you sitting at the counsel table?" I ask, and am relieved when he shakes his head.

"I thought I'd sit with you. If that's okay."

"It is," I say. Things have changed a lot between me and Ollie, but he has seen me through most every crisis in my life, and it feels right that he will be beside me now, too.

His smile is gentle as he lays a soft hand on my shoulder. His expression, however, is intense. "You're doing okay? I mean, you're not—you know?"

"I'm not," I say but I don't meet his eyes. "I'm good." I draw in a breath and fight the urge to cry, mourning the loss of those days when I would have told Ollie everything. How every day I've awakened expecting to battle the urge to cut, and every night I am amazed when I get back in bed beside Damien and realize that the compulsion never came. I am not "cured"—I know I never will be. I will always crave that pain to keep me centered. I will always be just a little astounded when I get through a crisis without putting a blade to my flesh. But I have Damien now, and it is him that I crave. Damien who is my release valve instead of turning a knife on myself. Damien who keeps me centered and safe.

And that, I know, is another reason I am afraid to lose him.

"Nikki?"

"Really," I say, looking into his face. "No blades, no knives. Damien is taking good care of me."

I see the way he flinches, and for a moment I regret my words. But it is only a momentary weakness. Ollie has been an absolute shit about my relationship with Damien, and although I will always love him, I am not going to forgive or forget that easily.

"I'm glad," he says, his voice formal. "You're going to be okay, you know. No matter what happens, you're going to get through this just fine."

I nod, but I also notice that he's said that I will be okay—not that Damien will. And a peculiar spark of anger tinged with sadness rushes through me, spurred by the simple truth that Ollie no longer understands what I need. If he did, he would realize that without Damien, I won't be okay. Not ever again.

We have been talking in the hall a few feet from the wooden double doors that lead into the courtroom. Now Ollie steps in that direction and holds one open for me. I hesitate only briefly, glancing down the hall where Damien and Maynard went, but they have not come out of the conference room. I draw a deep breath for courage, force my feet to move, and sweep past Ollie into the courtroom where the course of the rest of my life will be decided.

Though the gallery is already full of reporters who have come to watch the spectacle of Damien Stark on trial, the main area is empty with the exception of one man in a uniform who stands at attention and will, presumably, escort the three professional and two lay judges into the courtroom once the proceedings are ready to begin.

Unlike a U.S. courtroom, there is no bar separating the visitors from the action. Ollie and I walk up the middle aisle toward the rows of chairs behind the witness stand. As we do, the noise level in the room increases as the occupants whisper among themselves and shift their positions to get a better look at us. Despite the fact that I understand next to nothing in German, I can pick out the sound of my name and Damien's mixed in among the din. I concentrate on walking forward and on not turning around and slapping the reporter closest to me. On not screaming at the lot of them that this isn't entertainment—this is a man's life. This is my life. Our life together.

My back is still to the crowd when the room gets even noisier. I turn, certain of what I will see, and sure enough, the doors are pulled open and there is Damien standing at the threshold. He is flanked by Maynard and Herr Vogel, his German lead counsel, but they are little more than white noise in my vision. It is Damien I want, Damien I see. And now it is Damien striding toward me with such confidence and power it makes my knees go weak.

There are no cameras in the courtroom, so when Damien pulls me into his arms to kiss me, I know this moment will not be captured on film. I wouldn't care if it was, though. My arms go around his neck, and I cling to him, fighting not to cry, and then fighting to let go, because I cannot clutch him forever.

He releases me and steps back, his eyes burning into me as he gently brushes his thumb across my lips. "I love you," I whisper, and see the words reflected back in his dual-colored eyes. His smile, however, is sad.

His eyes shift, and I realize he is looking over my shoulder at Ollie. His expression is unreadable. After a moment, he nods in greeting, then turns his attention again to me. He squeezes my hand, then moves to sit at the defense table next to his attorneys who have already moved past him and are now opening their briefcases and pulling out documents and files and the other accoutrements of trial work.

I collapse onto my chair, suddenly exhausted. Ollie settles beside me. He says nothing, but I hear the silent question, and I turn to him with a wan smile. "I'm okay," I say, and he nods in response.

All too soon, the judges enter the courtroom and the proceedings officially begin.

After the judge runs through the preliminary matters, the prosecutor stands. He begins to speak. I do not understand German, but I can imagine what he is saying. He is painting Damien as a young, eager, competitive athlete. But more than an athlete. Because from a very young age, Damien was driven by ambition. He had a head for business, a passion for science.

What he didn't have was money.

Oh, sure, he started bringing in the prize money, but how much is enough for a young man with dreams of founding an empire? And isn't that exactly what he did? Isn't Damien Stark now one of the wealthiest men on the planet?

And how did he get that way? How did he earn that first million?

Did he take out a patent as a young man while still on the tennis circuit? Did he convince his father—who had control over his income as a youth—to invest his tennis winnings?

Or did he inherit that first million from the coach who had trained him? Nurtured him? Doted on him?

And how did Damien repay that attention and affection? He saw dollar signs—and he killed Merle Richter. That first million was blood money, the prosecutor is arguing. Blood money for which the German people now want Stark to pay.

That is the story, and without Damien testifying in counter to it, I am afraid that it is a good one.

The prosecutor seems to speak forever. I watch the faces of the judges. They do not look sympathetic.

When it's over, I realize that I have drawn blood on my knees. I don't remember taking a pen out of my purse, but I must have, because I have been digging the point into my flesh.

"Nikki?" Ollie's voice is sharp beside me.

"I'm fine," I snap. I lick my finger and try to rub out the spot of blood and ink. Damien will see it, and he will worry about me more than he worries about himself.

As the judge speaks I see Maynard whisper to Herr Vogel, who is reputed to be one of the best defense attorneys in Bavaria, if not Germany. He's a polished, practiced man, and I have been impressed with him so far, but now that we're in court, I'm going in blind and I'm nervous. He gathers his papers, readying himself for his chance to speak, when the tallest of the professional judges accepts a piece of paper from his clerk.

He reads it, frowns, and then speaks in rapid-fire German before standing. He aims a hard look at the prosecutor and then at Herr Vogel. Maynard turns to face Damien, and from where I sit I can see the deep lines of his frown.

I have absolutely no idea what is going on, and I don't think Damien does, either. As if he can feel my thoughts upon him, he turns. *What?* I mouth, but he only shakes his head, not in dismissal, but in confusion.

At the bench, the professional judges stand and the lay judges follow suit. They don't look happy.

The tall judge points to Herr Vogel and the prosecutor, and says a few more words in German. Again, I'm left clueless, but considering how quickly the two move to follow him through the heavy wooden door to the court's inner sanctum, I can tell that something important is going on.

Tense moments pass. Maynard leans over and says something to Damien. Damien shakes his head. The observers in the court-room shift and mumble, and I know that all eyes in the gallery are on Damien. I am clutching the bench upon which I'm sitting, ter-rified that if I don't hold on I will go spinning off into space. And equally afraid that I will dent the wood from my fingers pressing in too tightly.

Time has no meaning for me until the door finally opens again. The bailiff steps out. He speaks to another of the German attorneys, who then bends and whispers something to Maynard. I try to read his lips, but of course I cannot. I see Charles stiffen, though, and my own body tightens as well. Charles reaches for Damien, his hand closing over his elbow. He speaks low, but I manage to make out the words: "They want to see us in cham-bers."

I swallow as Damien stands, and without thinking, I reach for him. I don't see him move. I don't see him step toward me. But for the briefest of moments, his fingers close over mine. Electric shocks whip through me. He squeezes my fingers, his eyes meet mine.

I open my mouth to speak, but I don't know what to say. I am scared, so scared. But I don't want Damien to see that. He knows it, of course, but I want to be strong. I need to be as strong as he believes me to be.

And then he is walking away, moving through the heavy wooden door to the judges' chambers. Going where I cannot fol-low into a world I don't understand.

All I know is that trials are not usually interrupted in this way.

All I can see is the stern expression on the judges' faces and the blank control in the eyes of Charles Maynard.

All I know is that they have taken Damien from me.

All I feel is fear.

4

Ollie has moved to the defense table to sit with the legal team. I know he is trying to find out what is going on, but his absence makes me feel even more at loose ends. It has been over an hour now. I am alone and desperate for information. For the first time since I came to Germany, I truly feel what it is like to be in a foreign country, because I have no understanding of what is going on around me.

It's not the language, though. The fact that I do not speak German only exacerbates the illusion. The German attorneys all speak fluent English, and I can hear what they are saying to Ollie. And what they are saying is that they do not understand any more than I do. We have all stepped through the looking glass, and I'm afraid that what we will find on this side is something even worse than the spectacle we anticipated.

I press my hands to my chair, preparing to lever myself to my feet. But I force myself to remain seated. Pacing will only call attention to me, and I have already noticed how many of the people in the gallery are staring at me, whispering among themselves. In the absence of Damien, I stand as his proxy. It is not a role that I would mind under normal circumstances, but today I do not want to be in the spotlight.

When I am certain that I will go completely mad if even one more minute passes without any word, the door to the judges' chamber opens and the group files out. The professional judges come first, their expressions unreadable. Then Maynard, then Herr Vogel. The lay judges follow, and Damien brings up the rear.

I'm not sure when I stood up, but I'm standing when my eyes meet Damien's. My hands are fisted in my skirt, and I'm silently screaming at him to tell me what happened. He remains silent, and though I search his face, I can find nothing helpful in his expression. It is completely blank.

He slips in behind the counsel table, and he is only a few feet from where I stand. My heart lurches, because he is no longer looking at me, and a cold wave of fear settles over me. Then he shifts, his eyes once again meeting mine. I blink away tears.

It's bad, I think. Whatever it is, it must be very, very bad.

Damien looks away, and my sense of foreboding increases. He sits at the defense counsel table, and I take my seat, as well. There is already one witness—a janitor—who saw him arguing on the roof with Richter before Richter fell to his death. Could there be another witness? It is the only thing I can think of, and worry consumes me.

Then the judges are back at the bench and Ollie returns to the gallery. The presiding judge calls the proceedings to order just as Ollie sits beside me.

"Do you know what's happening?" I whisper.

"No." His forehead is creased, and he looks as confused as I feel.

The tall judge begins to speak in slow, controlled German, and although Herr Vogel and Maynard and Damien stay perfectly still, the other attorneys at the defense table begin to shift in their seats. They weren't privy to what was said behind closed doors, and from my perspective, they look like men about to explode.

Behind us, the spectators in the gallery begin to whisper. The gloom that has filled this space has lifted. I don't understand how or why, but I am sure that something shocking is happening. Shocking, but good.

I glance at Ollie, afraid that I'm seeing too much, but he meets my eyes and holds up his hand. His fingers are crossed, and in that one moment, I could kiss him. Whatever his issues with Damien in the past, right now he is on Damien's side. He is on *my* side.

And then suddenly the judge is finished, and he's standing, and he's filing out of the room with the other judges behind him. As soon as the door behind them has shut, the courtroom explodes into a cacophony of sounds, some cheers, some shouts, but some boos and catcalls. One of the attorneys takes pity on me. He turns and faces me. "The charges," he says in a thick German accent. "The charges have been dropped."

"What?" I say stupidly.

"It's over," Ollie says, pulling me into a hug. "Damien's free to go home."

He releases me and I stare at him, my body cold with shock. I'm scared to believe it. Afraid that I haven't heard right and someone is going to tell me that I've misunderstood and the trial will be recommencing any moment now.

I turn to face Damien, but his back is still to me. The prosecutor now stands in front of him, speaking earnestly, but in such a low voice that I cannot make out the words. Maynard stands beside Damien, his hand on Damien's back, the gesture almost paternal.

"It's true?" I ask the German attorney. "You really mean it?"

His smile is broad, but his eyes are soft with understanding. "It is true," he says. "We would not joke about such a thing."

"No, of course not. But why? I mean—" But he turns away in response to a question from another attorney. Then I see that the prosecutor has moved away from Damien, and a wave of pure joy sweeps through me and I no longer care how or why.

"Damien," I say, and my voice sounds light. His name feels delicious on my lips, and I want to capture this moment and hold it close to me. This singular instant when I got back the man I feared that I had lost.

He begins to turn, and I anticipate how he will look when I see his face. His eyes alight with joy, his features stripped of the worry that has been weighing on him since the indictment came through.

But that is not what I see. Instead of warmth, I see a chill in his eyes. And there is nothing joyous in his expression. Instead, it is flat and cold and desolate.

I frown, confused, then rise and hurry to him. "Damien," I say, reaching out to take his hands. His fingers close tight around mine, as if I am a lifeline in stormy waters. "Oh, God, Damien. It's over."

"Yes," he says, but there is a harshness in his voice that sends a shiver through me. "It is."

Damien holds my hand, but says nothing during the ride back to the hotel. He is shell-shocked, I think. Probably unable to believe that the nightmare is really over.

We are alone—the attorneys having hung back to take care of all the administrative stuff that goes on once a trial reaches its conclusion, and I can only assume that there is even more to do when the conclusion is unexpectedly premature. I let the silence linger until we pull up in front of the hotel, but then I can't take it anymore.

"Damien, it's finished. Aren't you happy about that?" Personally, I'm about to explode simply from the joy of knowing that Damien is free and safe.

He looks at me, and for a moment his expression is blank. Then his face clears as he smiles. It's not huge, but it is real. "Yes," he says. "About that, I couldn't be happier."

"About that," I repeat, confused. "What else is there? What's going on? Why were the charges dismissed?"

But now the valet has opened the door, and Damien is sliding in that direction. I mutter a sharp curse and follow. Damien reaches for my hand to help me out, then twines his fingers in mine as we walk the short distance to the hotel entrance.

I'm so wrapped up in my storm of joy and confusion that it takes me a minute to realize that the walkway is lined with reporters, and that the hotel staff are making a human barrier to let us pass.

Damien was news when he was on trial for murder. Now that the charges have been dropped, he's an even bigger story.

The concierge greets us with a stack of messages that I take since Damien seems utterly uninterested. They are all congratulations, and the concierge himself adds his own. Damien replies politely, thanking the man, and then steers us toward the elevator.

"I thought we could stop in the bar for a drink," I say. It's a lie. I hadn't thought that at all. But I'm trying to get some sort of reaction from Damien, and at the same time I'm hating myself for manufacturing a scenario where he'll be forced to actively make a choice.

"Go ahead if you want."

"Alone?" I feel a bead of sweat trickle from my underarm down my side. I'm starting to panic.

"Ollie will be along any moment. I bet he'd be happy to have a drink with you."

"I don't want to have a drink with Ollie," I say, proud of myself for keeping my voice calm, when all I want to do is scream. Because the Damien who would willingly park me at a happy-hour table with Ollie McKee is not the Damien I know and love. I take a step closer to him. "Damien, please tell me what's wrong."

"I just need to get up to the room." The elevator car arrives, and as if in proof of his words, Damien steps inside.

I follow, then frown as my gaze takes in his face. For the first time I see the beads of perspiration at his hairline. I see his blood-shot eyes and pale, waxy skin. "Jesus, Damien," I say, reaching out to press my palm against his forehead as the elevator whisks us up to the Presidential Suite.

He turns away. "I don't have a fever."

"Then what the hell is it?"

For a moment, he says nothing. Then his shoulders rise and fall as he takes a deep breath. "I'm just upset."

"Upset?" I hear my voice rising and force myself to keep it down. "Because the charges were dropped?"

"No. Not because of that."

The elevator door opens, and I follow him into the hall, then halt at the door of our suite.

"Then what?" I ask as he slides his keycard into the lock. My speech is unnaturally calm. "Dammit, Damien, talk to me. Tell me what happened today."

The light turns green and he pushes open the door and steps into the suite. I am not sure if it's real or my imagination, but he seems unsure of his steps, as if he's afraid that the floor is going to disappear out from under him. I have never seen him like this, and he is starting to scare me.

He may say that he's upset, but I don't believe him. When Damien is upset, he lashes out. That famous temper rises and he takes control of the surroundings. Hell, he takes control of *me*.

But right now he looks as though control is slipping through his fingers like sand. This isn't upset—this is damn near shattered. And I am terribly, terribly afraid.

"Damien," I repeat. "Please."

"Nikki—"

He yanks me toward him and though I'm startled, I almost cry out with joy. *Yes,* I think. *Kiss me, touch me, use me.* Whatever he needs, I will give. And he knows that—dammit all, he knows it only too well.

But he does nothing. Nothing except thrust his fingers into my hair and hold me tight.

"Damien." His name feels ripped from me, and I force my head up, then crush my lips against his in a bruising kiss. He responds immediately, his mouth hard and demanding under mine, his hands on the back of my head forcing me closer. The kiss is brutal. Violent. Our teeth clash, he bites down on my lip, I taste blood, and I don't care. On the contrary, I feel as though I am soaring, set aloft by the passion in his touch, by the desire coursing through him.

His body is hard against mine, and one hand has moved down to cup my ass. He holds me hard against him, and I can feel his erection straining against his slacks. I grind against him, almost melting from the white-hot relief that boils within me. *He's back,* I think. *He's back.*

But it's only an illusion, because suddenly he's shoving me away, his eyes wild and lost, his breathing hard. He reaches to steady himself on the back of a chair and tilts his face away from me. But it's too late, I've seen too much, and what I saw in his eyes was horror.

I stand frozen, not by fear, but by the knowledge that right then I am impotent. He has shut me out, and I don't know the way back to him.

"Don't," I whisper. It is the only word I can manage and I have to force it past my lips.

I think that he will ignore me, but he looks up, and I gasp at the gray pallor of his skin. Immediately, I am at his side. I brush my palm over his cheek. His skin is cold and clammy.

"I'm calling the hotel doctor."

"No." He looks right at me and I see pain in his amber-colored eye, but the black one is as empty and distant as the night. He moves to the sofa and sits down, his elbows on his knees and his forehead in his hands.

"Damien, please. Can't you tell me what's going on? Can't you talk to me?"

He doesn't move. "No." That simple word slices through me, not quick and neat like sharpened steel, but hot and raw and brutal. A serrated blade across unprepared flesh. *I could do it,* I think. *Just one quick motion. I could do it, and I could follow the pain back here. Back to Damien. I need the anchor. I need—*

No!

I flinch and look away; if he looks up, I do not want him to see the direction in which my thoughts have traveled. I do not want him to see the effort it takes not to move. Not to bolt to the bathroom and dig into his brown leather shaving kit. Not to unscrew the top of his safety razor and remove the fresh blade, so small yet so sharp. So sweetly tempting . . .

I focus on breathing—on finding my center. I've come to rely on Damien's strength, and now I can't help but wonder if I'll ever be able to do this alone again.

He shifts on the sofa so that he is lying back, but his eyes are open and he reaches a hand out for me. I go and kneel at his side, holding tight to him, my heart swollen to bursting. I am terrified—so afraid that happiness is only fleeting and that the universe is in the process of self-correcting, and is transforming our story from a romance into a tragedy.

"I love you," I say almost desperately. What I mean is, *You're scaring me.*

He draws my hand up and softly kisses my knuckles. "I'm going to take a nap." His lids are heavy.

"Yes. Of course." It's an excuse that makes sense, and I pounce upon it and clutch it tight. After all, we didn't get much sleep last night, and I know that he did not sleep well even when we returned. I know, because I didn't either, and every time I woke up he was either awake and staring at the ceiling or tossing in the bed. He was calm only when he held me close.

It's that memory that soothes me. I do not know what is going on with Damien right now, but at the heart of it all, I know that he needs me as much as I need him.

I give his hand a squeeze before releasing it. I slide off his shoes, then grab a blanket and gently spread it over him. His eyes are already closed, his chest rising and falling in time with his breathing.

I start to tiptoe from the room into the bedroom, but as I do, I hear the familiar buzz of his phone. I curse and sprint back to the couch, because I do not want the phone to wake him.

I find his phone in the inside breast pocket of his jacket, and I pull it out. I don't recognize the number, and I press the button to answer, planning to take a message.

"Damien Stark's phone," I say softly as I move away so as not to wake him. I hear something that sounds like a sharp breath, and then nothing. "Hello?"

And then there is simply the dead silence of a dropped call. I frown slightly, but don't think much of it. Then I switch the ringer off and leave his phone on the worktable where he can easily find it.

I go into the bedroom and take off the conservative Chanel outfit I wore to court. I change into a bright yellow dress, hoping that the cheery color will improve my mood. I keep the pearl choker, my fingers drifting to it as I recall the texture of Damien's fingertips as he fastened it around my neck that morning. I lie on the bed and try to sleep, but sleep is not coming and my mood is not improving. Finally, I can take it no longer. I have to have answers, and I can think of only one way to get them.

I pull out my own phone and send a text—It's Nikki. I need to see you. Are you in the hotel? Can I meet you?

I hold my breath as I wait for the reply, hoping he will answer and not simply ignore my plea. So much time passes that I'm beginning to think that's exactly what he's going to do. Then the reply comes, and I sag with relief.

Room 315.

I gather my things and hurry to the elevator. I want to get there before he changes his mind. I stand by the elevator call button, my finger repeatedly jabbing the down arrow even though the light is already illuminated. Finally it comes, and I join a teenage couple who stand next to each other, his hands in her back jeans pocket and vice versa. The sight makes me smile, and I turn away, afraid that the simple public display of affection is going to make me cry.

I get off before them on the third floor and take a moment to get my bearings. Then I turn and hurry down the hall until I'm standing at the door to suite 315. I knock and wait, then sigh in relief when Charles Maynard opens the door and ushers me in.

"Thank you for seeing me," I say. "Damien is—well, he's asleep." It's a euphemism for "he's a wreck," and I think Maynard knows it.

He gestures toward the sofa. "Sit down. You want a drink? I just walked in the door when you texted. I was considering ordering a late lunch."

"I'm fine," I say as he walks to the wet bar and pours himself a very large Scotch.

"You must be relieved," Maynard says, which is probably the most ridiculous thing anyone has ever said to me.

"Of course I am," I snap, with more irritation than I intend.

He glances at me over the Scotch bottle. "Sorry. That sounded patronizing."

My shoulders sag. "I came here because I don't understand what happened. And I need to know. I need to know because Damien—"

But I can't finish the sentence. I can't say—even to this man who has known Damien since childhood—that for some reason this non-trial seems to have broken him.

At the same time, I can't leave. Maynard is my only chance for answers, and I cannot leave this room without some.

So I wait, and the only sound between us is the hum of the air conditioner. I fear that Maynard will say nothing, and that I will be forced to tell him how Damien walked through the hotel like a zombie. How he now lays asleep on the couch. How he seems shell-shocked, like someone who just went through a battle.

I don't want to tell him, because in some small way it feels like I am betraying Damien if I do. Damien Stark is not a man who shows weakness, and that he has shown me is only more proof that he trusts me. I can't break that trust now. But that leaves me tongue-tied, with no way to explain why I've come here.

Maynard, thank God, comes to my rescue.

"He's tied up in knots, I take it?"

"What happened back there? Why was the case dismissed?"

Maynard looks at me for a moment, and I can see that he is weighing whether or not to tell me.

"Please," I say. "Charles, I need to know."

One more moment passes, and then he nods. Just one quick movement of his head, but it seems to change everything. I feel lighter. My breathing comes easier. I lean forward, no longer caring what it is that he's going to tell me, but simply needing to hear the truth of it.

"The court received photographs and video footage," Maynard says. "That was what happened after the opening statement. The reason for the in-chambers conference. The images were shown to the prosecution and to the defense. In light of that evidence, the court decided to drop the charges."

"The court?" I say. "I thought who gets tried was always up to the prosecutor."

"Prosecutorial discretion is a broad power in the States," he says. "Not in Germany. The ultimate decision was up to the court, and both the prosecution and the defense presented quick arguments supporting the decision to dismiss."

I nod, not particularly interested in the legalities of *who* had the power to let Damien walk. I'm still hung up on the *why*.

"All right," I say stiffly. "So tell me what the photographs and videos show."

Maynard focuses on the papers on the coffee table, then reaches out to idly rearrange them. "Exactly what Damien didn't want to testify about. Things he wanted to keep private." He looks up at me. "Don't ask me to tell you more, Nikki. Just telling you that much pushes ethical boundaries."

"I see." The words are hard to force out past the knot of tears that has formed in my throat. I may not know exactly what's in those pictures, but I get the general idea. And I understand why seeing them would wreck Damien.

I stand, because right then all I want to do is return to him. To hold him and stroke him and tell him that it will all be okay. That nobody else knows.

Then a horrible thought occurs to me. "Will the court release that stuff?"

Maynard shakes his head. "No," he says firmly. "Damien was given the duplicate set, and the court has ordered the file copy sealed."

"Good." I take a step toward the door. "Thank you for telling me."

"Give him time, Nikki. It was a shock, but this doesn't really change anything. There wasn't anything in those photos that wasn't already in his past."

I nod, my heart breaking for the boy who had to live through that nightmare. "Thanks," I say again, then step out into the hall and pull the door closed behind me. I take a deep breath and lean back against the door frame. A shudder cuts through me, and I sag to the ground, my legs no longer able to hold me up. I press my forehead against my knees, wrap my arms around my legs, and cry.

No wonder Damien is wrecked. The one thing in all the world he didn't want made public came out of the sky like a meteorite and smashed him in the head. And, yeah, the photos are sealed now, but the judges saw them and the lawyers saw them. And someone out there had them. And that someone must still have copies.

Shit.

I need to go to him. I need to hold him and tell him that it will be okay, and I rise to my feet and move slowly to the elevator. I press the "up" arrow to call the elevator to take me back to the suite, then immediately curse my own selfishness. *I* need to go to him? *I* need to hold him? What Damien needs is rest—he as much as told me so himself. What I want—what I need—can wait.

With almost painful brutality, I jam my forefinger against the "down" button, but I don't want to wait. I need to move, and if I'm not moving toward Damien, I need to be going somewhere else. I shift my stance in the hallway, feeling suddenly at loose ends. At the end of the hall, a lighted sign marks the stairwell. I hurry in that direction, then slip off my shoes. I hold them by the heels and run down the three flights of stairs in my bare feet. It feels good—it feels right—and when I reach the bottom of the stairs, I slip my shoes back on and exit the stairwell into the lobby.

I am not sure what I intend to do. It has been such a long day and I am so exhausted that the sun shining through the windows of the hotel seems like an anomaly. But it is still early afternoon on a stunningly beautiful summer day.

I turn toward the entrance, but I'm stopped by the vibration of my phone. I yank it out of my purse expecting Damien.

It's a text from Ollie. Turn around.

I do. He's standing behind me, a few feet from the entrance to the bar. He lifts his hand and waves.

Despite myself, I grin and wave back.

He lifts his phone, and I see him typing another message. A second later, my phone buzzes.

Hey, lady. Can I buy you a drink?

I can't help it—I laugh. A little early, isn't it? I type, but the message doesn't send because my phone is dead. *Shit.* I think back and remember that I forgot to plug it in when we got back from the lake last night.

I hold it up so Ollie can see it and then, with an exaggerated gesture, I drop it from two fingers into my purse, as if I'm discarding something useless and slightly gross. Then I start walking toward him. He goes in ahead of me, and when I enter, I find him already sitting at the bar. The bartender comes up to us and slides a martini in front of Ollie and a bourbon on the rocks in front of me.

"Thanks," I say, speaking both to the bartender and to Ollie. "It's a little early."

"Doesn't feel like it," he says. "Not today."

I take a sip of the drink. "No," I agree. "It doesn't."

He stirs the martini with the olive-skewered toothpick. "I'm glad Stark's in the clear. I am. I swear."

I study his face, because I do not understand where this is coming from. But it is like a bright shiny sparkle of welcomeness in a shitty day that should have been an incredible one. So I do the only thing I can do—I smile and tell him thank you.

"I figured you'd be locked away celebrating," he says.

"Damien's asleep."

"Must be exhausted," Ollie says. "I am. It's been a hell of a wild ride."

This is small talk, and I can't stand it. "Do you know?" I demand. "Do you know why they dismissed the charges?"

He tilts his head as he studies me. "Is that really a line you want me to cross?"

I think about it. About how shattered Damien seems. I've refused to hear what Ollie's had to say about Damien in the past, but now I'm afraid that if I don't know exactly what is in those photos, I can't help.

"Yes," I say firmly. "I want to know."

He exhales loudly. "Oh, hell, Nikki. I don't know. For once, I can't tell you a damn thing. I'm sorry."

The wave of irritation I expect doesn't come. Instead, a swell of relief washes over me. Whatever is in those photos, I don't want Ollie to know. "It's okay," I say, then close my eyes. "It's okay."

He takes a long sip of his martini. "So, you want to go grab a late lunch? Hang out? Make up conversations between the folks at the other tables?"

My smile is tremulous. Part of me wants to say yes—wants to try and mend whatever has gone wrong between us. But the other part . . .

"No," I say with a shake of my head. "I'm not ready yet."

The muscles of his face seem to tighten in what might be a flinch. "Sure," he says. "No problem. We'll do it when we get home." He runs his fingertip idly around the rim of his martini glass. "So, have you been talking to Jamie?"

"Not a lot," I admit. "I've been preoccupied."

"I guess you have. She tell you that fuckwad Raine got her fired from the commercial?"

My shoulders sag. "Shit," I whisper. "When?"

"Right after you left."

"She didn't tell me." I know that she didn't want to bother me with it, what with Damien's trial, but I still feel like I've made a major best-friend blunder. "So, how's she doing?" I ask. "Has she been auditioning? Any other bites?"

"Don't know. I haven't seen her since. I'm staying away from temptation." He doesn't quite meet my eyes.

"There shouldn't be temptation," I say. "Not if Courtney really is the one."

"Is that really true?" He looks hard at me. "Or is that just a romantic myth?"

"It's true," I say, holding an image of Damien tight against my heart. "It's the truest thing in the world."

"Maybe you're right," he says, and my heart breaks a little because those words shouldn't make him sad. Not when he's about to get married.

He shakes his head as if clearing out cobwebs, then polishes off the rest of his drink. "I'm going to go lay on my bed, close my eyes, and feel the earth rotate. How about you?"

I think of Damien. If I go back, I'll want to touch him, if only to reassure myself that he is there and real. But he needs to sleep, and right now that is the only thing I am capable of giving him.

"I'm going out," I say. "I'm in need of some retail therapy."

5

I exit the hotel and turn left, then wander aimlessly down this polished street that I have walked so many times with Damien. Like Rodeo Drive and Fifth Avenue, Maximilianstrasse has its own rhythm, its own pace. And like those equally famous streets, it also has the pristine sheen of money. Last week, I held Damien's hand as we strolled and shopped. This street was like a magical place, banishing the dark gloom of the trial and giving us a few moments of light all wrapped up with a bright, shiny bow of luxury.

Today, I desperately want to return to that state of mind. To let the polished brass door handles and crystal-clear windows with ornate displays fill my head so that there is no room for my worries. It's not working, though, and this street that held fun and fantasy when Damien's hand was in mine now seems like nothing more than a crush of grasping, gaping people who are pushing and shoving, moving through the world with too much time and too little to do.

Dammit. I should be celebrating. Hell, *Damien* should be celebrating.

I walk a few blocks, past Hugo Boss and Ralph Lauren and Gucci until I reach a small gallery that Damien and I had popped into on my third day in Munich. The manager, a reedy man with an easy smile, greets me immediately. Considering he'd flirted shamelessly with Damien but essentially ignored me, I'm surprised he recognizes me. "*Fräulein!* It is so good to see you. But why are you not celebrating? And where is Mr. Stark? I was so pleased to see that he has been cleared."

"Thank you," I say, and I can't help but smile at his effusiveness. This is the kind of reaction I'd hoped to see from Damien. "He's asleep, actually. It's been an exhausting couple of weeks."

The manager nods knowingly. "And what can I do for you?"

I had entered on autopilot, but now that I'm here, I realize that I've come with a purpose. "You can ship, right?"

"Of course," he says, and he's polite and well-trained enough not to scoff at my idiotic question.

"I want to look at those black-and-white prints," I say, pointing toward the room where Damien and I had spent over an hour gazing at the brilliantly executed photos from a local Munich photographer.

I followed Damien to Germany so quickly that I forgot to bring my own camera, and even though this is hardly a trip that rates a flurry of souvenir snapshots, there have been moments when I regretted not having it. For years, a camera has been my security blanket. First, the Nikon that my sister Ashley gave me during my freshman year of high school. More recently, the digital Leica that Damien presented me in Santa Barbara, an amazing gift that reflected just how well the man understood me—and how much he wanted to please me.

Now it is Damien I want to please. Though he isn't comfortable behind the camera, he has excellent taste in the resultant images, and we had both been impressed by the astounding composition and ethereal lighting of this series of photographs.

I pause in front of one that shows the sun descending behind a mountain range. Bands of light seem to shoot out from the image, and though the shadows are deep, every nuance of the stony mountain face can still be discerned. It is beautiful and dark and romantic and edgy. It reminds me of Damien. Of the times that he has held me close and softly whispered that between us, the sun is never going down.

Now I want to give him this photo. I want to hang it in the bedroom of his Malibu house, a reminder of all that is between us. I want us both to know that even in the dark there will always be the light, and that no matter what, we will continue on forever. I want an image that says *I love you*.

"It is a beautiful print," the manager says from behind me. "And a limited edition."

"How much?"

He quotes me the price and I come genuinely close to having heart failure. But except for the Lamborghini rental, I have spent none of my million on frivolous things, and besides, this image isn't frivolous. As I turn once again to look at the photograph, I realize that it feels strangely important, and I know that if I walk away I will regret it every time I look at the walls of the Malibu house and see that it is not there.

I shift again to smile at the manager, but end up looking out the window instead. A woman stands there, the brim of her hat pressed against the glass as if she is trying to peer into the gallery. There's nothing intrinsically odd about that—after all, most people do look through gallery windows—but there is something about her that looks familiar. And there is something in her stance that suggests that it's not the photographs she is looking at, but me.

I shiver, suddenly and unreasonably disturbed.

"Fräulein?"

"What? Oh, sorry." I turn my attention to the manager, but

my eyes dart back to the woman. She pulls away from the window and walks on. I exhale with relief, then mentally shake myself. I am being ridiculous. I aim a smile at my companion. "Yes," I say firmly. "I'll take it."

The manager only nods his head in polite acquiescence, but I am struck by the thought that inside he is leaping with glee, and I can't help my grin.

"The photographer will be in town this weekend. Would you like me to have him sign it to you and Mr. Stark?"

"That would be wonderful. Do you have a piece of paper?"

He does, of course, and while he inflicts serious damage on my credit card, I write out the shipping address and the notation that I'd like the artist to add.

"Have a good day, *Fräulein,*" he says as I leave. "And please tell Mr. Stark how happy I am for him."

"I will," I say, stepping back out onto the Maximilianstrasse. Less than an hour ago, this spectacular street had seemed gloomy. Now, everything seems a bit brighter. I continue my walk, this time paying more attention to the stores I'm passing. I pause in front of windows to look at purses and dresses and suits for Damien. Twice, I think I see the woman in the hat, but when I turn to look, I see no one. I frown, because I'm not prone to seeing phantom women, so I am certain that I am not imagining her.

I doubt very seriously that it is truly me that is of interest to her. Instead, I'm betting that she's a reporter. And she knows that if she follows me long enough, eventually, she will find Damien. I consider marching up to her and telling her that I don't appreciate the stalker vibe, but though I pay attention to the faces on the street and the reflections in the windows, I don't see her again.

I wander the main avenue and side streets for almost three hours before I can't take it any longer. I know that Damien needs to sleep, but I also need Damien. Selfish, yes, but I have held back for as long as I can.

I've almost reached the hotel when I remember a small boutique that Damien and I had noticed one evening as we were walking back from dinner, and I decide to squeeze in one more stop before returning. I wave to the valet as I pass in front of the Kempinski, then hurry across the street and down the two blocks to Marilyn's Lounge, a high-end lingerie store. I don't know if sexy lingerie will help wrest Damien from his funk, but I doubt it will hurt.

As I reach the store, I catch a quick glimpse of raven-black hair. *Damien?* I hesitate, then lift myself up on my toes, trying to see more clearly over the crush of people on the street, but I see no sign of him.

Still, Damien and the unidentified woman have become juxtaposed in my thoughts, and I can't shake the strange sense of foreboding. I frown, feeling foolish, and push through the door and into Marilyn's Lounge.

A willowy blonde with cat-like eyes approaches me right away, and when I tell her I'm looking for seductive sleepwear in which I don't intend to actually sleep, she flashes a brilliantly white smile. "You have come to the right place, Ms. Fairchild."

I manage not to react. By now, I really should be used to the celebrity factor.

She devotes her full attention to me, leaving her dark-haired companion to scurry between the half dozen other women who are eyeing these tiny bits of satin and lace. Some wear expressions of shocked interest. Others have the bland faces of veterans to the art of seduction. The youngest is looking only at white baby-doll nighties, and I immediately peg her as a bride.

I do not have time to bond with my co-shoppers, however, because my tour guide is a strict taskmistress. She whips out a measuring tape and orders me to stretch out my arms. Then she moves in and gets more intimate than anyone except Damien has in a long time. She announces my bra size—which I already knew—and proceeds to lead me through the store, plucking up camisoles with matching skirt-style garter belts, open cup bras, body stockings, baby-doll nighties, and even a variety of retro lingerie that makes me think of Rita Hayworth or the other classic movie pinup queens.

By the time she finally sweeps me into a dressing room that resembles a small hotel room, I have decided that I am not the expert shopper I always thought I was. She has completely exhausted me, and it is with both amusement and relief that I eye the bucket of ice that holds an uncorked bottle of champagne. There are two crystal flutes on a nearby marble table, along with a pitcher of orange juice. The juice is clearly to remedy the extreme drop in blood sugar brought about by too much exertion. The champagne is to loosen the wallet.

While I pour myself a mimosa—after all, my wallet was loose when I walked through the door—my personal shopper hangs negligees, nighties, and sultry camis on a bar. She places the monogramed canvas shopping basket on the floor. It is full to the brim with what might appear at first glance to be mere scraps of material, but actually constitutes a variety of sexy underthings. And should I become exhausted from climbing into and out of such decadent clothing, I can relax on the chaise lounge that dominates the back half of the dimly lit room.

If the lingerie business starts to stall, Marilyn's can just rent out their dressing rooms as high-end housing.

The first outfit is made from a sheer black material that is so soft it feels as though I am wearing a cloud. It's a little bit longer than a baby-doll style, hitting me just a bit higher than mid-thigh. It boasts a swishy skirt and a fitted bodice that manages to make my breasts—which aren't too shabby to begin with—look even bigger and perkier. I hold the thong-style panties up to see the effect, and I have to admit I like it. And though I'm technically failing Lingerie Etiquette 101 by doing it, I go ahead and step into the thong. Why not, since I've already decided to buy the outfit?

The thong is little more than a tiny triangle of material held in place by a stretchy black string. I twirl slowly, checking out the look in the Hollywood diva style three-way mirror that stands in one corner of the room. Honestly, it doesn't look half bad. More important, I think Damien will like seeing me in it—and seeing me out of it.

I'm grinning, and about to extricate myself from the bodice so that I can try on the next outfit, when the salesgirl taps on the door. "I found something else you might like. May I come in?"

"Sure. Thanks." I tug the top back down so that I'm fully covered—at least as fully covered as one can be wearing a see-through, low-cut, semi-baby-doll nightie—and watch as she opens the door. I expect frills and lace and silks and satins. What I see instead is Damien.

"Oh!"

His eyes are fixed on my face, the near-black one seeming to reach all the way into my heart, and the amber one so soft with apology that I think I'm going to cry. He steps inside the room and my head goes weak, as if all the air has been sucked out of the space. "I thought you might need a second opinion," he says, his mouth curving into a half-smile.

"I—yes. That would be great." I am a tongue-tied mess. My gaze darts to the salesgirl, who grins and backs away, shutting the door behind her. "Um, are you allowed to be here?"

"Apparently I am." He takes a step toward me, full of that Damien-esque arrogance I know so well.

I grin. In relief, in excitement, in joy.

"I'm sorry." His simple words seem to burst with emotion.

"You don't have anything to be sorry for," I say. His face doesn't change, but I see the smile touch his eyes, and my relief grows exponentially. "How did you know where to find me?"

He moves forward again, this time stopping only inches from me. My body thrums merely from his proximity. I want to launch myself into his arms, but I stand motionless. Today, it must be Damien who makes the first move.

"I've told you before that I'll always find you." His words are as soft as the silk on my body, and just as intimate. It occurs to me that the valet probably mentioned seeing me, but it doesn't matter. Nothing matters right now except the desire that burns in his eyes. It is more dangerous than the wildest flame, but I don't care. On the contrary, I am craving the heat. He may have doused that fire back in the hotel, but it is back tenfold now, and all I want is for it to burn free. To engulf the two of us and render us to cinders.

Slowly, his gaze skims over me and this barely-there outfit. He doesn't touch me, but that doesn't matter. My skin tingles anyway, and the tiny hairs on my arms and the back of my neck rise from the charged energy that crackles in this room. It's a good thing I'm buying these panties, because I am already wet simply from being near him. "We're going to end up in the tabloids again," I whisper.

He shakes his head. "I can be very persuasive when I try. She won't say a thing."

"Is that a fact? Just how persuasive were you, Mr. Stark?"

"Persuasive to the tune of a thousand euros." His eyes crinkle as he grins. "She'll ensure our privacy. From the press and from her own curiosity. Of course," he adds as he finally reaches out to touch me, "the more interesting question is what does she think is going on in this small, private room?"

"I'm sure she has a very vivid imagination," I say dryly.

"Really?" Damien appears to consider the possibility. "Maybe she thinks I'm touching you like this," he says as his fingertip moves slowly over the swell of my breast. I draw in a sharp breath, fighting the riot of sensations that threaten to overwhelm me. The black nightie is designed for maximum lift, and is cut so low that it barely contains me. I'm breathing hard, and that only increases the illusion that I'm about to spill out over the cups. My nipples are hard beneath the material, and when he slides his hands down and catches them between his thumbs and forefingers, I have to bite back a small cry of pleasure.

"Or maybe she's imagining my mouth on your breasts," he murmurs, his lips caressing me in potent illustration of his words. "Or maybe she's a bit more naughty, and she's picturing my hand sliding down your abdomen, your skin quivering beneath my fingers, your breath coming faster and faster until my fingertip finds the tiny bit of elastic that is holding those panties up."

His fingers slip ever so slightly under the band of the thong, and my breath hitches. "Damien." His name is barely a word. It's a sigh, a groan. Hell, it's a demand.

His hand is inside the thong now, the other supporting me at the small of my back, because without that insistent pressure, I will surely collapse. "Does she wonder if I'm easing my hand down, if my finger is skimming lightly over your damp pubic hair? Does she know how hard your clit is, how turned on you are?"

My body shudders in silent answer.

He bends forward, his finger still teasing my clit as his lips brush my ear. "Does she know how wet and ready you are for me? Does she know how much you want to come for me?"

In time with his words, he thrusts his finger inside of me. I cry out and arch back, my body tightening around him. "Is this what she's imagining?" he asks, his voice as erotic as his touch. "My fingers inside you, playing with you, making you just a little bit crazy?"

I can't answer. I can barely think past the electrical storm that is building inside me, much less form words. I am lost to his touch, lost to the rising pressure of an inevitable and explosive release. I'm so close, and Damien's hands upon me—his finger stroking me—feel so good. I want to stay like that, lost in this sensual limbo, and at the same time I want the crescendo. I want to explode in the circle of Damien's arms.

"Come on, baby," he demands. "Come for me."

His mouth closes over mine as his finger slides deeper inside me, the pressure of his thumb upon my clit increasing. It's as if he's hit some magic combination, and I feel the hot sparks of my orgasm shooting through me, so wild and violent I wonder if I will spontaneously combust.

Slowly, he withdraws his fingers, and I can't help but whimper. "Was that what she's been imagining?" he whispers. "That salesgirl who knows there's something naughty going on behind this door?"

I shake my head, forcing uncooperative words to my lips. "Not quite," I say. "She's imagining your hands on her, not on me."

"Is she?" His brows lift slightly as if the possibility hadn't even occurred to him. I can't help but laugh. Damien knows damn well the effect he has on women. "Well, she can have whatever fantasies she wants." He pulls me closer and holds me tight. "You're my reality."

"And you're mine," I say, feeling right then like the luckiest girl on the planet. Damien is safe and this afternoon's funk seems like nothing more than a bad dream. Most of all, I am in his arms. There may be other shit going on, but all that can wait for later. For right now, I am content.

"Of course, there is one small matter we need to discuss," Damien says, his voice suddenly stern. I look up, not certain if he's serious or teasing, but his eyes reveal nothing. He hooks a finger under the elastic and lightly snaps the band of my thong. "I seem to recall a certain agreement that ensured unfettered access whenever and however I wanted."

I force my expression to remain as bland as his. "Unless I was imagining all that just happened, I think it's fair to say that these panties don't fetter in the least."

I step back, then run the tip of my forefinger lightly over the soft skin between my pubis and my thigh, tracing gently along the edge of that minute triangle of material. I aim my most sultry look at him. "Besides, what's the point of having rules if you don't break them on occasion?"

"You make an interesting point." He looks me up and down, the slow inspection making my body tingle again. Then he moves to the far side of the dressing room and squats down to look at the contents of the canvas shopping basket. His back is to me, but he is at an angle, so I can see his muscular legs straining against the now-tight denim of his jeans. The material curves the cup of his rear, too, and I imagine that I have moved behind him. That I am lowering myself until my lips are pressed to the back of his neck, the short bit of hair that brushes his collar teasing my lips. I close my hands gently and let my fingertips graze my own palms as I imagine my hands cupping his rear, not just to balance myself, but because I am compelled to touch him. And because I want to turn him on.

I swallow, lost in the fantasy, but not yet ready to move to him and make it reality. I am enjoying the anticipation too much, not to mention the decadent pleasure of watching Damien's body straining against that lucky, lucky denim.

He lifts his hand, a lacy thong dangling from his finger like an enticement. "Interesting," he says, then repeats the process, pulling out the expensive scraps of silk and satin that constitute underwear and bras in all shapes and sizes. Some barely there. Some that create more cleavage than the law should allow. Some that would have my breasts spilling out over the tops. Some that, if the gleam in Damien's eye is any indication, are very intriguing indeed.

He stands, a red thong and matching red push-up bra hanging from two extended fingers. "I think perhaps it's time to amend our deal, Ms. Fairchild. As much as I appreciate the possibilities associated with complete access, there is something to be said for the pleasure of the journey." He extends his empty hand to me. "Come here," he says, and I comply obediently.

"I'll go with you anywhere," I whisper. "I'll do anything for you. You know that, right?"

With a violence I'm not expecting, he tugs me to him, capturing me within the circle of his arms. We are tight together, my breasts against his chest, my nipples hard. I feel the press of his erection hot and hard against my very scantily clad body, and that rush of tactile pleasure is accompanied by an even greater one. The pleasure of knowing that I am his and that he is mine.

He tilts his head so that his forehead presses gently against mine, then sighs deeply. "I thought you'd gone."

I blink, confused, and ease backward, then wait a single heartbeat for him to lift his head and meet my eyes.

"I woke up and you weren't there," he says in explanation. "I talked to Charles and he told me you'd come by. That he'd told you about the photos and videos." He shakes his head and laughs without humor. "I thought you were so disgusted by them that you'd left me."

I look at him hard. "I wasn't the one who went away," I say, my voice level and firm. "You're the one who left. I stayed." I swallow and blink back tears. "I stayed because I knew you would come back to me."

"I will always come back," he says, and in those simple words I hear both understanding and apology.

I nod, then clutch his hand. "I didn't see the photos," I say.

"But no matter what is in them, I would never have left you. I just thought you needed sleep." I look away, not meeting his eyes. Because the words that I am biting back are just too damn selfish. *I didn't think you needed me.*

"I wanted you, Nikki," he says, as if in answer to my thoughts. "I wanted to pull you close and strip you naked. I wanted to tie you up and run my fingers over every inch of you. I wanted to bury my face between your legs and bring you to the brink over and over again, never quite letting you come."

I swallow. I am suddenly very, very warm.

"I wanted every sensation you experienced—every spark of pleasure, every hint of pain—to come from me. I wanted to fuck you until you begged me to stop and then I wanted to fuck you some more. Everything you felt, everything you wanted, everything you desired—I wanted it to be wrapped up in my touch, in my bed. I wanted to fuck you until there was nothing left but you and me. Until the whole goddamn world was erased."

"Why didn't you?" My mouth is dry and I have to force the words out.

He doesn't answer.

I take a step closer, pushing through the thick, charged air that fills the space between us. "Whatever you need from me, all you have to do is take it. You know that."

"I couldn't," he says, and his voice is harsh. "I couldn't bear to have you in my arms when those images were in my head."

"I—oh." I am not sure what to say to that, so I say nothing. Just settle my cheek against his chest and listen to his heartbeat and the steady rhythm of his breath.

After a moment, he continues, his voice eerily steady. "Those images are like scenes from a horror movie. They show what Richter did, and how he did it. They show degradation and they show pain, and I will never, ever put those images in your hands. I won't let you look at even one of them. Imagine what you want, but I don't want the reality of my past haunting your present the way they haunt mine."

"All right," I say, because I don't want to see them any more than he wants to show them. I stand a bit straighter. "But, Damien, if it will help you, then show them to me. I can handle it."

"No," he says with a slow shake of his head. "I don't want you to have to handle it. That's the horror of my past. But you . . . you're the reality of my present. You're the proof that I survived. The prize in the cereal box," he adds with an impudent grin, but it quickly fades. "Hopefully you won't see them anyway."

"Why would I?"

"Whoever sent that evidence to the court must still have copies." It is the bland, unemotional quality of his voice that tells me how much he hates that simple truism.

"But surely that person will protect them, right? I mean, those pictures have existed for almost two decades. They only surfaced when you were in trouble."

"In my experience," Damien says, "unearthed things have a tendency to remain unearthed."

I have no counter to that. "Do you have any idea who it was?"

"No." The answer comes a little too quick.

"There can't be that many people who know about—" I cut off my words. Though we are talking all around his abuse, I don't want to voice it. "Your father, maybe? He was desperate to keep you from being tried." Jeremiah Stark wasn't concerned about Damien's neck, but his own well-being. The end result, however, was the same.

"It's possible," Damien says. It's clear he doesn't want to talk about this.

"I just want it to be over for you," I say, more than happy to drop this topic for the time being. "You deserve happiness, Damien."

"So do you," he says, looking at me with such intensity that it almost seems like he is imagining each of my scars in turn.

"Then it's lucky we found each other," I say, because I don't want to think about the past that I have worked so long to leave behind. I'm only interested in the future with Damien.

His hands slide over my back, then up under the flimsy outfit to caress my bare skin. Slow, heated caresses that go on and on until I just want to rip the damn nightgown off and feel his hands over every inch of me.

"Do you know what I want right now?" he murmurs.

"Probably the same thing I do," I say, then skip back out of the circle of his arms. "But we're still in a dressing room."

He steps closer, his eyes darkening. "I believe I explained how much privacy a thousand euros can buy."

"You explained very well," I concede. "But we have a lot of celebrating to do. And you deserve more than a fast fuck in a dressing room."

"As it happens, it's not a fast fuck that I want."

"Oh?" I ask, innocently hooking my arms around his neck. I press my hips against him and move in a lazy grinding motion. "What exactly do you want?"

His hands slide slowly down over my ass, stilling me, but also pressing me up hard against him. I feel his erection straining against his jeans, hot and demanding. "You," he says simply. "I want you naked, Nikki. Naked and hot and wet for me. I want to hear you moan. Hell, I want to hear you beg. And I promise you, baby, there will be nothing fast about it."

6

"There," he says, as soon as we are back in our suite. He is pointing to the area in front of the window, and I go without hesitation. The drapes are open, and the window of our fifth-floor suite overlooks the Maximilianstrasse. "That's it," he says. "I want to watch as the sky darkens and the city lights rise behind you. I want to see the sunset reflected on your skin and the glitter of the nightlife shining in your hair."

He strides toward me, all strength and power and a confidence that borders on arrogance. This is not the man who spent weeks at the mercy of the German court system only to have his freedom lobbed at him by a stranger. No, this is the man who built an empire. A man with strength enough to beat back the demons I saw this afternoon.

I look at him and feel no chill lingering from the nightmarish shadows that obscured him from me. There is only Damien now. The man that I know—the man that I crave.

This is the Damien who takes charge—who simply *takes*.

Tonight, all I want is for him to take me.

My body trembles as he approaches, his eyes never leaving

mine. He reaches out, and his fingertips brush my neck, flicking lightly over the pearl necklace that I still wear. It is the slightest of contact, but it reverberates through me like an explosion.

I suck in air and tilt my head to the side, elongating my neck for him. My breath is ragged, my skin on fire. He leaves a trail of goose bumps on my neck before his fingertips gently graze the weave of my dress along my shoulder, and then once again stroke my sensitive skin to travel down my bare arm.

He breaks contact and steps away, and I want to weep from the loss.

"Yes," he says, as if in answer to some question of his own. "This is how I want to see you, standing naked before the world. I want to look at you and know that you are mine."

"You know I am." My words are soft, barely a whisper.

"Say it," he says.

"I'm yours," I say, because I mean it. More than that, I understand why he wants to hear it. He's taking back the control that had been wrenched from him—and he's taking it back through me.

He moves his hand to the zipper at the back of my dress, then slowly tugs it down. Slowly, he brushes the dress off my shoulders. It falls to the floor, the circle of yellow like the petals of a flower. I am left in my newly purchased underwear. A demi-cup bra in a deep purple and matching thong panties. Damien looks me up and down, and there is no mistaking the heat in his eyes.

"Come with me." He takes my hand and leads me a few steps closer to the window. It's not floor to ceiling, but it's close. We are right up against it. Another step and the window ledge would hit me just above the knees. Damien is behind me, his hands on my shoulders and the denim of his jeans rough and cool against my bare ass. In front of us, Munich is spread wide.

Slowly, Damien reaches around and unfastens the front clasp of my bra then eases the straps off my arms. He drops the garment to the floor as I instinctively try to cover myself. "No," he says simply as he slides his arms down along mine, then holds me firmly at the wrists, my arms now at my sides.

"But the window," I say, looking out at the stores and offices that rise around us. "The other buildings."

"No one is watching. The glass is tinted, and there are no lights in here. No one can see."

I relax infinitesimally.

"But even if they could . . ." His voice trails off as he releases my wrists. His hands stroke my body, one trailing up until he finds my breast and the tight, puckered skin of my areola. The pad of his thumb flicks roughly over my nipple, and I gasp from the deep, decadent pleasure. His other hand slides down until his fingers sneak under the band of the thong to brush over my damp, trimmed pubic hair. He teases me, his fingers forming a V as he glides over my folds, coming so tantalizingly close to my clit that I want to cry out in frustration and beg him to please, just touch me.

"What if that's what I wanted?" he whispers. He presses his lips to the back of my neck, then lowers himself to trail kisses down my spine, leaving me shivering in the wake of his touch. The sun has dipped below the horizon, and the world outside is fast darkening, turning our window into a mirror. I meet my own eyes in the reflection, and see my features soft with desire.

"What if I want you naked before the world, your legs parted, your cunt wet for me?" He is behind me, his hands stroking the curve of my hips. His breath teases the small of my back as much as his decadent words tease my imagination. I have never fanta-sized about exhibitionism, but right now, I am having a hard time thinking of anything but Damien touching me, Damien fucking me. I don't give a damn about the windows, tinted or not. I don't care who sees, I only want to surrender to Damien's touch. His hands on me, his tongue stroking me, his cock deep inside me.

"Damien—" The word feels wrenched from me.

"Does it excite you?" he asks as he slowly stands, his body sliding against mine as he rises, the brush of his clothing rough against my skin. "Not knowing who might be watching, but knowing that I want you like this? That I want the whole god-damned universe to look down on us and know that no matter what, you belong to me?" He rests his left hand on my hip, his thumb hooked in the thong's band. The other hand brushes over my belly, then eases down under the triangle of silk again.

I'm desperately wet, almost painfully turned on, and I silently pray for his touch, but once again it doesn't come. Instead, I hear only his words. "I want you to tell me, Nikki. Does it turn you on?"

God, yes. I have to fight to speak. "Keep going," I manage. "Touch me and see for yourself."

I hear his smile reflected in his chuckle. His fingers brush my skin, but he's not going south. "Not unless I hear you say it."

"Yes," I breathe.

His lips are in my hair, and I feel the reverberation of his words as he whispers, "Me, too."

I close my eyes, expecting his touch. Craving it. But still it doesn't come. Instead, I feel the brush of his fingers over the band of this brand-new thong—and then the pressure as he rips it at the back seam. I gasp—surprised, yes, but also aroused by the violence of the action and by the rush of cool air against my damp sex as he pulls the panties away.

"What are you—?"

"Shhh," he says. "Lean forward, hands on the window. No, don't argue. Beautiful," he adds when I comply, then punctuates his words by stroking my now completely bare ass. "Now spread your legs for me. Oh, God, Nikki," he groans. "Do you have any idea how much I want you?"

"You have me."

He slides his hands up over my hips, trailing up the curve of my waist. He presses his body against mine, his torso against my back and his hands upon my breasts. "I do," he says. "But I'm not taking you. Not yet."

A tremor runs through me, part frustration, part anticipation. I am so hot, so ready, and I do not know what to expect or where he is taking this. I only know that I want to find out.

He stands upright again, then circles me, finally stopping near my right hand, still splayed out against the window. "I like this," he says, reaching out to run his finger along the pearl necklace that is the only thing I still wear. "It is said that oysters are a potent aphrodisiac, but I think that pearls are equally enticing. It's rumored that Cleopatra crushed one and drank it in wine in order to render herself irresistible to Mark Antony. But I think I prefer them as an adornment. For that matter, I can think of a few other adornments that I would like to see."

"Damien—" I stop myself because I don't know what I want to say other than to beg.

"Stay put," he says. "Don't touch yourself. Don't put your legs together. You'll come when I let you, Nikki, but not before. Break my rules, and I promise you won't like the punishment."

I swallow and nod. "But where are you going?" I call as he disappears into the bedroom. I get no answer, and I close my eyes in frustration, hyperaware of every inch of my body. Of the dampness at the back of my neck along my hairline. Of the tiny hairs upon my skin, standing up as if electrified, caught up in this storm that is Damien. Mostly, I am aware of the aching in my cunt.

I do not touch, though I desperately want to, and I am aware of every movement of my body, every brush of air. I can feel my pulse beating in my sex, and my muscles clenching with longing. I am need personified—and what I need is Damien.

He is only gone for minutes, but it seems like I am waiting for hours, lost with my own reflection. A nude woman against a shiny surface, a dream world of city lights blazing behind her. I am like a woman from one of Blaine's paintings, forever captured by his brush in a state of arousal, never quite able to reach satisfaction.

No, I think. Please don't let Damien be teasing me like that.

When he returns, he has something in his hand. He sets it on the table behind me. I can't see what it is, but I think I hear the clink of metal upon metal.

"Damien?" I ask, my voice wary. "What are you doing?"

He comes around in front of me, then gently takes my hands off the glass, easing me back up straight. A slow grin lights his face, and I see both amusement and heat in those beautiful eyes. I expect his answer before he says it—"What I want, Nikki. Always, what I want."

I lick my lips. "And what is that?"

"To give you pleasure." He moves behind me, to the table, then returns with something in his hand. "Do you remember this?"

He opens his hand to reveal a silver serpentine chain connected by two rings, each with two small metal balls on them. The balls pull apart, creating an opening, then snap back together when the pressure is released. They are nipple clamps, and I shiver from the memory of that exquisite bite of pain mixed with pleasure.

He brushes his thumb over my now painfully erect nipple. "Oh, yes," he says. "I think you remember just fine."

I moan as he slowly caresses my breast. "How did those get here?"

His chuckle seems to roll over me. "It's been almost a month, Nikki. I had Gregory pack and ship a few things. Including the small leather case I keep in my closet."

"Oh." I wet my lips. "That was very efficient of you."

"I'm a man who likes to plan ahead." He catches my nipple between his thumb and forefinger, then squeezes tight. I gasp, relishing the sharp sensation, the pleasure edging toward pain. With his fingers tight, he rolls the hard nub and I bite down on my lip as electricity sparks through me, racing from my breasts to my wet, throbbing cunt.

"Damien." I'm not sure what I'm demanding. I can barely form thoughts, much less words. All I know is desire. All I want is more.

Hell, all I want is everything.

As if in answer to my demand, Damien spreads the rounded ends of the ring, then gently releases it, causing the cold silver to clamp against my nipple. There's more pressure now than Damien had applied, and I suck in air, surprised at first by the fiery pain. It fades soon, though, and I moan in pleasure at the warmth that ripples through me as my body adjusts to the tantalizing torture.

"We've gone so far together, Nikki," he murmurs as he attaches the other one. "I'm going to take you even farther. I want to balance on the edge with you, and see you open and wide and wild."

My breathing is ragged. I'm hyperaware of my breasts, of his touch. And when he slides his hand down between my ass cheeks, his fingers finally—*finally*—finding me hot and wet and wanting, I cannot help but moan aloud.

"I want to give you everything, Nikki," he says, as his thumb brushes my anus, and I feel the slick lube of my own arousal. "I want the universe spread wide before you. And I want to be the one who sends you tumbling over, shooting off into space, without control, without inhibitions." I feel the firm increase of pressure, then gasp as something small and well-lubed slips inside my rear.

"And, Nikki," he says, his voice rough with passion, "I want to be the one who tethers you and brings you back."

"You are," I whisper. I am as unraveled by his words as I am by the riot of sensations storming through me. "Oh, God, Damien, you know you are. I'm lost without you."

He moves to face me, then strokes my cheek. With a fervency I don't expect, he pulls me close. I gasp as my raw, chained nipples rub against his shirt, but he silences me with a long, almost violent kiss.

"Please," I beg when he releases me. I am helpless, I am melting. The pressure on my nipples sends shocks arcing through my body. That wicked plug fills me, opening me, making me hyper-aware of every movement and sensation.

"Please what?" he whispers. "Tell me what you want, Nikki."

"You, Damien. Always you—only you. I want you to touch me." I reach for him, fisting my hands in his T-shirt. "I want you to fuck me because I'm not entirely sure I can survive without feeling you inside me right now."

"I want that, too," he says, and I sag with relief. "But we're going to have to risk your imminent demise," he adds with a very wicked grin. "Because I have something else in mind first."

According to the concierge at our hotel, Club P1 is one of the hottest nightclubs in Munich. The venue is huge and crowded, and the patrons are as polished and bright as the modern interior. It's funky and fun—and at the moment, I couldn't care less. My body is too on fire, too teased by Damien's sweet torture.

The limo ride was bad enough, with Damien demanding that I sit with my knees apart and my hands on either side of me, palms on the soft leather of the seat. He'd dressed me in a shelf bra before we left, leaving my still-chained nipples exposed. In the limo, they brushed against the black silk of my beaded tank top, the sensation making me squirm. And *that* caused all sorts of other shocks and quivers and pulses to ricochet through my body.

Damien sat across from me, sipping Scotch and watching me

with such raw passion that I spent the entire ride in a constant state of unsatisfied arousal.

The ride, thank God, was short, but now that we are here I want nothing more than to go back to the hotel. Dancing, drinking—none of that holds any appeal. All I want is Damien's mouth on mine, his hands on my bare skin, and his cock deep inside me.

Unfortunately, I don't think I'll be getting what I want anytime soon, and so I draw in a breath and try to focus despite this sensual haze in which I am currently living. "You're glowing," Damien says, his mouth curving into a self-satisfied smile.

"Glowing?" I repeat. "Jesus, Damien, I'm practically radioactive."

"Mmm," he says, looking me up and down. "So I see." He pulls me to one side so that my back is up against a smooth wooden wall. He presses his hands to either side of me and leans in close. "A bit on edge, Ms. Fairchild?"

"Just a tad." I catch the scent of him—the whiskey on his breath, the deep, spicy musk of his arousal—and it works upon me like the most potent of aphrodisiacs. In addition to my sparkly black top, I am decked out in a black leather miniskirt, thigh-high stockings, a tiny red thong, and very high, very fuckable heels. I take one step away from the wall and lift myself on those heels, gripping Damien's shoulders for balance. "I'm still trying to decide if I should thank you for this," I whisper. "Or if I should figure out a way to get revenge."

"While I'm very intrigued by the possibility of being at your mercy," he says, "we both know that you're as turned on as I am." He slides an arm around my waist and pulls me toward him. Our hips meet, and I can feel his erection pressing hard against my belly.

"I am," I admit, sliding my hand down between our bodies to stroke his cock through his jeans. The corner is dark and secluded, but I think I would have stroked him even if we were on the dance floor. I am intoxicated by lust, emboldened by passion. And since Damien isn't shifting my hand away, I know that he is, too.

"I'm hot and horny and desperately wet," I murmur, moving my hand in time with my words. I feel him grow even harder and I smile with the knowledge of my own power. "Do you know what I wanted in the limo, Damien? I wanted you on your knees in front of me. I wanted your hands on my thighs spreading me wide, and I wanted your tongue on my clit."

He is close enough that I can feel the quickening of his pulse and his quick shallow breaths. "I wanted to feel my nipples tighten when you tugged on this chain, and my body tense around this plug when you made me come, so hard and so fast that you'd have to carry me into this club."

"Holy fuck," he whispers, his voice so soft I can barely hear it.

"So yes," I continue, as if I hadn't even heard him. "I am turned on." I stroke his cock slowly, because at least for this one moment, I have turned the tables on Damien Stark. "But what I wanted I didn't get. And *that,* Mr. Stark, is why I want revenge."

"You make a very sound argument, Ms. Fairchild."

"I pride myself on my sharp business skills."

He steps back from me, his eyes gleaming mischievously, then holds out his hand. "Come with me."

"Where are we going?"

"Come with me and find out."

He leads me through the crowded club full of beautiful people who are much more interested in each other than us. I'm relieved. We do not look like the Nikki and Damien who have been in the German news. I'm in my Girl Goes Clubbing outfit and Damien is casual in jeans and a light jacket over a T-shirt, not to mention a day's worth of beard stubble. That's not to say that I haven't seen a few heads turn when we pass, but I think that is more a product of Damien's astounding good looks than his status as either a celebrity billionaire or as a man who narrowly escaped a murder charge.

As far as I can tell, the club has two main rooms, both filled with bright colors and shiny surfaces. The DJs spin an eclectic mix, but the theme seems to be techno-club, and while the music isn't anything I recognize, it is deliciously danceable.

At the moment, however, dancing is not on the agenda. Instead, Damien leads me to the terrace, and we step outside. I pause a moment to take it all in—the candles that illuminate the patrons in a surreal glow. The plush leather sofas and love seats that dot the terrace. Some are in clusters near colored lights and provide a place for energetic dancers to have a drink and get a second wind. Others are secluded, tucked away in dark corners for lovers to curl up together and soak in the atmosphere.

The bouncers downstairs made it clear that no one gets into this bar if they look shabby, and here under the starlight, that policy is obvious. Everything glows, including Damien and me. There is a polish to everything that I see, but I know better than anyone how tarnished something shiny can be underneath, and I can't help but imagine this place come morning. The sofas stained with spilled drinks. Cigarette butts stamped out on the stone floor. The ethereal candles revealed as nothing more than globby clumps of wax.

Nothing is as it appears. Not this club nor its patrons nor Damien. And certainly not me.

We weave among the other patrons to one of the love seats tucked in a darkened corner. Damien sits, and I start to sit beside him. "No," he says, then pulls me into his lap so that I am straddling his leg, the hard muscles of his thigh pressing enticingly against the hard knot in my ass as I face him.

I exhale, making a little *ah* sound as shimmers of awareness crash through me.

"Trouble, Ms. Fairchild?"

I lift a brow and rock my hips, grinding my rear against him and making this hedonistic tempest crackle and pop inside of me. And—if his face is any indication—my lap dance is driving Damien a little crazy, too.

"No trouble, Mr. Stark," I say, as primly as I can manage despite my body being on fire.

"Christ, Nikki . . ."

He tugs me forward so that I am still straddling him, but now I can feel his denim-clad erection against the bare skin of my thigh above my stocking. I meet his eyes, my heart pounding wildly, then moan when his mouth crushes against mine. One of his hands is around my waist, holding me in place at the small of my back. The other slides under my skirt, his fingers finding the thin strip of silk that makes up the thong, then beginning to move in slow, easy circles calculated to drive me crazy.

"Damien," I whisper. "Someone might see."

"I want you. Right now. I want to watch you explode in my arms."

"But—" I look around. There doesn't seem to be anyone paying attention, and in the dark it's not obvious where his hand is hidden.

His fingers curve inside me, and whatever protests I might have raised die right then. His thumb presses against my pubic bone as if my body is a handle, and I gasp as he roughly pulls me closer. "Now," he repeats. "I want you coming in my arms."

"Yes," I say, because I am too wrecked, too wanton, to say anything else. Right then I think I'd let him lay me out on the dance floor and fuck me with the crowd cheering us on. He wouldn't, though, and deep inside, under this haze of passion and lust, I know that. We're still in our bubble, hidden in the dark, buried in the corner.

But Damien needs this. This man who once told me he doesn't do public sex. Because that's not what this is about. Instead, he needs proof that I am really here. That I didn't leave after talking with Maynard. That the demons of his childhood haven't pushed me away.

He needs me to get lost in his arms as much as I need to lose myself to him. To know that he is back—and that he is still mine.

"Yes," I repeat, because it is the only word I can manage through my jumble of thoughts and emotions. "Oh, God, Damien, please, yes."

"Good girl," he says, sliding his hand off my back. I'm vaguely aware that he has thrust it into his pocket, but that is not the hand that interests me. Instead, all of my thoughts are centered on the fingers that are teasing me under my skirt, playing with my clit, making me bite my lip so that I don't rock back and forth with these building sensations. I'm just a girl sitting in her boyfriend's lap, after all. Not like a woman about to come like she has never come before from the intimate way that said boyfriend is fingerfucking her.

Just a girl sneaking a brief kiss. Just a girl—

"Oh, God!" I cry, but my shout is swallowed by Damien's hard mouth over mine. The orgasm rips through me—not just because Damien's expert fingers have played me so well, but because of the surprising, shocking, totally mind-rocking vibration of the plug with which Damien has filled me. I want to scream with delight, to writhe and make the sparks build again and again. I want this whirlwind of pleasure to keep pulling me up and up, and the fact that I can't—the fact that I need to stay quiet and still—only increases the fever that is burning through me.

All too soon—or possibly hours later—rationality returns to

me. My heart is pounding against my rib cage. I feel as though I have sprinted a mile. And when I lick my lips, I taste blood.

I rub my mouth, but it's not mine, and it takes me a second to realize that I bit down on Damien's lower lip. "Are you okay?"

"Baby, you can bite me anytime."

"Oh my God," I say. "Oh my God." And then, "You didn't tell me it did that."

He pulls his hand out of his pocket to reveal the remote control for the plug. "A man has to keep a few surprises."

I sigh contentedly, then slide off him. I curl up next to him on the love seat, discreetly adjusting my clothes. "Wow," I say. "That was kind of kinky."

His grin is as playful as my words. "And is kinky good?"

"Yeah," I say. "Kinky is very good."

His arm is around me, his hand resting on my hip. After a moment, his lips brush over my ear, and I shiver from the butterfly-soft touch, then immediately laugh when I hear his words—"Your ass is vibrating."

I lift my brows. "Is that a euphemism for what you just did to me, Mr. Stark?"

"Complaining?"

"Hell, no," I say.

"Good. But no, it's not a euphemism. It's your phone."

Shit. I realize that he's right. I'd charged it in the room, then left everything except it and my passport in the hotel. Damien has my passport tucked into the interior pocket of his jacket, but I have my phone in my back pocket, right under Damien's hand. He plucks it out and hands it to me, but when I answer it, there's no one there.

"Must have kicked over to voice mail," I say with a frown. As I wait for the little icon to show a waiting message, I look back at the call information, but I don't recognize the number. Since the voice mail still isn't pinging, I assume it was a wrong number and slide the phone back into my pocket. "That reminds me," I tell Damien. "You got a call earlier. Right before I went to see Maynard. I thought it might be one of the German attorneys, so I answered it, but there was no one there. Did they call back?"

He shakes his head. "Probably not important," he adds, even as he pulls out his phone and begins to scroll through his call information. I see the instant his face changes. It is subtle and quick, and if I didn't know his features in such exquisite detail I might not have even noticed. And when he meets my eyes again, there's no hint that he was surprised or disturbed.

I wrap my arms around myself, fighting an unexpected chill. Once again, Damien is locking his secrets away.

"Who was it?" I say, keeping my voice light but resolute. "Does it have anything to do with the trial or with those pictures?"

"No." The word is both too fast and too firm. And there is a distance in his voice that bothers me. I tell myself it is only the distortion from this thrumming club, but I don't believe it.

"Do you want to talk about it?" I ask, which is really the stupidest question in the world, since if he did want to, he wouldn't be speaking in monosyllables.

"I don't." He must see something in my face, though, because a moment later he sighs, then lightly strokes my cheek. "I promise you. It's nothing."

A shudder runs through me, desire, yes, but it's mixed with something else. Something darker. I had thought that after everything we'd been through there would be no more secrets. But now there are the photos. And this call. And I realize that I was foolish to have even entertained the possibility that Damien's walls had truly come tumbling down. Damien Stark has many layers, and while I am enjoying the process of slowly revealing the deliciousness at the center of the man, I cannot deny the frustration that goes along with the territory.

Damien squeezes my hand. "Don't look so worried."

I manage a teasing smile. "I can't help it," I say. "I may not be the jealous type, but if you're getting calls from old girlfriends looking to pull you back into their web . . ." I am joking, of course, and I expect him to laugh and pull me close as the tension slides off him. I am not prepared for his answer.

"Getting the calls and taking the calls are two different things."

"Oh." I thought the call was about the trial or whoever sent those damn pictures or even some business issue. An old girlfriend was not on my radar at all, and I'm certain I look as shocked as I feel.

"I told you I used to fuck around. And I'm sure some of those women want back in my life." He stands, then takes my hand and eases me to my feet before softly kissing my palm. "I also told you I wasn't serious about any of them. There's only one woman I want."

I cock a brow as I glance at his phone. "Do they know that?"

"I know it," he says. "And so do you."

For a moment, there is only silence between us. No, that isn't true. Where Damien and I are concerned, there is never just silence. There is heat and electricity and lust and need, all harnessing the power of the universe to pull us together. And how can I be expected to fight physics?

I step toward him, sliding comfortably into the circle of his arms, right where I belong. "Do you want to dance?" I ask.

"No," he says, his tone sending ripples of heat through me. "I want to take you to bed."

7

"So you're really taking me to bed?" I ask Damien as we speed down Prinzregenstrasse in the back of our limo.

"That's my current plan," he says. "Unless you want to file an objection?"

"An objection? No." I'm leaning against him, and the space between our bodies hums with sensual energy. The orgasm that rocked me at the club didn't take the edge off at all. Instead it just ramped up my appetite like a fine wine before dinner, leaving me feeling slightly intoxicated and ready for the main course.

I flash a mischievous smile, then shift my position so that I am kneeling on the floorboard of the limo, my hands resting on his thighs. "But perhaps I might file one tiny change order?" My fingers make swift work of the button fly of his jeans.

"Nikki . . ." His voice is full of heat and amusement and a hint of warning.

"What? I mean, fair is fair. You've never fingerfucked me in a club in Munich before tonight. And unless I'm mistaken, I've never gone down on you in a moving limo in Munich, either. That's one of those oversights I want to remedy right now."

I slide my hand into his jeans, relishing his low groan as I stroke and tease, working my way into the fly of his briefs. He's deliciously hard, and I only have to shift his cock a little before it springs free, as excited about the possibilities as I am. Slowly, I bend my head, but lift my eyes, so that I am looking at Damien's face as I gently brush the tip of my tongue over his glans.

I see the shudder that runs through him, and something swells inside me. Lust, power, possessiveness. *Control.* I know it drives him insane not to be firmly in charge. And I also know that of all the people in his life, I'm the only one to whom he willingly abdicates that control. In small doses, yes. But I still get my moments.

This is one of them.

"Dear God, Nikki," he says, his voice tight. "Sometimes you surprise the hell out of me."

I only smile. I want to taste him, to touch him, and there is nothing keeping me from taking exactly what I want. Gently, I circle the base of his cock with my hand, the sensation like soft steel against my palm. I press my lips to the head of his cock, then draw him in, my tongue teasing him as I piston my mouth in time with the strokes of my hand against him.

He is already desperately hard, but I feel his body responding, tightening. I hear his low groans. I feel his fingers twining in my hair, then the tension filling his body as he comes closer and closer, and I know that I am doing that to him.

The knowledge empowers me, and I think of my earlier fears about reality sneaking in and breaking through our perfect little plastic bubble of a life. In this moment, though, my fears seem a million miles away.

A ripple of passion cuts through him, and I feel the corresponding pressure in my sex as my body responds to his desire and to the knowledge that I have brought him to the brink.

A sensual hunger courses through me, my own arousal as potent as if his fingers were stroking me. I writhe a bit, wriggling my hips in time with the need growing inside me. I am smug with satisfaction and ripe with the knowledge that Damien is as turned on as I am.

And then I'm shocked as hell when his hands close around my ribs and he lifts me up—then dumps me back on the seat and hooks my legs over his shoulders.

"What are you—" But I don't bother to finish the question. I know exactly what he's doing, and I'm proven right when he leans forward, his hands stroking my thighs in time with the movement. His laves his tongue over the delicate skin right next to the edge of my thong.

A tremor runs through my body. "Damien," I moan. "Holy shit."

"Hold still." His breath burns hot upon my sex. "Don't move," he demands, and then ensures that there is no way I can obey when he simultaneously flips on the vibrator in my ass, but also nips at the thong with his teeth, teasing my clit in the process.

I cry out and arch up, both in surprise and from the nearly unendurable sensations that are ricocheting through my body.

"Naughty," Damien says as he turns off the vibration, then cups my ass with his hands. "Let's see what we can do about that."

I see the devious gleam in his eye and swallow. "I'll be still."

"Too late," he says, then removes the plug, sending another wave of sensations rolling through me as my body rocks in protest. He smiles as he wraps it in a handkerchief and slips it in his pocket. "I think someone likes my toys," he says. "I'll have to think of more ways to play."

"Oh, God, yes," I say impulsively, eager for whatever he wants to bring on.

He slides down my body, trailing kisses along my left leg as he eases down my stocking until he reaches the strap of my shoe. "This should do nicely."

I bite my lip, uncertain what he has in mind. "You realize that if you mess up my shoes, you're in serious trouble."

"Even if it gets you off?" He strokes my foot along the side of the arch, which is exposed in these shoes.

I close my eyes, trying to think despite this assault upon a deliciously new erogenous zone. "Some things are as sacred as sex," I say. "Shoes among them."

He chuckles. "Touché, Ms. Fairchild." I feel his lips press where his finger once was and have to bite my lip in order to remain still as ordered. "I'll be gentle."

My eyes widen as he takes the seat belt and wraps it around my ankle. He clicks the buckle into place, then tightens the strap. After that, he flashes me a smug grin. "One down."

I am speechless. I'm also unable to move my left leg. "Damien," I begin, but there's no point in protesting. He's not going to stop. And the truth is that I don't want him to.

"Now let's see what we can do about this one." I remember that this limo is part of the Stark International fleet when he moves without hesitation to a camouflaged floor panel. He pulls it open and removes a white box emblazoned with a red cross.

I prop myself up on my elbows. "First aid? What exactly are you doing?" I'm teasing, of course. Well, mostly teasing.

His eyes meet mine and he slides his hand slowly up my thigh, then cups my sex. "Surprising you."

Oh. I swallow. Had I really believed that I'd had even an iota of control? Whatever control I'd had when we'd started this adventure is gone. I am Damien's to do with what he pleases—and that simple fact only makes me even more excited.

"Lay back, baby. Lay back, and trust me."

I comply, because I do trust him. I watch as he unrolls an ace bandage, then carefully winds it around my ankle, just below the platinum and emerald bracelet. He threads one end of the bandage through some part of the seat frame that I can't see, then makes a knot. I try to move my legs, but I can't. I'm completely trussed up. I'm completely open. And I'm completely turned on.

"Damien." My voice is low and gravelly with desire. "Damien, please."

"Please what? Please touch you?"

Just the thought of his hands upon me is enough to make me squirm with anticipated pleasure. "Yes," I say. "God, yes. Touch me. Fuck me. Please, Damien, I want you." Tonight has been one long tease, and I have crossed the line to desperate.

"Mmm." He shifts position, rising from the floor to perch on the edge of the seat across which I am spread. I reach for him, craving his touch against my now exposed sex, but just before I can place my hand upon his leg, he shakes his head. "No. Arms above your head. There you go," he adds, when I stretch out as ordered.

He reaches out, his hand hovering over my breasts. Beneath the beaded tank, my nipples are already tight and erect and deliciously sensitive from the clamps with which he had adorned me earlier. I bite my lower lip, craving his touch. The slightest brush against my breast. A soft caress upon my nipple. Anything to relieve the growing, heavy pressure.

Of course he denies me. Instead, he moves his still-hovering hand slowly down the length of my body—my breasts, my belly, my very aching cunt, then all the way down my legs until even my toes are wiggling in a futile attempt to draw him closer. It doesn't work. He never touches, just skims along over a pocket of air that is burning hotter and hotter, as if I am trapped beneath an electric blanket with no way to throw it off and cool down.

Not even the air-conditioning is blowing between my legs. The only sensation is the tiny brush of material over my sex brought on by the motion of the limo and by my own pulse, which is pounding so hard that it is making my clothing quiver with each beat of my heart.

His voice is little more than a murmur. "So tell me, Nikki, can you imagine the touch of my fingertip upon the inside of your thigh? The way your body would tighten in response to a touch that is neither a caress nor a tickle?"

"I—yes."

My words are so low that I doubt he has heard me. It doesn't matter, though. He continues on. "A sensual dance, like the brush of a feather over your panties. A hooked fingertip to tug them aside. And then what, Nikki? What kind of touch do you want then?"

I don't answer, because he has moved—not between my legs to where my sex now throbs in response to both his sensual tone and the erotic nature of the words themselves, but higher, so that his hip is near my chest and his hands are cleverly twining my wrists with the nylon webbing of the farthest seat belt.

"Damien, what—"

But I don't bother to finish the question, because he has finished and I know what he was doing. He was binding my hands as he has done my legs so that I am fully strapped down, bound to this long, leather bench in the back of a limo.

"Do you want it, Nikki? Do you want me to fuck you?"

"You know that I do." I keep my voice calm even though I want to scream—*Yes, yes, goddammit, yes.*

He cocks his head. "What was that?" he asks, and I almost cry with frustration.

"Yes," I say. "Please, sir."

His smile is slow and a little too self-satisfied. He moves toward me and I see that he has a small pair of bandage scissors in his hand. He slides a blade under the lace of my thong, snips twice, then rips the material free.

I arch and shudder, my body begging as much as my words. "Please, Damien. Please, please fuck me."

"Believe me, Ms. Fairchild, there's nothing I'm looking forward to more. But no. I don't think so. Not yet."

I actually whimper.

He bends forward to whisper in my ear. "What if I told you to touch yourself? Ah, but you can't do that, either."

I tug at the belt that is binding my hands, but I'm not going anywhere. I can shift right and left a little, but for the most part, where he bound me is where I'll stay.

He reaches down and plucks up the hem of my shirt, managing the maneuver without actually touching my skin, despite the way my back arches up, as if my body is determined to try even though my mind knows it's futile. After a moment, he has my shirt pulled up, exposing the lacy bra and the serpentine chain that stretches between my very erect nipples. He runs his finger over the chain, then gives it a gentle tug, causing me to arch up as hot threads of electricity sizzle through my body, racing from my breasts to my throbbing cunt.

"Oh, baby," he murmurs. "I love how hot you get, how your body responds. Do you know what it does to me, knowing that you've given yourself over so fully to me? No barriers, no inhibitions. Just mine. To touch, to tempt, to tease."

"Anything you want, Mr. Stark." My voice is raw with passion. "Anything you need."

"I'm very glad to hear it," he says, as he moves away from me to sit on the bench that runs the length of the limo, perpendicular to this long backseat across which I am strapped. "Right now, I just want to look at you. The flush on your skin. Your cunt, swollen and wet and begging for me. Your hard nipples and the rise and fall of your chest as you try to control your breathing. It makes me hard, Nikki, so goddamn hard to see you like this, laid out and wanting, and knowing that I am the one who brought you there."

I can only moan. Words are impossible, the power of speech obliterated by the violence of the emotions raging through me.

He leans over and punches the intercom button, then asks the driver how close we are to the hotel. We're just a few blocks away, and I don't know whether to be relieved or frustrated when Damien tells the driver to circle the block until he says otherwise.

Then he clicks off, smiles at me, and pours himself a shot of whiskey over ice. His eyes never leave my face as he tilts the glass back and takes a long, deep swallow before moving back to my side, the glass still in his hand.

"Open," he says.

I open my mouth, and he takes out a cube of ice, holding it between two fingers and his thumb. He brushes it gently over my lips, and I open wider, reaching out with my tongue to taste the smooth liquor. It's gone too soon, though. Because he eases down until he is holding the ice cube over my belly, and three fat drops fall from the cube to land upon my overheated flesh. The sensation is electrifying, and I arch up, gasping. Wanting. The droplets swirl on my skin with the motion, leaving a cool trail down to my pubic bone. My skin quivers, my need like a palpable thing.

Damien meets my eyes, then slowly—too damn slowly—trails the cube between my thigh and the sensitive skin of my sex. My body bucks, and I'm not certain if I'm trying to escape because it is too much to bear or if I am desperate for more. All I know is that I cannot escape. I am bound, tied down, and right now, Damien can do with me whatever he wants.

"Oh, God. Damien, what are you doing?"

"Unless I'm doing it wrong, I'm getting you very, very worked up. And, my dear," he adds, as he tosses the tiny shred of ice that remains back into the glass, "I think I've succeeded."

He eases back over to his seat and presses the intercom button. "Once more around the block," he says. "Then you can take us to the hotel."

It is then that I am certain that, at least for now, he is not taking this any further. *Well, damn.*

"Are you punishing me?" I ask. "Because right now, I'm really not above begging."

He chuckles. "Punishing you? I was simply following your lead."

"My lead?" I haven't got a clue what he's talking about.

His eyes twinkle with amusement. "You said you'd never gone down on me in a moving limo in Munich. I assumed you'd never been tied down half-naked in a limo. In Munich or elsewhere. Or was I mistaken?"

"Not mistaken," I say. "And I've never been fucked in a limo in Munich, either," I add, almost petulantly. "But you seem to have overlooked that."

"Complaining, Ms. Fairchild?"

"Hell yes, Mr. Stark."

"You know, I'm tempted to keep you like this forever." His gaze trails slowly over every inch of me. The inspection is slow, lingering upon my breasts, then my bare abdomen, and then my sex. I shudder as the muscles of my vagina clench with need of him. "We could tour Europe by car, you splayed out in the back of a limo, open to my pleasure."

"Or we could go back to the hotel this very second, and you could have your wicked way with me." I glance up at him and smile. "Your call, Mr. Stark," I say, shaking my bound hands. "But at the very least, you have to untie me."

We move through the lobby of the hotel with blinders on, heading straight for the elevator, which seems to open magically upon our arrival, as if this hotel understands just how desperately we need to get upstairs.

We have the car to ourselves, and I lean against Damien, relishing the way his arms go automatically around me. Right then, it feels as though nothing can go wrong in our world.

Then we're on our floor and the doors open and we step out. Immediately, I feel my phone vibrate, and the corresponding *ping* signals an incoming text. I frown, mentally flipping a coin between Ollie and Jamie. I have no intention of texting with either of them, but my phone is set to repeat buzz incoming texts three times so that I don't miss any, which means that at the very least I have to open the messaging app.

I do—and then freeze in the hallway when I see the text. It's not from anyone I know, the phone number is unfamiliar.

The message, however, is something I've seen before: Bitch. Slut. Whore.

I recall the anonymous letter that arrived for me care of Stark International and tremble as a finger of foreboding creeps up my spine. I had thought that letter had been prompted by the fact that I'd accepted money to pose nude. Now I wonder if it's about something else.

"Nikki?" Damien has turned to face me, his forehead creased with worry. "What is it?"

I don't want to show him the text—I don't want the magical bubble of this evening to pop. But I know that it already has. More, I know that Damien needs to know.

Wordlessly, I hand the phone to Damien, my entire body tightening as I wait for the explosion I see building in his eyes.

"Is this the first time you've received a text like this?" His voice is steady and firm and cold as hell.

"Yes," I say flatly. Once again I feel the weight of the real world pressing in around us. The thin glass of our protective bubble is starting to crack. I don't know what will happen when the pressure is too much and those tiny fissures finally explode under the weight of the world. I fear, though, that I'm going to find out.

And when the explosion comes, I hope I can resist the urge to pick up one of the shards and grind it into my own smooth flesh.

A shudder runs through me. "Just delete it," I say harshly. "Just make it fucking go away."

"No. We're going to trace it."

"Later," I say. "Please, Damien. Leave it for later. I don't want to think about it now."

He studies me for a moment, then he turns off my phone and slides it into his pocket.

I cross my arms over my chest.

"Trust me, sweetheart, you won't need it tonight."

I can't help my responsive grin, especially when he pulls out his own phone and turns it off as well. "Now it's just you and me."

"Just how I like it," I say, taking Damien's hand and letting him pull me back into the protective circle of his arms. He slides his card key into the lock and I watch as the light flicks from red to green. My body is tight with anticipation. I am expecting lust and passion and Damien's hands upon me, his cock inside me.

I am expecting to slide back into that magical fantasy where there really is nothing but the two of us.

But when he opens the door, I realize that the real world can follow us anywhere.

Because right there—sitting on the couch where Damien has fucked me so many times—is a woman I never thought that I would see again.

A woman who used to be in Damien's bed.

8

Carmela D'Amato is tall and blond and so stunningly beautiful that it is almost painful. I've hated her from the first moment I saw her six years ago when she took Damien away from me.

Granted, at the time I had no claim to Damien, but I'd wanted to lash out at her nonetheless. I'd been competing in Dallas at the Miss Tri-County Texas pageant, and tennis star Damien was the celebrity judge. I'd never met him before, but he'd come over to where I was staked out by the buffet table, wondering if I could get away with eating cheesecake without my mother finding out. At the time, I'd thought it was my imagination, but even then the connection between us had been electric. He'd taken my breath away. Hell, he still takes my breath away.

Just standing there talking to him had sparked decadent fantasies. If he'd suggested it, I would have taken his hand and run away and never once looked back. But he didn't suggest it. And it wasn't me he left with, but Carmela.

I'd never expected to see her again.

Then again, at the time I'd never expected to see Damien again, either. Apparently we've now come full circle.

Instinctively, I take a step closer to Damien. He reaches down, his fingers automatically twining through mine.

Carmela's eyes flicker down to our joined hands, and I have to bite back a triumphant smile. *Ha. Take that, bitch.* The thought is petty. But it's heartfelt.

"What are you doing here?" Damien's voice is cold, his body tense. I can feel the irritation rolling off him in waves.

"Damie, darling, don't be angry." She stretches, cat-like, as she reaches for a glass of wine on the table beside her. She takes a sip, looking perfectly at home.

I want to go slap her face.

"How the *hell* did you get in here?" Damien demands.

Her eyes widen, then she glances at me. "After all the times I've shared this room with you, I'm like family. I just asked one of the room service boys to let me in."

"It didn't occur to you that you were costing the boy his job?"

She laughs. "Why would it? I thought we could celebrate your victory together. And when have you ever kicked me out of your room, Damie? When have you not been happy to see me?"

"Now," he says.

I'm watching her face as he speaks, and am startled to see that there is no reaction. She doesn't flinch. She doesn't blink. She is neither angry nor hurt.

In other words, Carmela came here knowing exactly how this would play out. What a goddamned bitch.

"Get up," I say. "Get up and get the hell out of here." *That* gets a reaction out of her. A tight, condescending smile that only pisses me off even more.

Beside me, Damien squeezes my hand, but he says nothing. Somehow he knows that this is my fight now.

"You're Nichole, aren't you?" she says, though there is no doubt in my mind that she knows exactly who I am. "You're the little girl who caught his eye in Texas at that ridiculous pageant."

"I caught more than his eye, Carlotta," I say, deliberately getting her name wrong.

Her eyes narrow. "Are you sure? Reality so rarely lives up to expectations. I hope you're prepared for the day he realizes that you are not the woman he wanted, after all."

I flash my best pageant smile and conjure a honey-sweet Texas twang. "Sugar, I think you have us confused. I'm the one he's taking to bed. It's you he doesn't want." I imagine a stadium of people leaping to their feet and applauding. "Now get the hell out of here."

I know my blow struck home from the way her eyes dart to Damien, as if he will soothe the wound. But Damien is not her salvation. "You heard the lady," he says. "Go."

For an unpleasant moment, I think she's going to argue. Then she rises to her feet. She moves with deliberate slowness as she takes the last sip of her wine and then hooks her purse over her arm. It seems to take forever, but she finally steps over the threshold and out into the hallway, the weighted door slamming shut behind her.

I turn to Damien. I can see the rage in his eyes. The rising fury. But it's tempered by something else. Regret. And apology. *No, I think. No way in hell is he apologizing for that bitch.*

"Nikki, I—"

"You what? You didn't know she would be here?"

"You know I didn't." His voice is hard. Firm.

"Do you think I'm going to be jealous, knowing that there was a time when she had free run of this suite?" I ask, making my voice even harder. I have a point to make, and I'm damn well going to make it. I cock my head, considering. "Just how many hotels around Europe is she intimately familiar with?"

"Goddammit, Nikki."

"One? Three? Five?"

He stalks toward me and I take a corresponding step back,

then another until my back is against one of the pillars that divides the sitting area from the kitchen and dining area. "Did you take her here? Like this? Hard against a wall?"

"What the fuck are you doing?" Anger curls in his voice and I know that I've almost pushed him too far.

"What do you think I'm doing?"

"Pissing me off," he says, then kisses me hard, the force of his lips upon mine knocking my head back. I open my mouth to draw him in even as I hook one leg around him and curl my arms around his neck. I want him hard against me. I want to feel him—to feel our connection. Because nothing—not Carmela, not anybody—can break that.

Roughly, he wrenches his mouth off mine. I hold him tight though, so that I feel his breath upon my face when he speaks. "You're the only woman in my life now, Nikki."

I am breathing hard, my eyes never leaving his. "Don't you think I know that, too?"

I see the exact moment when he realizes that I have been playing him.

"Unless I find you in bed with one," I say, "don't you even think of apologizing for another woman. Believe it or not, Damien Stark, I was not under the impression that you'd taken a vow of chastity before sleeping with me."

He looks me up and down, his eyes filled with a dangerous kind of heat.

"What?" My voice is wary.

"I think, my very dear Ms. Fairchild, that you are in for a much-deserved punishment."

"Oh." I feel the tightening in my body simply from the thought of his hand smacking hard against my ass. Still, though . . .

I try to take a step backward, but am blocked by the pillar. "Why? Because I pushed your buttons? That doesn't seem quite fair."

"No," he says, "it doesn't. And not because of that."

"What then?"

"Do you really think it's in the realm of possibility that you would ever find another woman in our bed?"

"No," I say.

"Well, there you go."

I cross my arms over my chest. "But you know I don't believe it and didn't mean it."

"I do," he says. "But I'll tell you a little secret. It's the best excuse I have for bending you over and feeling the sting on my palm."

I lick my lips. The room turns suddenly warm, and I feel beads of moisture at the back of my neck and between my thighs. I reach back, holding on to the pillar to steady myself. "Is that something you want?" I keep my voice low and even; it's damn sure something *I* want.

"Right now," Damien says, "I want it more than anything."

He uses the pad of his thumb to trace lightly along my jawline. I close my eyes and draw in a breath, suddenly unable to concentrate.

"Why?"

"You know me better than anyone, Nikki. You know why."

I do know. He needs me like I used to need a blade—like I now need him. In a day when he's been blindsided by horrific pictures of his past and bitchy ex-girlfriends, he needs to know that I will surrender utterly to him. That it is Damien who controls my pleasure even by controlling my pain. He needs to know that he can take me to that limit. And he needs to know that I want him to.

And I do.

Everything has spun out of control. Not just Carmela's appearance in our room, but the whole day. Ollie's appearance in Germany. The horrible photos. Damien's reaction to the dismissal of the murder charge against him.

Too much noise, and it all bubbled up inside of me, so much so that when it knocked Damien flat, I'd craved the feel of a blade in my hand. I'd fought it, though. I'd fought and I'd won. I didn't need to cut, but I still needed Damien. *Do* need Damien. I need to feel his hands upon me and the rise of pleasure accompanied by the sharp sting of pain. I need the release to keep me anchored. A safety valve preventing me from exploding.

I need it—and so does Damien.

"Take off your skirt." His voice is tight.

"I—"

He cuts me off with a quick shake of his head. I get it; we're through talking. We're moving on. We're leaving the trial and Carmela and the photographs behind. We're saying fuck you to the real world and sliding back into our bubble, which is just where I want to be.

"Your skirt," he repeats, his tone broaching no argument.

"Yes, sir," I say, and his slow, approving smile slides over me as intimately as his hand upon my sex.

Slowly, I reach behind my back and unzip my skirt. I wriggle my hips and use my hands to ease it down until it falls in a circle at my feet.

"Step out of it," Damien says.

I do.

"Now the top. Pull it off. Toss it over there."

Once again, I comply. I feel the rush of air against my newly exposed skin, the sensation even more enticing considering how sensitive my nipples are from the clamps and how heavy my breasts feel simply from the minimal weight of the silver chain. I shiver, not from the chill of the air, but from the anticipation of what is to come. I do not know exactly what Damien has in mind. I only know that I want it, and that it will be spectacular.

I move my hands to the front clasp of my bra, but he shakes his head. "No. I'll do that." He steps closer, and I find it suddenly hard to breathe, as if the air has become as thick as liquid. I should be used to this by now—to the way he makes my body hum, the way molecules seem to shimmer when he is near me. I should be able to draw a breath without trembling, and stand beside him without feeling as though I will swoon. But I cannot, and so help me I hope that day never comes. I am in thrall to this man, and I do not want anything about that to change.

His hands brush the swell of my breasts as he detaches the rings. I gasp, surprised by the rush of sensation back to my nipples that is at least as enticing as the initial shock of contact when he put them on. He sets the chain and rings on the bar, then removes my bra, sending shocks of anticipation shooting through me. I close my eyes, expecting to feel his mouth close over me, his teeth grazing my nipple. But that sweet sensation doesn't come. Instead, his palms stroke down my arms and his fingers close around my wrists. Gently, he raises my hands above my head. "Keep your eyes closed," he whispers.

Satin twines gently around my wrist before tightening, the pressure pulling my hand flush with the pillar. "What are you—"

"Hush," he says. A moment later, I feel that same constriction around my other wrist. I try to move my arms, but they are bound in place, and I realize that Damien has used my bra to tie me to this pillar.

"Clever," I say.

"Enticing," he retorts. "Can I trust you not to peek?"

"Yes," I say.

"Mmm." From his tone, I'd have to say he doesn't believe me, and I open my eyes to find him frowning at me. I grin sheepishly, but he says nothing. Just turns and goes into the bedroom, leaving me tied to a pillar in the living room, wearing nothing but my thigh-high stockings, high heels, and a conservative strand of pearls.

I twist my head, trying to see what's he's doing, but it's impossible. I listen, but I hear nothing.

I close my eyes and say a silent prayer that he's not leaving me here. Unfortunately for me, I know damn well that I can't discount the possibility. "Damien?"

There is no answer.

"Mr. Stark? Sir?"

Again, the room remains silent. And I, alone and essentially naked, can't help but wonder just how long he'll be gone. For that matter, I can't help but wonder what he'll do when he returns. This may be my punishment, but I know that the reward, when it finally comes, will be astounding.

"And here I thought you had more patience." I hear his voice, but there is no Damien.

"And here I thought you were going to fuck me. At the very least, you were going to spank me."

Then he steps in from the bedroom, his stride long and easy, his back straight, his expression that of a man who knows damn well that the earth will rotate whichever way he tells it to. All that power, and right now it is focused entirely on me. "Frustrated, Ms. Fairchild?"

"Maybe I'm feeling a little cheated," I say.

"I promise you won't by the time I'm through with you," he says with such heat in his voice that it's a wonder I don't melt right there, and slip out of my bond like butter. "I didn't get to take you as far as I would have liked during our limo ride. I intend to remedy that now. Slowly, and very, very thoroughly."

He has something in his hand, and it takes me a minute to realize it's one of his ties. "Your eyes are open," he says.

"Ah." I can hardly argue, as I'm looking right at him.

"Close them," he says, and I do. I feel the brush of silk over my eyes, then the tug as he tightens the tie around the back of my head. His lips brush the corner of my mouth. "Nice," he says. His lips brush my ear. "Now everything you hear, everything you feel, every bit of pleasure, every hint of pain will come from me. So tell me, Nikki. Does that excite you?"

"You know it does."

His lips graze my neck, and his one simple word seems to reverberate through me. "Why?"

I swallow. It's not a question I expected. "Because—because you know me. Because you know what I can take. You know what I want. You know my limits, Damien. And because you push them."

"Good girl."

He reaches up and traces his finger lightly along my collarbone, then over the strand of pearls. A moment later, he has removed the necklace, and I hear the *clink* of pearls against pearls as he crunches the strand in his palm, then cups his hand over my breast.

I tilt my head back and suck in air as he rubs small circles over my nipple, massaging me with the hard, slick surface of the cluster of pearls. Then he opens his hand more and I feel the brush of the necklace as he untangles it, then rubs the strand enticingly against the swell of my breast, my puckered areola, and my oh-so-sensitive nipple.

"Damien," I murmur as he trails the tip of the strand down my belly, careful to let only the smooth surface of one stone touch my skin. The sensation is intoxicating. The cool brush of the gem. The sweet anticipation of not knowing where the next touch will fall.

I jump a little when the necklace grazes my pubis, then bite down on my lower lip, willing myself to stand still.

"Should I crush these as Cleopatra did?" he whispers.

"I don't need an aphrodisiac," I retort, my voice breathy.

"No, I don't think you do. I can see the flush on your skin, I can breathe in the scent of your arousal. When I touch you, I know I will find you desperately wet for me. Won't I, Nikki?"

"Oh, God, yes."

"Good." I hear the smile in his voice. "Now spread your legs for me."

I do, then moan when he draws the strand of pearls between my legs, back and forth, the strand becoming slick with my own arousal. Each perfect gem glides over my clit, and the sensation is maddening, right where I want it, and yet at the same time not quite there. Not quite *enough*. I squirm, shameless, wanting more. Hell, wanting it all.

"Shhh," Damien says. He is right in front of me, and he pulls the strand free, making me whimper in protest. Then I feel his fingers on me, stroking and opening me.

"Yes," I say. I need to feel him inside me. I need to come, to explode, to release this maddening pressure.

I hear the crunch of the pearls in his hand again, then he rolls the cluster enticingly over my desperate sex. I am being bombarded with sensations, buried in heat. I am on edge, desperately aroused, and on the verge of simply crying out and begging.

What I'm not expecting is for him to stretch me wide and slide the pearls inside me.

"Damien! What the—"

He silences me with a kiss. "Quiet," he says. "And stay still."

And then he's gone and I'm left naked and exposed and unsatisfied, my sex heavy from the knot of pearls tucked inside me, my body desperate for his touch, and my mind spinning with possibilities.

"Damien?"

At first I don't hear him. Then I detect the slightest rattle from behind me. I strain against the bond that keeps my hands tight above me. I want to take off this blindfold. I want to see.

I want Damien.

It's no use, though, and all my struggles do is shift the pearls even more. Little shock waves burst through me, but not enough to bring on the explosion that I so desperately crave. Damien—damn him—has brought me to the edge and left me there.

And this, I think, is part of the punishment he promised.

The pillar with which my ass is now on such familiar terms is the line of demarcation between the living area and the suite's kitchen. We've eaten out or ordered room service most nights, so we haven't had to rely on the kitchen for anything other than the storage of wine and ice cream, the latter being a late-night splurge about a week ago. I checked it out my first night in Germany, though, and was impressed to find it fully stocked.

I hear him moving about, but I can't tell what he's doing. There is the thud of a drawer. The clatter of cutlery. And then there is the even rhythm of Damien's steps as he moves toward me. "Do you have any idea how beautiful you look?" he asks. "Your skin flush. Your nipples hard. Your lips parted as if waiting for my kiss."

"I am waiting," I say, and am rewarded by the briefest touch of his lips upon mine. Brief, yes, but oh so powerful. Much like the butterfly effect in chaos theory, that minuscule sensation has set off a chain reaction, sending sparks humming and dancing throughout my body. It's deliciously sweet, but it isn't enough.

"Turn around," he says.

"Um . . . ?" I tug on my hands, still bound to the pillar above me.

"Cross your wrists and turn," he says, and though I'm dubious, I manage. Now I am facing the pillar, though with the blindfold I can see nothing, and my back is to Damien. "Good girl. Now slide down a bit. That's it," he adds as I try to ease my hands down. I have to scoot back to manage, and I end up with my torso almost parallel to the floor. The position shifts the pearls, and I draw in a shuddering breath.

He runs his palm over the curve of my rear, and I bite my lower lip in anticipation of a firmer touch. "Beautiful," he whispers, then slides his fingers down. I'm so wet and so ready, and his low moan of satisfaction sends another shiver through me. I swallow, expecting him to thrust his fingers inside me, but then he withdraws his hand, and I find myself whimpering—and hear Damien chuckling.

"Soon. I have something else in mind, first. Your legs," he says, tapping the inside of my thighs gently. "A bit wider."

I comply again, my brow furrowed. That wasn't his hand upon my leg just then, but I'm not sure what—

"It's interesting how many things one can find in a kitchen that entice," Damien says, interrupting my thoughts. "This, for example, seems quite intriguing."

I feel something warm and flat press gently against my rear. The surface is slightly rough, and I cock my head without thinking, trying to figure out what it could be.

"A simple wooden kitchen spoon," Damien says, as if in answer. "Who knew it could be so tantalizing?"

I feel a rush of cool air when he removes the spoon, but it is gone almost immediately, replaced by the sting of wood against flesh. I cry out, my ass stinging, then immediately soothed by the firm press of Damien's hand against my rear. All too soon, his hand is gone, and he swats me again—not too hard, but hard enough that it feels as though a million pinpricks of pleasure are rushing to the spot.

I squirm a bit, wanting more. Wanting the pain to center me—and wanting Damien to launch me off into the stars.

"That's it, baby," he says. "You're glowing, but your ass is on fire."

I can't speak. I just want more. But I'm not expecting the next blow—not on my ass, but on my sex. One light, upward thrust with the back of the spoon, barely brushing my clit. But it sets off little sparks inside me. Then another spank, this one firmer, and I cry out as I come closer to the edge. I bite my lip, wanting another—just one more. One more to take me over.

But instead of the thwack of wood against my sex, there are Damien's fingers inside me, Damien tugging the pearls. I arch up and cry out in surprise and release as he draws the pearls out of me, each tiny round bead rubbing against my sensitive clit. Each pearl heightening the sensation. Each millimeter sending me spiraling off until a cry is ripped from my throat and my body bucks and quakes, unable to withstand the force of the ecstasy that is spinning out of control inside me.

"Oh, yes, baby. Yes—"

And then I hear the soft thud as the pearls fall to the floor. I hear the brush of material against flesh as Damien steps of out his jeans. I feel his hands stroke my hips, my ass. Then his fingers are inside me, opening me, readying me—though that's hardly necessary at this point.

I suck in a breath and moan with pleasure as the head of his cock presses against my folds. He thrusts forward, entering me, going deep, so deep that it feels as though this will never end, that we will tumble off into each other.

His hands release my hips and he leans forward to cup a breast with one hand, the pressure of his fingers on my nipple as he moves my body back to his in time with his thrusts, so that it is as if we are wrapped in a web of current, sizzling and alive.

His other hand reaches around, finding my overly sensitive clit. He strokes me ever so lightly until all I know is a bone deep pleasure, so consuming that I lose all sense of where the sensations come from, but know only that they are there. That I am pleasure. That I am electricity. That I am Damien's.

The second orgasm hits me just as fast. It's an explosion, and I cry out, my body contracting around him, the touch of his finger against my clit now so intense it borders on pain. He doesn't relent, though. Instead he draws it out and out and out, until his own release comes even as my body is still quivering and shaking—and if I weren't tied to the pillar, I would surely be collapsed on the ground.

"Damien." It's all I can say. It's enough.

"Shhhh." He unties my hands, but doesn't remove my blindfold. Gently, he carries me into the bedroom and lays me on the bed.

"I want to see you," I say, as he begins to trail slow kisses up my body.

"You see me better than anyone," he says, then gently removes my blindfold. I open my eyes to find Damien smiling down at me, and all of my own emotions are reflected there on his face. He kisses me, deeply and gently, his mouth claiming mine.

"I think I'm destroyed," I say with a smile. "I don't know that I can ever move again."

"No? That's too bad." He moves down my body, gently stroking my skin with his fingers, his lips. When he reaches the scars on my inner thighs, he traces a fingertip over the worst of them then lifts his head to look at me. I draw in a shuddering breath, done in by everything I see reflected in his eyes. Love, desire, respect.

"Destroyed or not," he says, "I have to have you again."

"Take me," I say, reaching for him and tugging him up my body, spreading my legs and lifting my hips in invitation at the same time. He enters me slowly, filling me, and we move together in a sensual rhythm that makes me want to cry out with pleasure as he fills me.

I arch up and draw his mouth to mine, connecting myself fully to this man. "Turn over," I beg when I break the kiss. "I want to see you under me."

He raises a brow but complies, and I shift my hips as I straddle him, taking him even deeper as I rock slowly, then ease myself up and down to tease his steel-hard cock. My eyes are open and I'm watching his face, his beautiful face that I have seen through so many emotions—humor and ecstasy, anger and frustration, and on and on and on. Right now, though, he just looks happy, and something I think might be pride swells within me. Damien Stark is a complicated man. And yet I am what he needs.

Despite my bliss, Carmela's words come back to me, and I cannot help but be struck by how they mirror my earlier dark thoughts. That once reality pokes its head in, things start spiraling out of control.

"What is it?" Damien asks, his eyes intent upon my face.

I do not want to bring a dark cloud between us, but I also don't want to hide my fears from Damien. Not when I know that he is the only one capable of soothing them.

"Stupid stuff," I say. "I was thinking about what Carmela said. About reality."

"Carmela's a cold bitch. And the only reality I know is you. Don't tell me you doubt that."

"I don't," I say emphatically. "But, Damien, all the noise outside of us. I don't want to feel like we're living in a fantasy bubble, but sometimes I think that we are, and that reality keeps trying to break through. The trial. Stalker mail and texts. The press. And now your old girlfriends."

"Fuck them," he says.

"Damien, I'm serious."

"So am I," he says, his expression as intense as I have ever seen it. "At the end of the day, it's just you and me. We make our own reality, Nikki. And no one can take it from us."

9

As we head down in the elevator the next morning with the bell-man and a cart full of luggage, I keep glancing back, unable to shake the feeling that I've forgotten something.

"I keep that room on a permanent lease," Damien says. "If you left something behind, the hotel will ship it to us."

"You own the room?" I don't know why I'm surprised; after all, he owns much of the known universe. And I was already aware that he keeps a permanent suite at the Century Plaza hotel for clients who travel to Los Angeles.

"Enough clients visit the Stark International office here to jus-tify the expense." He speaks casually, as if it's no big deal that he leases one of the most expensive rooms at one of the most expen-sive hotels in Europe for three hundred sixty-five days out of the year. "If the maids find anything, the concierge will call our cor-porate liaison. Don't worry."

I nod, hoping there is no call—and then do a mental head-thwap as I realize what I've forgotten. "My phone," I say. "We do need to go back." I try to picture where I left it, but nothing comes to mind. Maybe it's charging on the bar?

"I still have it," Damien says, then pulls it from the leather messenger bag that is doubling for a briefcase.

"Oh." My stomach churns unpleasantly. I'd completely forgotten about my stalker text from last night, and I'm not overly thrilled with the reminder. "Were you able to learn anything?"

"Not yet. I forwarded it to my team. Hopefully they'll have news by the time we arrive back in the States. In the meantime, don't delete it."

"Okay," I say, although I'm not really keen on seeing that number pop up every time I open my text messages.

Since Damien had powered the phone down, I hit the button to wake it back up so that I can check my texts, emails, and voice messages. I don't expect there to be much—Ollie is here and knows I'm traveling—but Jamie or Evelyn or Blaine might have buzzed me, especially once they heard the news that Damien's case was dismissed.

Sure enough, I have an emoticon-filled text from Jamie consisting of balloons, confetti, and about a dozen smiley faces followed by CWTSY and another round of balloons. I roll my eyes at her goofiness, but the truth is that I'm smiling. I text back that I can't wait to see her, either.

Evelyn and Blaine left an actual voice message telling me how much they're looking forward to our return, and that I should give Damien a hug from each of them. "And feel free to plant a kiss on him from me," Evelyn adds.

I also have two emails. The first is from my mother, and just seeing it makes me cringe. I have finally reached a point in my life where I don't feel the constant pressure of being under her thumb, and I know that I should simply delete the email and declare a victory for sanity. That, however, is one baby step too far. Instead, I move it unread to an archived folder. Someday I'll either delete it or read it; the only victory I can claim today is simply that I dealt with it.

The second email is much more pleasant. It's from Lisa, a woman I recently met, but who I'm hoping is going to land firmly on the "friend" side of the equation. I skim the message, and can't help but smile.

"Good news?" Damien asks.

"Maybe. It's from Lisa." I'm about to continue, but we've reached the lobby, and as we step out of the car into the open area, I see Ollie leaning against a wall, deep in an animated conversation with a lithe brunette. I tense, immediately wary. Ollie is finally engaged to his on-again-off-again girlfriend, Courtney, but he's not the most devoted fiancé, as evidenced by his recent romp between the sheets with Jamie.

I relax a little when the girl shifts and I see her face; she's one of the associates at Bender, Twain & McGuire, and I crossed paths with her a few times during the whole trial prep period. I tell myself that she and Ollie are just friendly colleagues, then let out a barely audible, "Well, shit," when she reaches out and rubs his arm intimately before turning away from Ollie and heading toward the elevator bank.

"Talk with him later," Damien says, and I realize he's been watching me watching Ollie. "You'll want to cool down first."

I start to tell him that I don't want to cool down at all. What I want to do is chew out my horndog of a friend. But I know Damien is right; now is not the time, and I continue at Damien's side, following in the wake of the bellman and our luggage.

It's Ollie who changes the plan. Ollie, who must not realize what I saw when he hurries up to us. "Nikki," he says and pulls me into a hug. "You heading out today?"

"We are," I say. My voice is tight, and I know damn well that Ollie will pick up on that. He knows me too well.

"Right." He shoves his hands into his pockets. "So I'll see you on the flip side?"

"Sure," I say. "We'll do drinks."

"Hell, yeah, we will."

Silence hangs between us, awkward and full of ghosts from the past. I can't help but remember a time not too long ago when we couldn't stop talking once we got together. And God forbid we should go out for drinks. Invariably we'd lose track of the time and end up getting kicked out when the staff needed to shut the place down.

But those memories are shrouded and soft. Nothing like the sharp, dangerous reality that now fills the space between us.

I reach for Damien, and he squeezes my hand, giving me strength even before I have to ask for it.

I see something that might be regret flicker in Ollie's eyes before he turns his attention to Damien. "Congrats again, man. I'm really happy it worked out for you."

"I appreciate it," Damien says. "And thank you for all your hard work." There's tension in his voice, but sincerity, too, and for that I am glad. I don't expect miracles, but I also know that if Damien and Ollie can't find a way to coexist, then my friendship with Ollie will have no chance to heal.

We say our goodbyes and continue outside to the valet stand. "Maybe I was imagining it?" I say to Damien once we're safe outside. I'm talking about the girl, of course, and it's obvious that Damien has followed my thinking. I want to believe that it was all innocent, but there was a definite flirt vibe going on, and I have a feeling that if I'd gone to meet Ollie for a drink in his room one night, the odds were good I wouldn't have found him alone.

"You weren't," Damien says, "and it's going to bite him in the ass. Maybe not because of this girl, but because he's living in a fantasy world, and eventually reality is going to catch up to him."

"I know," I say. "Ollie's always been a master of denial."

The limo arrives and the valet holds the door open while the bellman moves to the end of the car to load the trunk with our luggage. Damien lingers to tip the staff, but I go ahead and get in, my mind still on what he said about reality. Because he's right. Eventually reality catches up with everyone. The only question is, can you survive when it does?

The moment Damien gets into the limo, I can tell that he knows what I'm thinking. His expression softens, and he settles in next to me, silently taking my hand. He doesn't say anything until we are off of the city streets and on the A9 heading toward the airport. The gap in the conversation doesn't matter, though. I understand exactly what he's talking about when he turns to me and says simply, "Different realities, Nikki. You and I are together, and we can withstand whatever the world throws at us."

I draw in a deep breath, forcing myself not to ask the questions that seem lodged in my throat, begging for release: *Are you sure? Can we survive? Can we really make it after the bubble bursts?*

Damien goes on, either unaware of or ignoring my unspoken words that seem to me like such an elephant in the room. "Ollie has the chance to have what we have. To be part of something special. But he's scared and now he's sabotaging his own happiness." He reaches out and strokes my cheek with the back of his hand, the gesture so sweet I am certain that I will cry. "I'm not scared," he says. "Not about that. And neither are you."

I nod, because he's right. There are still a lot of things that I am afraid of, but being with Damien is not one of them.

"What did Lisa have to say?" Damien asks, and I have to once again marvel at how perceptive this man is. I am not afraid of being with Damien, but I still have sharp bouts of fear with regard to running my own business. And as a business consultant, Lisa is not only a friend, but also a potential colleague.

"She says one of her clients is moving to Boston and wants to sublet a space in Sherman Oaks at a pretty steep discount."

"That's excellent news," Damien says.

"Maybe," I say. "I'm still not sure I need it." My start-up

business has been a frequent topic of conversation between Damien and me throughout our time in Germany. Not only did I legitimately want his thoughts—after all, who better to take business advice from than a self-made billionaire?—but talking about my entrepreneurial adventures kept the focus off the trial.

Damien is convinced that I should go ahead and set up shop somewhere and hire myself out as an app designer for small businesses while I work on larger projects. I see his point, but that doesn't mean I'm not nervous.

"At the very least, you should meet with her and talk about the possibility. She's sharp and has a good reputation and a solid client base. She can help you."

I make a face, but I know he's right. I know, because we already had this argument after he told me that he had his office run a background check on Lisa, just to make sure she was legit. I'd aimed a few choice curses in his direction and told him that I'd handle my own goddamned due diligence. He told me to say thank you for taking that burden off my shoulders.

The night had ended in a bath with candles, but that didn't mean I hadn't been irritated.

The bottom line, though, is that I like Lisa. The times we've talked, we've hit it off. And I'm new enough to Los Angeles to crave the addition of a few more friends to the small circle I've gathered since I've moved to LA. Resolved, I email back that I'd love to meet with her. Then I drop my phone into my purse and try not to hyperventilate.

Beside me, Damien laughs. "You did good," he says. "I'll even take you out to lunch to celebrate. How do you feel about fish and chips?"

"Fish and chips?"

"I need to make a stop in London."

"All right. Sofia?"

"Do you mind?"

"Of course not." I don't know much about Sofia other than that she had a rocky childhood, and that she and Damien and his friend Alaine were tight during his tennis days. I know that she's been in and out of trouble recently, and that Damien has been frustrated by her inability to get her shit together, as he puts it.

I also know that she was the first woman he slept with, but they've been only friends for a long time.

"Is she okay?" I ask.

"I don't know," he says, then runs his fingers through his hair. "She's missing again." He looks ripped, but he reaches for my hand, and I squeeze it tight.

"Whatever you need," I say. "Anytime, anyplace."

I have never been to London, and I can't say that I'm seeing much of it on this journey. We went straight from Damien's jet to his limo to his office. During the course of that ride, I saw traffic and people and buildings that are significantly older than any we have in either Texas or Los Angeles. But I didn't see the Tower Bridge or Buckingham Palace or even a British pop star. In a way, I'm glad. This is hardly a vacation stop. On the other hand, who knows when I'll be back this way again?

Now we're at the London office of Stark International. It's located in the Canary Wharf business district, and Damien's office takes up one half of the thirty-eighth floor. The building is ultra modern, as is the furniture. Damien spent most of the short plane ride at my side, organizing a plan for locating Sofia while I made some notes about a smartphone app I've been pondering and sent Jamie and Evelyn both emails telling them we were on our way home and mentioning that I am—gasp—seriously considering leasing office space.

Now I'm alone. I stand idly by the window and stare out into this dreary, overcast day. I have a view of the Thames, but not much else, and even that famous river doesn't really draw my attention. My thoughts are twisting and turning when Damien comes back to his office, flanked by two efficient-looking women carrying electronic tablets and taking diligent notes.

He dismisses the one on the left and continues the conversation with the remaining woman. She's in her late fifties, tall and slim and with the look of someone very capable. He introduced me to her earlier as Ms. Ives, his permanent London assistant. As far as I can tell, one of her primary duties is acting as the liaison between Sofia's residential treatment facility and Damien.

I'm still fuzzy on why such massive resources are devoted to Sofia's mental health. I understand that she's a friend, but as far as I know, Damien doesn't assign assistants to keep tabs on all of his friends.

"Let me know the moment you get through to Alaine," he says to her. Alaine is now a chef in Los Angeles, but since he and Sofia and Damien were tight in their youth, Damien is hoping that he's heard from her. He moves behind his desk and glances down at the neat piles of paper. "And since I'm in town anyway, bring me the projections on the Newton project."

"Of course, Mr. Stark." She pauses in her exit to nod at me. "It was a pleasure to meet you, Ms. Fairchild. I'm sorry the circumstances couldn't have been more pleasant."

"A pleasure to meet you, too," I say. I remain by the window until the door shuts behind her, then I move to Damien's side. "Any luck?"

"Unfortunately, no. She checked herself out of the most recent rehab facility about a week ago, and no one's heard from her since."

"Oh. I'm sorry."

He grimaces. "It's not the first time, but usually she turns up after a few days back in her apartment in St. Albans, drunk or stoned off her ass and ready to go get dried out again."

"How old is she?"

"Twenty-nine. A year younger than me."

I nod, digesting the information. "And she's in rehab voluntarily? I mean, a judge didn't put her there?"

"Sometimes I think it would be easier if one did," he says flatly. "But no, it's voluntary."

"I see," I say, but of course, I don't. His desk is the size of the bathroom I share with Jamie, and made of chrome and glass and polished teak. I hop up on it, letting my legs dangle as I think about what he's told me—and about what he hasn't. "I get that you're worried something happened to her," I say. "What I don't understand is why. She's an adult and she checked out legitimately. Maybe she just decided to travel. To go hang with some other friends. They said she was almost dried out, right? Maybe she wants to prove to herself that she can operate sober on her own."

I expect him to shoot me down. To tell me—rightfully—that I don't know a thing about this girl. Instead, he seems to seriously consider my words.

"She may have done just that," Damien says. "But if you suddenly couldn't find Jamie, what would you do?"

Considering that happened not so very long ago, he knows exactly what I would do. Completely freak out. "Point taken, Mr. Stark."

"There's another reason, too," he says. His voice is casual, his movements equally so as he moves to the window where I was standing only moments before. I join him, and we both look out over this industrial section of the city. But it's not the view that has captured my attention. It's the reflection of Damien's face in the glass. His voice and manner may be casual; his expression is not.

I don't say anything, and after a moment, he continues. "She and I had an agreement. I'd foot the bill, and she'd finish the treatments. I don't like having my conditions ignored."

I nod. Knowing what I know of Damien, what he is saying makes perfect sense. The only thing I don't understand is why, and though I'm almost certain he will shut me down, I decide to voice the question. "Why are you paying for the treatment? And not just this one round. There've been others, too, right?"

The silence that hangs after my question seems unusually heavy, and I am not sure how much longer I can stand the weight of it bearing down upon me.

When he finally speaks, the words are soft, but there is a harshness to them that I don't understand. "I've been paying Sofia's way for as long as I've had the money to do so."

My question is once again "Why?"—and it bursts past my lips before I can think better of it.

I am looking at him now, not at his reflection. But Damien is still looking through the glass, and I can't help but wonder if he's seeing the city or the past. Is it me that he is standing beside? Or is Sofia next to him?

I squeeze my hands into fists, because I do not want to be jealous of a ghost, and yet I feel those tiny green seeds begin to sprout inside me.

Damien still hasn't answered my question, and I think that perhaps I have gone too far. But then he finally speaks, and I am suddenly cold—chilled to the bone for Damien, and for the innocent girl who was his friend.

"She was Richter's daughter," Damien says. "And he didn't leave her a dime."

It takes me a minute to fully comprehend what he is saying. "Sofia is Richter's daughter, but he left all of his money to you?"

"He did," Damien says.

"So that's why you take care of her? Why didn't you just sign the money over to her?"

"That wasn't an option," he says. "For one thing, she had issues even back then. She's brilliant but impulsive, and she doesn't make the best choices. So I set up a trust. She can access money for her needs. I bought an apartment for her. I pay for her treatment. The bottom line is that she has a life and property because I didn't give her that money. If I had, she probably would have died from an overdose. At the very least, she would have either drunk, injected, or snorted it away."

I nod because that all makes sense.

"But the truth is that I would have helped her even if there had been no inheritance." For the first time since he has started speaking, he turns to face me. "She knew about what he did to me. Her friendship helped keep me sane."

"Oh, God." I'm not sure if he can hear the words through the hand that I have pressed against my mouth. But I am certain that he can see the horror—and the sadness—in my eyes. "She knew what kind of a monster her father was."

"She did," he says. "And we survived him together. In the end, I was better suited at survival than she was. But dammit, Nikki, she was there for me."

I am nodding, tears trickling down my cheeks. "Alaine, too?"

Damien shakes his head. "He didn't know anything. I value his friendship, of course. But my relationship with Sofia runs deeper."

I take his hand and hold it tight. Those tiny green tendrils have completely shriveled up. There is no jealousy. Instead, I am as desperate to find this woman as Damien. This poor girl who shared what little strength she had with Damien, and suffered through her own kind of hell simply from knowing that the blood of a monster flowed through her veins.

"You'll find her," I say. "When have you ever not gotten something you want?"

As I had hoped, that draws a small smile to his lips. He pulls me into his arms and holds me tight.

"The trial must have been hell for her," I say. "Her father. You." I keep my cheek pressed against his chest as his reply rumbles through me.

"We didn't talk about it. She didn't like to think about the fact that Merle Richter was her father. I spoke to her a few hours before you arrived in Germany, actually. I kept expecting her to bring it up. She never did."

I don't know what to say next, so I am relieved when Ms. Ives's voice comes across the intercom, telling Damien that she has Alaine on a video call, and does Damien want her to put it through to the wall screen?

Damien tells her to go ahead, and immediately a decorative mirror on the far side of the room turns opaque, then blue. And then, suddenly, I see Alaine's face.

"Damien," he says, "I was so pleased to hear about the dismissal."

"Thank you. You remember Nikki?"

"Of course. It is a pleasure to see you again, Nikki. Hopefully next time it will be in person with a glass of my best wine."

"I'd like that." When I met Alaine, I hadn't been able to place his accent. Since then, Damien has told me that he grew up in Switzerland. It's still not an accent I would recognize easily, but listening now, I can hear the influences of both French and German.

"I'm sorry I wasn't available when you called earlier. Your message said it was about Sofia?"

"She's gone again," Damien says. "Checked herself out a few days ago and took off. I haven't been able to find her, and I thought she might have called you."

"You are in luck, my friend," he says. "I know exactly where she is."

I meet Damien's eyes and see the flash of relief. "Where?"

"Shanghai."

"Shanghai?" Incredulity laces his voice. "Why? When did you talk to her?"

Alaine's brow furrows. "Three—no, four days ago. Do you remember David, that drummer she was intrigued with a few years back? Apparently his band is booked for a week in a club there. She said she might be in Chicago, too, if a job the band is hoping for comes through."

Damien presses his fingertips to his temple. His expression is an odd mix of softness and concern. It's a paternal expression, the kind I imagine I'd see if he was worried about our own kids one day.

Our kids? I stiffen, but in surprise, not fear. The thought came unbidden, but it is not terrifying. On the contrary, it's soothing, as if I've been given a sneak peek into the future, and it is a future with Damien and a family.

"She called you?" Damien asks Alaine. "I've been trying to reach her by cell, but it just rolls over to voice mail."

"It was a video call," he says. "I asked if she'd talked to you, but she didn't want to bother you during the trial. I'm surprised she hasn't called you now that it's over, but knowing Sofia, she hasn't seen the news."

"Can you conference her in through the account she used?"

I see Alaine's eyes shift up, as if he's examining the various options on his computer monitor. "I think so. Hang on." Alaine's image stays on the screen, but a smaller box appears in the corner. It's a snapshot of a girl with spiky black hair tipped with red. She has a multi-pierced ear filled with tiny silver rings. Her elven face is small and delicate and her skin is unnaturally pale. Her deep brown eyes are ringed with pitch-black kohl. The only color comes from her lips, which are wide and full and striking with bloodred lipstick. It's hard to tell her age, but even though Damien said that Sofia is almost thirty, she looks barely twenty to me. Then again, I have no idea how old this image is.

"I think this will do it," Alaine says, then almost immediately adds, "Well, damn the girl."

It takes me a second to understand what has happened, but then I see that a red X has appeared as a watermark over the image. "What is that?" I ask.

"She's closed her account," Damien says. "You don't have another contact number?"

"Other than her cell phone? No." Alaine's mouth is curved down into a frown. "I swear I don't know what she's thinking half the time. But she said she'd call after Shanghai and let me know where they're going next."

"Tell her to call me, too. For that matter, hook me into the call."

"Will do. And, Damien, don't worry. She will turn up. She always does. And we both know that she is a mercurial soul."

"She's a disturbed soul," Damien says.

"Aren't we all?" Alaine says, but there is a sparkle in his eyes, and it's obvious that he doesn't understand the fundamental truth of his words.

As soon as the screen goes blank, Damien calls Ms. Ives back in and gives her a list of instructions, including searching the file for David and then tracking his current band to Shanghai. She takes meticulous notes and promises to contact him the moment she has information. As soon as she's left, Damien folds me into his arms.

"Are you okay?"

"Frustrated," he says. "But I'm fine."

I see the worry etched on his face, but when he looks at me and smiles, it all seems to fade.

"Thank you," he says.

"For what?"

"For everything."

My answering smile is so broad it's almost painful. "Anytime, Mr. Stark."

"I think I'm done here for now," he says. "You've never been to London, have you? Do you want to stay the night? We could go to Harrods. Catch a show in the West End. See a few sights."

"No," I say. "I just want to be with you. I just want to go home."

"And that's another reason that we are perfect together," Damien says. "I want exactly the same thing."

10

"Welcome aboard, Mr. Stark, Ms. Fairchild. Would you care for a glass of champagne?"

"Yes, thank you," I say, taking the glass gratefully. Damien and I are seated side by side in the rich leather recliners. There's a polished table in front of us and equally shiny wood trim throughout the interior of the very large cabin. The seats are so comfortable I'd happily have them at home. The flight attendant is tall and slim, with a mass of curls piled on her head in a way that manages to look both cute and professional.

I sip the champagne, sigh, and have to admit that there's something to be said for the billionaire lifestyle.

"What happened to the other plane?" I ask Damien. We'd flown from Munich to London in a small jet, similar to the one he keeps hangared in Santa Monica. While comfortable, it pales in comparison to this one.

"This is the Lear Bombardier Global 8000," he says. "We're crossing the Atlantic, remember? Not to mention all of the United States. I thought traveling in a plane with sufficient fuel capacity made sense. Plus it's easier to get work done with an actual office.

And sleep in an actual bed," he adds, trailing his finger lightly up my leg and giving me shivers.

"This thing has an office and a bed?"

"There's a bed in the stateroom," he says.

"Wow." I want to get up and explore, but the attendant has already asked that we fasten our seat belts as the plane is now taxiing toward the runway.

Now she's standing next to the jump seat. She's speaking into a headset, presumably communicating with the pilot. A moment later, she hangs up, then walks toward Damien and me. "Mr. Stark, you've had a telephone call from Mr. Maynard. He tried to reach your cell, but apparently the call didn't connect. When he realized you were on board, he called the tower and asked that we get a message to you to call him at your earliest convenience."

"Can we hold on the runway?"

"Yes, sir."

"I'll call him now," he says, then pulls his phone out of his pocket. I watch from beside him, frowning as he's put through to Charles. I can't imagine why Maynard would be calling—could the court have changed its mind? Is it even allowed to do that?

I study Damien's face, but his expression gives me no clues. It's gone completely blank and totally unreadable. A boardroom expression designed to give nothing away to competitors—or to me.

After a moment, Damien stands, and though I reach for his hand, he doesn't reach back. Neither does he meet my eyes. He heads to the back of the plane and disappears into what I assume is the office.

I try to focus on my book, but it's impossible, and after I've read the same page over at least three dozen times, Damien finally returns. He nods at the attendant, who radios the cockpit, and by the time Damien has fastened his seat belt we are once again readying for takeoff.

"What happened?" I ask.

"Nothing to worry about." He stills wears that bland, corporate mask and I feel my heart constrict, as if a giant fist is squeezing it tight.

"But I am worrying. Charles wouldn't radio the tower unless it was important."

He smiles, but it seems forced, and I see no corresponding humor in his eyes. "You're right. He wouldn't."

"Then what is it?"

"There've been some time-sensitive developments on a couple of matters that I've been chipping away at." His voice is level, his words perfectly reasonable. I, however, don't believe a word of it.

"Don't shut me out again, Damien."

"I'm not," he says firmly. "Not everything is about us."

I tense, the sting of his words as potent as a slap. "I see." I finger the book in my lap. "Well, never mind."

"Nikki . . ." His voice is no longer cold.

I tilt my head to look at him, my own mask firmly in place. "It's fine," I say.

His eyes search mine, the near-black one seeming to see so deep into me that it is almost dizzying. I hold his gaze for as long as I can before I have to look away or else risk him seeing too clearly that I'm certain his words are all bullshit. What I don't understand is why.

I turn my head, ostensibly to look out the window as the plane gathers speed, rushing forward to its inevitable climb. And as the wheels lift off, I can't help but think that we have reached the point of no return, Damien and I. Like this plane, we will either continue to move forward, or we will crash.

There are no other options.

And as I glance sideways at Damien with his papers spread out and his face a mask of secrets and fears, I cannot help but be very, very afraid.

*   *   *

I'm sitting cross-legged on the narrow bed in the stateroom, feeling hollow. I brought the empty champagne flute back with me, and now I hold it like a baton—one hand on the base, and one hand on the rim, the fragile stem stretched out between my hands.

It would be so simple, I think. Just a contraction of muscles. One quick movement and—*snap*.

One second, maybe less, and I'd have the stem in my hand, its top raw, the edge of broken glass as sharp as a knife.

My skirt is hitched up so that I can sit like this, and beneath the material that is stretched taut across my legs, I can see the marred flesh of my inner thighs. I can imagine tracing the stem along the edge of the most jagged one. The pain as I press the glass into soft flesh. The release as I tug it down, my skin yielding and the horrible pressure in my chest finally lessening as the valve is open and all this shit that has been building can finally explode out of me.

I want it—oh, God, I want it.

No.

I squeeze my eyes tight, desperate for Damien's hand. But he is not here, and it is just me, and I am not certain that I can do this alone.

Slowly, I run the rounded rim of the flute against my thigh. Just one snap—just a little pressure—

No, no, goddammit, no.

I will *not* do this, and I lift the glass, prepared to hurl it away from me, but a firm tap on the door startles me and I jump guiltily. I don't expect it to be Damien—he returned to the jet's office as soon as we reached altitude two hours ago, and I haven't seen him since. Instead, I assume it's Katie, the flight attendant, who promised to wake me when dinner was served.

"I'm not hungry," I call. "I'm going to sleep a little longer."

But then the door bursts open and he's right there. *Damien.*

And there I am holding the goddamn flute.

I shift my position so that I'm sitting with my legs out and my back against the polished wood siding. I casually put the flute on the nearby table, hoping that he doesn't realize the dark direction in which my thoughts were traveling.

He stands there for so long, I fear he isn't going to say a word. His face is firm, his eyes sad. "You should have called me out for my bullshit," he finally says, and I allow myself the tiniest bit of relief. He didn't see the glass; he didn't realize what I was thinking.

"Of course it's about us," he continues. "There's nothing in my life that isn't about us. How could there be when my world revolves around you?"

"Don't," I say, still unbalanced and edgy. "Don't shift the focus by plying me with romantic platitudes."

I see the spark of anger fire in his eyes as he crosses the stateroom in three long strides, the door clicking shut behind him. "Platitudes?" he repeats, his tone hard. "Jesus, Nikki, are you telling me you don't know what you mean to me?" He reaches out to touch me, but stops with his fingers only inches from my face. "Haven't I told you every single day that we've been together?"

I can feel the heat rolling off him. A violent passion. A sensual need. I close my eyes and draw a shuddering breath as my blood pounds through me in response. Oh, yes. I know how he feels about me; I feel the same way. Alive in his arms. Lost out of them. He is everything to me.

And that is why I am willing to fight so hard.

Slowly, I open my eyes and tilt my head to look at him. "I know," I say. "But that doesn't make it relevant. Maynard didn't call about stock prices or your corporate logo or what they serve in the goddamn lunchroom at Stark Tower."

He's staring at me as if I've gone mad, and maybe I have a little. But dammit, I want him to understand.

"We're not attached at the hip, Damien. Everything's *not* about us. And that's fine. Hell, it's good. I don't want to steal your autonomy any more than I want to hand you mine. But I have memorized every line of your face, and I recognized the shadows I saw in your eyes. So don't trivialize something that really does affect us by making it sound like some minor irritation that's going to require us to reschedule dinner next Thursday."

He raises an eyebrow as he looks at me. "Well," he says, and that simple word holds both surprise and acknowledgment.

After a moment, he takes the last step toward me and sits next to me on the bed. He gently takes my hand and uses his fingertip to trace lightly upon my skin. He says nothing, though, and the silence hangs heavy between us, full of both questions and hope.

I remember my thought as we took off—that we are either going to keep moving forward, or we are going to crash. Finally, I can take it no longer. I reach for him, then stroke my hand down the side of his cheek. "I love you," I say, though the words seem too big for my throat.

"Nikki." My name sounds as though it was wrenched from him, and when he pulls me close and holds me tight, I close my eyes, wanting—no, needing—to hear the words back. He has not said that he loves me since my first week in Germany. Not since the trial prep began in earnest and the attorneys warned him that he was risking jail and his future if he didn't testify.

I need to hear it now, though. I desperately need him to say those three little words. Not because I doubt that Damien loves me, but because I cannot shake the fear that we are on a collision course with the real world, and that those words are our only shield once our shiny, protective bubble shatters.

He says nothing, though. He simply holds me, his arms closing tight around me as if that is all the protection I need.

When he does speak, his words surprise me. "The press has been going hot and heavy suggesting that I bribed someone to get the charges dropped."

I stiffen and pull back so that I can see his face. "Those fucking bastards."

The corner of his mouth lifts. "I agree completely with your assessment, but the truth is I've been accused of worse." I search his face and see nothing of my own anger. Whatever is bothering him, it isn't this ridiculous accusation. That's just one part of the story.

"Okay," I say. "Go on."

"Apparently the prosecutors and judges weren't thrilled with the allegations. The prosecution released an official statement that the charges against me were dropped after additional evidence was brought to the court's attention."

Considering that's exactly what happened, I'm still not seeing the problem. But I say nothing, content to wait.

"Now the press is pushing to see the evidence."

Oh . . .

I squeeze his hand tight. "Damien, that's—" I cut myself off, because I don't know what to say. Horrible? I think of how wrecked he was after the dismissal and try to magnify that a million-fold if those photos are released to the whole goddamned world. My chest constricts and my skin feels prickly merely from the thought. I can't even imagine how Damien must feel—or how brutally the release of those photos will rip him apart.

I suck in air and try again. "Surely they won't. The evidence is sealed, right? What did Maynard say?" I'm babbling, but I know nothing about the law, and even less than that about the law in Germany. Does the press have a right to see the evidence? Will the court or the prosecution turn the photos over to save its own reputation?

"Vogel is on it, and Charles is staying in Munich to work with him. He's optimistic, but it's too early for me to have any real sense of the outcome."

"I see." I want to tell him that it will be okay, but I can't quite bring the lie to my lips. Because if those photos are released, it will rip him apart. And, yes, Damien is strong, and I know that he will heal. But like the cuts on my thighs, that wound will never go away. Part of him will have died, and nothing will be the same again.

"I'm sorry I hurt you," he says as he brushes the pad of his thumb across my lips.

I open my mouth, drawing him in, then close my eyes and savor the taste of him. "Aren't you the one who told me that pain and passion go hand in hand?" I murmur when I finally release him.

I watch as his eyes darken, then gasp as he pushes me back onto the narrow bed. Desire—hot and heavy—slams through me with such force and power it makes me dizzy. I need him—I need his hands upon my breasts and his body against mine. I need his tongue in my mouth and his cock deep inside me.

I need to feel the connection between us. I need to revel in it, to bathe in it.

I need to feel what I already know—that Damien is mine, and that I am and always will be his.

His hands are holding fast to my wrists, keeping my arms stretched above my head. He holds me tight, and I wince from the pain of my skin twisting in his grip, then cry out again when he violently kneads my breasts through my thin cotton shirt. "Do you like that?" he asks.

"Yes, oh, God, yes."

He lowers his mouth to my breast, suckling through my shirt before shoving it up, then tugging my breast free from my bra. He is straddling me at the hips, and I am breathing hard, unable to move as his hands hold me down and his mouth closes over my now-bare breast. He draws the nipple in between his lips, sucking so intensely that I arch up, then cry out when he bites down, his teeth drawing tighter than the little silver rings from the night before.

He pulls away, tugging the nipple with him, and I arch up, wanting more—wanting that sensual bite, that seductive sting.

"Tell me what you need," he demands.

"You," I say. "I need you."

"Goddammit, Nikki," he growls, "that's not what I mean. Tell me what you need."

And that's when I realize—of course he saw the flute. Of course he knew what I was thinking. Damien knows; hell, he always knows.

"I need you," I repeat hoarsely. "That's all I need. I wasn't going to do it, I swear. I thought about it, but I wasn't going to do it."

"Oh, baby." His mouth closes over mine, and he is kissing me, wild and hungry and with so much fervency I feel as though we will both get lost in it. His hands move over my body and I writhe under his touch, every sense firing. "I'm sorry," he says. "I brought you there, and I'm so fucking sorry."

"No," I say. "It's me. Only me. And you're what keeps me strong. Oh, God, Damien, please," I add, because I cannot have his hands on me and have this conversation at the same time. "Now, please, I need you now."

"*Nikki.*" My name is an anthem as his fingers thrust aside the negligible material of my thong and his fingers sink deep inside my already dripping cunt. "Oh, baby."

I shift my hips and struggle against his hand that still holds me fast. Whatever anger or hurt I'd felt moments ago has completely evaporated. This is Damien, the man I love. The man I need, and

I want him inside me. I want him touching me. I want—dear God, I simply want.

He releases his hold on me to unfasten his pants and free his cock. I tilt my head up, then suck in air when I see him, thick and hard. I shift my arm, my fingers itching to stroke him.

"No," he says, and I have to bite my lower lip to hold back my cry of disappointment as I comply, keeping my arms stretched high above my head.

"Hurry," I beg. I spread my legs wider, desperate for him. I am liquid flame. I am hedonism personified. I am lust and need and passion.

And then he is above me, his mouth upon mine, wild and wet even as the head of his cock slides over my sex, cruelly teasing me but never entering me.

I arch and writhe, begging him with my body, and when that doesn't work I nip his lower lip with my teeth and demand, "Now, Damien, fuck me now."

And then I moan as he thrusts hard inside me. My skirt is around my waist, my thong shoved to one side. He balances with one hand beside our joined bodies. The other hand is twined with my fingers above my head.

The plane hits a pocket of air, and I cry out in alarm and pleasure as we free-fall, then slam back at altitude, the motion thrusting Damien even deeper inside of me. I want my hands to be free—I want to cup his ass and push him hard inside me—but he is giving me no leeway. He breaks the kiss and as he balances above me, he looks deep in my eyes. Our bodies are touching only where his hand circles my wrist and where his cock is thrusting so enticingly in and out of me.

"That's it, baby," he says, going deeper with each stroke, his body rubbing my clit with each motion. "I want to watch your face as you explode. I want to know that I've taken you to the brink, and then I want to go over the edge with you.

"Come on," he urges as the storm rises like a wellspring of colors inside me. "Come on, baby—oh, yes," he groans as my body explodes around his. The orgasm ripples through me, making me arch up and cry out and writhe with wanton desperation. I'm not sure if I'm trying to escape this riot of sensation or if I'm trying to make it go on and on. All I know is that Damien has not stopped thrusting and the muscles of my sex are still spasming around him and I am clawing at the cover on this bed and arching up and trying to breathe and—

"Oh, God," I cry as one final, violent jolt of electricity cuts through me just seconds before Damien finds his own release. I collapse, limp, onto the bed and though my eyes are heavy, I cannot pass up the joy of watching pure sensual satisfaction play across his face. Then he smiles at me, his expression so tender that I can think of nothing more than curling up next to him.

As if in answer to my thought, he lowers himself beside me, and the hand that just a few minutes ago held so fast to my wrist now traces lazy strokes down my arm.

"Welcome to the Mile High Club," he says, and I burst out laughing.

I roll closer and nestle against him, sated and satisfied and happy. "You are what I need, Damien. You're all that I need."

I have surrendered to this man completely, and now, once again, it feels wholly right. Between Damien and me, sex is as necessary as conversation. It is our method of discovery. Our sharing of trust. And our ultimate surrender.

It is, I think, his "I love you" spoken with his body, if not with his words.

I'm drifting, neither awake nor asleep, when Damien's words bring me fully back to myself. "No matter what the German court decides, there's a good chance those pictures are going public."

There is no emotion in his voice, and that chills me more than anything. I don't move. We are spooned together, my back against his chest, his arm draped over my waist. I keep my eyes closed, as if that somehow makes the words less real. "Why would you say that?"

"I think your earlier thought was right," he says. "I think my father might be the one behind this."

"Damien, no." I roll over now—I have to see him. "Do you really think so?"

"It makes sense. If I go to jail, his asset stream dries up." Despite the fact that Damien's father makes my mother look as sweet and cuddly as the Easter Bunny, Damien has continued to support the man.

"Even if you're right, that only explains how the court got the photos. Why on earth would you think that he'd make them go public?"

He rubs his fingers together, symbolizing money.

I shake my head, not following.

"Tabloids. Internet sites. So-called news programs. They'll all pay a lot for information if they think it will sell ad space or papers."

"Shit," I say, because he is right, and that pretty much sums it up. "Maybe it's not him."

"Maybe not." But I can tell that he doesn't believe it.

"What will you do?"

"I'm still thinking about that," he says, and there is a dangerous edge to his voice.

"Will you tell me when you decide?"

He presses a kiss to my forehead. "Yes," he says. "I promise."

I breathe in deep, wishing I could somehow make everything better for him, but knowing that's just not possible. "How much longer before we get home?" Part of me wants the plane to land right now. Part of me wishes we could stay in flight forever.

"A few more hours," he says, idly stroking my bare arm, the

touch feather-soft and sweetly enticing. "But we're not going home. Not right away."

"We're not? Where are we going?"

"One of my favorite places," he says, brushing a kiss across my hair. "I think you'll like it."

11

The narrow mountain road twists and turns so much that I am beginning to feel a bit nauseated. It's late, but the full moon casts a glow over the towering pines that grow so thick along the side of the road that it seems as though we are traveling through a tunnel. We are in a Jeep Grand Cherokee that someone from Damien's staff left for him at the Ontario airport just outside of San Bernadino. It's the least sporty car I have ever seen Damien drive, but he looks perfectly at home. In fact, I can't remember a time when Damien has ever looked out of place. It's that cool confidence that lets him slide into any situation, and I amuse myself by thinking of him going from a high-powered board meeting to a survivalist weekend retreat.

"You're grinning," he says.

"I'm picturing you in a loincloth holding an atlatl," I admit. "Damien Stark, the leader of the tribe."

"Please tell me this isn't a retreat you're planning for us," he says. "Not unless it involves you in a Raquel Welch–style fur miniskirt for a weekend."

"Even then you wouldn't like it," I tease. "I believe the women were in charge of the cooking back in the caveman days."

"Good point," he says with a wicked grin. I don't bother to take offense. We both know that my cooking skills take a nosedive once you get past "peel back plastic cover and set microwave for five minutes."

"Are we getting close?" He has told me only that he wants to take me someplace before we head back to LA. Beyond that, he is giving me no clues.

"Just around this bend." As the Jeep curves to the right, the trees break for a moment and I see the water of Lake Arrowhead sparkling like a diamond in the moonlight. I've only been up in the San Bernadino Mountains once, and that was when I came to visit Jamie one Christmas. Snow had come early that year, and we rented a car with snow tires and made the slow trudge up the mountain to Big Bear. In the end, neither of us had actually put on skis, but we'd had a fabulous time sitting in the lodge, sipping Irish coffee by the fire, and watching all the guys in tight snow pants.

A few more curves, and the view of the lake disappears. I'm totally turned around, but it's obvious that Damien knows exactly where he's going. He hasn't told me a thing, though. So although I've clued in to the general concept of a mountain retreat, I don't know if we're going to a resort, a hotel, a friend's house, or yet another property that Damien owns.

The beam of the headlights glance over a wooden sign indicating a private drive, and Damien turns onto it, then follows an even steeper, even more narrow road. The trees are closer on both sides of the Jeep, and in the dark I'm actually starting to feel a bit claustrophobic. Then we are cresting the rise, and all I see is an Alpine chateau looming in front of us, nestled among the towering pines. It is a stunning property, with wooden shingles and stone chimneys, and the kinds of angles and turrets that give the impression that we haven't left Bavaria. Or perhaps that we made a wrong turn on the way home and ended up in Switzerland.

Damien slows the car at an intricate iron gate, then rolls down his window and punches in a code, thereby destroying all illusions that this extravagant place is either a hotel or a bed-and-breakfast or a mountain spa resort.

"You own this?"

He eases the Jeep through the slowly widening gap in the gate. "I wanted a weekend getaway. Something I could drive to at the last minute. Something out of the way."

"Palm Springs not appealing? Your Santa Barbara hotel too long a drive?"

"The condo in Palm Springs is on the golf course," he says, "and since I'm not much of a golfer, I let my staff reserve time as a perk. As for Santa Barbara, it's an exceptional property, but sometimes a man just wants to be alone. Or not alone," he says, reaching over to squeeze my hand.

I squeeze back, amused. "You know those computer apps where you can put a little flag on a map for every town you've lived in or where all your Facebook friends are from, or whatever?"

"Sure."

"We need to get one of those for all your properties."

His answering grin is smug. "I'll get right on that. And then we can start working our way through them, one by one. Only a few of my properties have been properly christened."

"Is that so? Well, then. Maybe we should start with your Arrowhead property," I say. "Maybe we should start tonight."

"I can't think of a better way to spend the evening. Or the morning. Or the afternoon."

I grin as I take another look at the massive structure. "This place is huge. I say we christen these rooms first and then we can move on to other locations. That will take us, what? A year?"

"It's not that big," he says. "Only nine thousand square feet."

"Practically an efficiency apartment," I say, deadpan.

"Eleven thousand if you count the guest house," he says, pointing to the smaller building that is connected to the main house by a covered walkway. "The caretaker and his wife live there. I told them this was a relaxing and informal week and to leave us to fend for ourselves."

"Sounds good. I'm all about relaxing."

"The property has a pool, a hot tub, an outdoor grill, and access to some of the county-maintained hiking trails. It also," he adds, with a devious grin, "has a number of very comfortable beds. Depending on the kind of relaxing you'd like to do."

"I'm big on variety," I say. "A bed . . . a hot tub . . . so long as I'm not relaxing by myself, I'll be a very happy girl."

"I do love the way you think." He kills the engine on the Jeep and turns in his seat to face me. "That's not the only reason we're here," he says seriously. "I thought about what you said. About reality catching us off guard. And I thought that it might be good for both of us to ease slowly back into the real world."

"We can go as slow as you want," I say. "You won't get any complaints from me." Then I remember my plans, and grimace. "Except that I have to be back in LA by ten Friday morning. That's when Lisa is going to show me the sublet."

"Fair enough. Friday marks our return to reality. A sad, mournful day."

"Don't even," I say. "You're going to fire up that Bluetooth headset and start cooking up some deal before we even get through that door, and you know it."

"I won't," he says with a familiar gleam in his eye. "I have plans for when we walk through that door."

"Do you? I bet I can guess what." And I have to confess that I'm looking forward to it. Where Damien is concerned, I'm always looking forward to it.

We get out of the car and walk over the wide wooden bridge to the massive front door. I hang back as Damien opens it, but the second I step over the threshold, I'm accosted by a very loud, very familiar scream—*Jamie*.

Behind her, a wide white banner hangs across the entrance hall and dozens of helium-filled balloons float and bump up at the ceiling. My eyes meet Damien's, and I realize that he is as surprised as I am.

"You didn't know?" I ask, as Jamie launches herself at me and wraps me up in a tight hug.

"About Jamie, yes," Damien says as Jamie shifts her hug from me to him. "I couldn't think of a better way to ease you back into reality than to bring Jamie out here. She's about as real as it gets."

I can't help but laugh in agreement, especially when Jamie sticks her tongue out at him.

"But the decorations? I didn't have a clue."

"Oh, please," Jamie says. "It's a celebration. Banners, balloons, food, drink." She turns her focus to me, her eyes as wide as if she'd just stepped into heaven. "This place is so well-stocked you wouldn't believe."

I cock my head toward Damien and grin wickedly. "It's Damien," I say. "Excess is an art form."

"Watch it," he says, then lightly smacks my bottom before hooking an arm around my waist and planting a bone-melting kiss on me right there in front of my best friend. "Fuck reality," he whispers when he releases me. "I want to stay in our bubble as long as we can."

Yes, I think as I press my back to his chest and hold on tight to the arms he has wrapped around me. *So do I.*

"And where exactly are we going?" Damien asks from the Jeep's passenger seat.

"It's a surprise," I say. "Now shut up before I kill us." I'm not used to driving so big a car, especially on narrow, winding roads, but the surprise Jamie and I cooked up would be much less of a surprise if we told Damien where we are going.

He eyes me suspiciously. "The good kind of surprise where I get to slowly strip you naked? Or a bad kind of surprise?"

"Oh. My. God," Jamie says from the backseat. "I'm going to just melt back here."

I bite back a grin and focus on Damien. "Does any surprise that doesn't end with me naked fall within your definition of bad?"

"Pretty much," he says, and in the rearview mirror, I see Jamie clamp her hands over her ears.

I laugh. "Then I guess we're deep in the land of horrible."

He leans back in the seat at an angle so that he can stretch his legs out and examine me. He twines his fingers behind his head. He looks relaxed as sin and sexy as hell. "All right," he says slowly. "Tell me."

"You tell him," I say to Jamie. "It was your idea."

"We found a bar in Crestline that has a karaoke night," she says.

"Did you?" he asks blandly.

Actually, Jamie found it, but I enthusiastically agreed to this night out. After the news he got on the plane, I am operating on the theory that the more fun the better. Or I was. Now, I'm not so sure. Because despite everything I have learned about Damien Stark, I cannot read his expression.

"Are you going to serenade me?" he asks.

"Nope."

"Are you going to serenade Jamie?"

"Double nope."

"I see," he says.

My grin falters a bit. Jamie and Ollie and I used to get a huge kick out of karaoke bars, and they were always a cure for a bad week. But Damien is not Jamie or Ollie or me, and considering his current stony expression, it's more than possible that I misjudged the appeal of this evening's entertainment.

I meet Jamie's eyes in the mirror and see her tiny shrug.

I am just about to announce that I was joking and that we are really on our way to a five-star restaurant where we'll discuss business theory and stock prices, when his mouth twitches and his eyes begin to light with his slowly growing smile. "And here I thought you loved me," he says.

I force myself not to sag with relief. "I do."

"And you thought that singing bad seventies songs in public would be a good way to show it?"

I pause at a stop sign, and take the opportunity to glare at him. "Are you mocking me, Mr. Stark?"

"Never," he says, but his eyes are dancing.

"Mmm. I was actually thinking along the lines of the Rat Pack oeuvre, but I'll go with bad seventies if that's what you want. I'm more than willing to compromise."

His expression is pure sin. "I'm very glad to hear it, Ms. Fairchild."

"There it is," Jamie says from the backseat. She is pointing to a brightly lit building just up the block. "That's it, and thank God. It's getting just a little too warm in here."

I bite back a retort. As far as I'm concerned, with Damien, it can never be too hot.

Whatever heat there might be in the Jeep, however, has nothing on the interior of the bar. It's cramped and smoky and so warm it feels sticky. And, frankly, that's part of its charm. I can see from Damien's approving expression as we walk through the wooden double doors and into the dark interior that he agrees.

"It's definitely got atmosphere," he says, his hand pressed lightly to my back as he scans the room.

"What about that table?" Jamie asks, and Damien and I follow her across the room to a four-top near the stage. "Order me something fun," Jamie says, then disappears toward the ladies' room.

Karaoke night is already going strong, and as we get settled, a teddy bear of a man with a lumberjack beard belts out Gloria Gaynor's "I Will Survive" with at least as much energy as Gloria herself ever put into it.

I slump a bit in my chair and press my hand over my mouth in sympathetic embarrassment.

Damien notices and laughs. "Not planning to jump up and burst into song yourself?"

"No," I admit. "At the moment, I don't need the pain."

I can tell that Damien knows I'm teasing, but he still cocks his head and studies my face. I roll my eyes and take his hand, squeezing tight. "Sorry," I say. "I shouldn't joke about that."

"I don't mind the jokes," he says, "so long as you don't mind me second-guessing them to make sure there's no hidden agenda."

I turn my head away so that I do not have to meet his eyes. I can't help but think how close I came on the plane to breaking that damn glass and dragging the raw edge of the shard into the flesh of my thigh.

I didn't, though. And it is the fact that we are both aware of my victory that gives me the strength to turn and look back into his eyes, expecting to see reproach on his face. But all I see is love.

"I will always worry," he says gently. "There is no off switch, no pause button. You are the thing in this world that means the most to me, but we both know that I have come close to breaking you more than once. So get mad at me if you want, but don't tell me to stop being concerned or second-guessing you. I won't. I can't."

Slowly, I smile. "It's not about my pain," I say lightly, intent on refocusing our evening to its proper perspective. "It's about the pain of all these people were I to get up on this stage."

"Oh, but you're going to," he says, grinning wickedly.

"Um, no. No way."

"Mmm." He stands and eyes me for a moment, then nods. "All right," he says. "You don't have to get up on the stage."

I exhale in relief even as he bends to kiss my cheek, but then he walks away toward the guy who is emceeing this evening. A little finger of dread shoots up my spine as I see the emcee's eyes widen in recognition. Then he nods and starts to type something into his machine as Damien takes the stage. My chest tightens, and suddenly I'm having a little trouble breathing. Damien, however, doesn't look nervous at all. He's standing there in front of the screen upon which some lyrics will begin to flash, the lights from above shining down on him. He's wearing jeans and a casual linen shirt, and I can't help but think that he's the sexiest man in this bar. And he's all mine.

He taps the mic, and a soft *pop* reverberates through the room, making me jump. I shift in my seat and see Jamie hurrying over, her eyes as wide as mine feel.

On stage, Damien focuses on the crowd, looking as cool and confident as if he were in his own office about to give a presentation to a client. "I'd planned on doing Elton John and Kiki Dee's 'Don't Go Breaking My Heart,' but I'm having a little trouble working out the logistics of a duet." I feel the eyes of the pub's patrons as they turn to look at me. I'm not hard to find, especially considering Jamie's hoot of laughter and then her fingers aimed shotgun-style in my direction. I cup my hand over my forehead and duck my head to hide my blush, not certain if I'm amused at Damien or desperately pissed off.

Then again, I got myself into this mess. It may have been Jamie's idea to start out with, but I adopted it fully. I should have known he'd find a way to turn it around to his full advantage.

I draw in a breath, drop my hand, and lean back in my chair as Damien continues speaking.

"So I'm going to go with a serenade." He looks right at me. "For you, baby."

I brush away the tears that have welled and give him a shaky, happy smile. The music starts, and I'm enough of a fan of big band music and the Rat Pack that I recognize the song right away. The tears that I'd brushed away return immediately as Damien begins to croon the lyrics to Dean Martin's "You're Nobody Till Somebody Loves You." It's not a perfect voice, but it's strong and on-key, and he has captured the audience.

Then he's stepping off the stage, the mic in hand, and coming to our table, his voice filling the place, even rising above the claps and catcalls from the patrons who are loving every second of this spectacle. Half of them are holding up smartphones, and I'm certain that this will be all over the Internet by tomorrow, but when Damien reaches his hand out for me, I suddenly don't care. I take it, the world falling away. He's casting a spell over me, and for a brief, wild second, I think that Sinatra's "Witchcraft" would be more appropriate, because I am completely enchanted.

I'm not sure how it happens, but suddenly I'm standing up, and Damien's eyes are fixed upon mine, and everyone else in this pub has been swept away. It is only Damien and the music and me. He's singing as if he means it, and as the famous lyrics come out of his mouth, I melt.

Then it's over and I'm crying and the crowd is applauding. Damien's arms close around me and I'm vaguely aware of the applause and the camera flashes and the cheering. None of that matters, though. All that matters is Damien.

Beside us, I see Jamie smiling tremulously, her eyes wistful but happy. *He's a keeper,* she mouths.

I nod in reply and cling tight to Damien. *I know,* I think. *I know.*

12

It's late when we get back from the bar, but the cool night air and Damien's terraced stone patio are too enticing to resist. It looks out over a manicured lawn leading down to a private dock and the smooth surface of the lake. The sky is clear and the moon is full. It reflects off the sails and hulls of the various boats dotting the shore, adding a wash of muted color to what would otherwise be a gray tableau.

Jamie immediately flops down on the huge daybed. The waitress had suggested flavored vodka in response to Jamie's query as to what would be fun, and now she is in a whipped-cream-vodka-induced fog. I glance at Damien, then head into the house to get sparkling waters for all of us. When I return, Jamie's humming "Come Josephine, In My Flying Machine" and staring up at the stars as Damien looks on, bemused, from where he sits on the nearby love seat.

I meet Damien's eyes. "She loves *Titanic*," I say, by way of explanation.

"I hope this doesn't mean you're drowning," he says to Jamie.

She just smiles and slowly shakes her head back and forth. "No, I'm in a happy place. This is so nice. Y'all are so nice." She pushes herself up on her elbows. "Maybe we should go clubbing."

"Great idea," Damien says, as I gape. "But I've got a better one. How about we stay in?"

She cocks a finger at him. "Yes. *Yes.*" She looks at me. "He's so smart. *And gorgeous, too,*" she adds in the world's loudest stage whisper.

"I know," I say, half-embarrassed for my friend and half-amused by her.

She squints at Damien. "I bet I can totally whup your ass at poker," she says.

Damien grins at me. "Who am I to decline a challenge like that?"

"She's good," I warn. She and Ollie and I spent a lot of long nights playing poker. "Of course she's better when she's sober."

Jamie's grin is lopsided. "Maybe I am sober. Maybe this is all just one big bluff."

After four hands of five-card draw, it's starting to look like maybe Jamie really is sober. I'm losing spectacularly, Damien isn't doing much better, and Jamie has a huge pile of chips in front of her.

"You should know that all of my illusions are shattered," I tell him. "I don't know if I can stay with a man who loses at poker."

"But I do it with such charm," he says.

Jamie lifts her hands in a what-can-you-do gesture. "I'm just that awesome," she says. "Don't say that I didn't warn you."

Damien leans back on the small love seat that he and I are sharing, his feet kicked out in front of him and his cards face down on the small glass table. "You both do realize that poker is a game that develops over time. It's not about just a few hands."

Jamie and I exchange glances before she looks back at Damien. "In other words, you're sizing me up."

I raise my brows. "He better not be," I say archly.

We all laugh, but Jamie tosses down her cards, then flops backward onto the chaise. "Yeah, well, then the joke's on you, because I think I have to pass out now."

I wait, expecting her to say something else, but all I hear is a soft snore.

"Jamie?" I say stupidly.

"She's out," Damien says.

"It's the whipped-cream vodka," I say. "That stuff's dangerous."

"Shall I move her inside?"

I consider getting a blanket and letting her sleep outside, but decide she'll be better off with a mattress and real sheets and no sun blasting on her face first thing in the morning. "Can you lift her?"

"She's tiny," he says. "I think I can manage." He picks her up easily, and she tilts toward him, curled up like a little girl against his chest. I hold the door open for him, and she wakes up just long enough to smile sleepily at him. I expect her to say something flirtatious and trademark Jamie. Instead, my heart squeezes when I hear her soft, "You're so good for her. You know that, right?"

"She's good for me," Damien replies, squeezing my heart a little bit more.

"That's what I mean," Jamie says—and then she's out again. Lost in her whipped-cream haze.

I pause in the doorway before shutting her door, looking back fondly. As much of a wreck as Jamie can be, she's still my best friend, and it's times like this that I remember why.

"So tell me, Ms. Fairchild," Damien says as I follow him to

the master suite. "How much whipped-cream vodka did *you* have?"

"Too sweet for me," I admit. "But I ordered quite a few shots of Macallan."

"Did you? That can increase a bar tab pretty quickly."

I step close to him, relishing the way the air thickens with our proximity. "Well, maybe you can win it back at poker."

"That's an interesting wager," he says. "I propose a small amendment."

I cock my head. "Negotiating, Mr. Stark?"

"Always." He takes another step toward me. He's right there, so close that my breasts will brush against his chest if I do nothing more than take a deep breath. He leans forward until his lips are near my ear. We still do not touch, but his breath when he speaks sends shivers down my spine. "Strip poker, Ms. Fairchild."

The heat in his voice matches the fire in his eyes, and I start to melt a bit. But this opportunity is too delicious to squander and I match his gaze inch for inch, my lips curving into a smile when I see the bulge of his erection beneath his jeans. I lift my eyes slowly to meet his and find them smoldering. He cocks his head as if to say, *oh, yes.*

I swallow. "All right, Mr. Stark," I say, then turn and head toward our bedroom. I pause in the doorway and smile. "Prepare to get naked."

My threat, however, turns out to be hollow, and twenty minutes later I have lost my flip-flops, the light sweater I was wearing to ward off the chill from the lake, and my T-shirt. I'm left wearing a short pink skirt, a pale purple thong, and a matching demi-cup bra that is cut so low that my very erect nipples are straining against the decorative lace that lines the top of each minuscule cup.

Damien is still fully dressed.

"Are you sure you don't cheat?" I ask.

"As a rule, no. In order to see you naked, I would be sorely tempted."

"Aha!" I aim a stern finger at him.

He laughs. "Fortunately, your massive consumption of Scotch saved me the trouble. You're not playing your best, Ms. Fairchild."

I raise my brows. "Have you considered that I'm just setting you up?"

"Are you? Well, that's interesting information." He nods at the cards I hold in my hands. "Let's see what you've got."

I lay my cards down, feeling smug. "A pair of kings, ace high."

"Not bad," he says. "Too bad I have the other three aces."

"You do not," I say, but he lays the cards down and, sure enough, two red and one back ace wink up at me.

"Off with it," he says.

I reach for the clasp at the front of my bra.

"Oh, no," he says, then makes a twirling motion with his finger. "The skirt. I'll get the zipper for you."

I scowl, but comply, turning around to give him access. He presses his palm against my skin, his hand curved to cup my waist. With the other hand, he slowly tugs down the zipper. "Up," he says, and I rise to my knees, then close my eyes and try not to tremble as he slowly eases the skirt down, his fingers grazing oh so softly on each bit of bare skin that he reveals during the process. "There you go," he says, as I twist around to sit back down, pulling my legs free from the skirt as I do.

I'm dressed now only in the tiny bra and even tinier panties. It's cool in the room—we've opened the door to the private patio—but my skin is burning. "Deal," I say, trying to control my breathing, because with each breath my breasts rise and fall, and with each motion my nipples brush the lace. The sensation is driving me crazy. It's rough and teasing and I can't help but imagine the light nip of Damien's teeth, the soft pressure of his mouth as he suckles me, the warmth of his hands as he cups my breasts. And the insistent press of his cock as he presses his body full against mine.

"Nikki."

"What?" I jerk my head up, reality returning. Considering the way Damien is looking at me, I think he knows exactly what I was thinking.

"Your cards."

I glance down and realize he's already dealt. "Oh. Right." I see the corner of his mouth twitch. "What?" I demand.

"I didn't say a thing," he says. "But if I had, I probably would have told you to move."

I tilt my head. "To move?" I'm sitting on my heels, my knees and thighs together.

"On your bottom," he says. "Your legs crossed."

"I—why?"

"Because I want to see you," he says.

I raise my brows. "Is that part of the game, Mr. Stark?"

"It is now. I want to see how wet you are. I want to know how much it turns you on sitting here across from me, slowly losing bits of your clothing, becoming more and more open to me. And all the while knowing that soon—very soon—I'm going to bury myself in you."

"Oh." My heart stutters in my chest, and I'm certain he can see the beat of my pulse in my neck.

"Now, Nikki," he says. "You know the rules."

"Is that a command, Mr. Stark?" My sex feels swollen and I am desperately wet. He must know it, but soon he will also see it.

"It most definitely is."

"So if I don't, I'll be punished?"

His lips twitch. "I don't think you'll like the punishment I'd
render tonight."

"No? Why? What would you do?" I can imagine the sting of
his hand upon my ass. The thrill of a cat-o'-nine-tails upon my
sex. I try to imagine what naughty treat he could have in mind,
but my mind isn't working particularly well at the moment. I am
needy and hot, and not just because of the Scotch or because I'm
half naked. It's because of Damien. Because he does this to me.
Because I want him right now. "What would you do?" I repeat.

"It's what I wouldn't do," he says, and that's when I get it.
Disobey, and he won't touch me at all.

"That punishes us both," I say.

"Rules are rules," he says. "And I can be very strong when I
want to. But if you think I'm bluffing . . ." he adds, glancing at
the cards as if in illustration.

I get the message. I've been losing at poker all night. Do I
really want to lose at this, too?

I don't. I shift my position so that my legs are in front of me.
Slowly, I draw in my feet and spread my legs until I'm sitting
cross-legged in front of him, my sex wide open. I can hide nothing now, and the truth is that I don't want to.

I follow the line of Damien's gaze to the damp spot on my
thong. The telltale sign of just how wet—just how incredibly
soaked with desire—I am for him. Slowly, I lift my eyes to his. I
see the heat, and feel a corresponding power. He may be the one
making the rules, but I'm the one making him a little crazy.

I arch back a bit, my hands behind me for support.

"I like the view," Damien says. "I like seeing how much you
want me. How wet you are for me."

"Am I?" I say innocently. I shift my weight to one arm, then
lift my other hand. I trail my fingers up my own thigh, then trace
it lightly over the silk of the thong.

"Jesus, Nikki," Damien says, his voice ragged. But I show no pity. I run my fingertip along the side of the thong. I tilt my head up and meet Damien's eyes. And then, slowly and deliberately, I slide my finger under the scrap of material and into my very wet, very swollen cunt. I gasp from the rush of pleasure as a shudder runs through my body, as if it's a preview of an explosion to come.

And then, with Damien's eyes still on me, I draw my finger up to my mouth and taste my own arousal. "Yes," I murmur. "You're right. I'm very, very wet for you."

"Fuck poker," Damien growls, sweeping his arm over the bedclothes and knocking the cards to the ground even as he grabs my thighs and tugs me toward him. The motion counterbalances me, and I fall backward so that I end up flat on my back, my legs spread, and Damien between them.

"Are you conceding the game, Mr. Stark?" I ask, my voice full of laughter.

"I am," he says.

I raise myself upon my elbows. "I guess that means you lose."

"No," he says as he eases himself up over my body, then uses two fingers to flip open the clasp of my bra. "I assure you it means that I win."

His mouth closes over my breast even as his hand slides down to stroke my clit through the soaking wet silk. The sensations coursing through me are incredible, a flurry of sparks originating from his hand and from his mouth, and I arch up, lost in the violent storm that Damien is creating inside me.

"You're wrong, Mr. Stark," I say, struggling to form words while I still have the power. "Tonight, we both win."

I wake to a perfect morning. The man beside me. The sunshine streaming through the open door that leads to the master bedroom's private patio. The light breeze blowing in from over the lake. The smell of pine and—

I frown and draw in another deep breath. *The smell of what?*

"Damien, wake up." I shake his shoulder. "Either we really set the sheets on fire, or something out there is burning."

He is up immediately, grabbing a pair of jeans off the floor and heading toward the door. I pull on a robe and follow him so closely that I almost slam into him when he stops in the now-open doorway. "It's not a fire," he says. Now that I can smell it better, I agree. It's an almost sickly sweet smell, like Christmas fudge that has burned to the bottom of the pan.

"I think I know what it is," I say, then lead the way to the kitchen, where Jamie is frantically flipping pancakes on a griddle. She looks up at us, her expression a little bit wild, a little bit contrite.

"Sorry! I thought I'd make breakfast, but—" She indicates the stove and nearby counter as if that's all she needs to say.

I force myself not to laugh. "I don't think that pancakes are supposed to be served blackened," I say, deadpan.

She tosses a dish towel at me. "I had a little trouble incorporating the chocolate chips."

Damien pours himself a cup of coffee and leans against the counter. "As they say, it's the thought that counts. So I hope you don't mind if I just think about eating those."

Jamie smirks and looks between the two of us. "Great. I'm trapped in the mountains with a couple of comedians."

"Your choice," Damien says in his corporate-problem-solving voice. "We either clean up and start over, or I'll take you ladies out to breakfast."

"You're out of chocolate chips," Jamie says. She grabs up the plate of burnt discs that bear no resemblance to pancakes and tosses them in the trash. "Give me fifteen minutes to shower and change."

It actually takes us thirty to get out the door, because Damien makes the mistake of telling us that the restaurant not only makes fabulous waffles, but is also located in Arrowhead Village, an outdoor shopping center with both regular stores and high-end outlets. And, obviously, neither Jamie nor I can properly shop if we're not properly dressed.

Damien, of course, is ready in five minutes, decked out in faded jeans and a short-sleeved linen shirt over a plain cotton tee. His hair is vaguely mussed, as if he's been standing in the wind. He looks sexy as hell—like a guy who just stepped off the pages of an ad for men's cologne.

"He cleans up well," Jamie says, with a deliberately lascivious gleam in her eye.

"He does," I say, moving between them and hooking my arms through theirs. "And he's mine."

As the crow flies, it isn't far to the village. Since we are not crows, however, we have to deal with the twisty, turny, tiny streets, and it takes about half an hour. I don't mind. The area is charming, filled with A-frame houses tucked into the mountainside and spectacular views that take your breath away. The village is located on the lake, so technically we could have taken one of the boats moored at Damien's dock. The restaurant itself— The Belgian Waffle Works—sits right on the water, with a huge patio of outdoor seating. I catch a whiff of batter cooked to a crispy golden brown as we approach, and breathe in deep.

"That's more what I was going for," Jamie admits. "But, hey, you can still thank me. If I hadn't completely trashed breakfast, we wouldn't have a shopping morning."

"We're deeply grateful," Damien says, sliding his arm around my waist.

Thirty minutes later, I'm even more grateful, because we're not only seated on the patio with a view of the water, but we each have a plate overflowing with a giant waffle, eggs, and enough bacon to feed a small army.

"I'm going to fall into a food coma," I protest.

"We'll work it off by walking the shops," Jamie announces. She turns to Damien, her smile wide. "You really are awesome, you know. Thanks for inviting me. I was having a shit week."

"Anytime," he says, then leans over to give her a light kiss on her cheek.

She fans her face, making me laugh.

"Hang on, you two." I pull out my iPhone and motion for them to scoot their chairs closer together, then take a couple of snaps. "I'd take some of the view, too, but the phone won't do it justice."

"I think I can assure you we'll be back," Damien says.

"Or you can just buy a new camera," Jamie says. "For that matter, get one for each of his houses. That should ensure that Leica never goes out of business, right?"

"Not a bad idea," Damien says, with a playful gleam in his eye. "I like the idea of spreading you around all my properties. Hell, I like the idea of you naked in all my properties."

My face heats, and I widen my eyes and shoot a glance at Jamie, who has leaned back in her chair with a *whoop*.

"Don't you guys ever give it a rest?" she asks.

"Not really," Damien says, surprising me by pulling me to him and planting a bone-melting kiss.

"God," Jamie says. "I am so freaking jealous. Do you have a brother?"

"Afraid not."

"Figures," Jamie says as Damien slides his chair closer to mine and hooks his arm around me. I lean against him, wishing things could always be this calm, this happy.

"It sounds sappy as shit, but you two know how lucky you are, right?"

"Yes," Damien says sincerely. "We know."

"Good," she says, then sighs deeply. "Damn, but I needed this."

"Why didn't you tell me about getting fired from the commercial?" I ask.

She shrugs, looking embarrassed. "You were a little preoccupied, and it's not like there was anything you could do, especially not from Germany." Jamie had recently been cast in a national commercial, but before shooting began she started dating her costar, an up-and-comer named Bryan Raine. When that ended badly, Raine apparently decided that Jamie's commercial career needed to, as well.

"There's something I can do," Damien says.

She shakes her head firmly. "No, you helped me get the job in the first place. That was more than enough. They paid me for the gig anyway—they had to the way the contract was written—so I'm good. I just need to think about how I'm going to get my shit together."

"You will," Damien says.

Jamie reaches across the table and takes both our hands. "Thanks. Really."

"You're welcome," I say. "And you know I love you, right?"

"What's not to love?" Jamie asks with the kind of shit-eating grin that tells me that the morning melancholy has passed.

She tightens her grip on my hand before letting go. "You know people are staring at us, right?"

I glance around and see that she's right. Not everybody, but there are more than a few people sharing the patio with us who look guiltily away when my gaze sweeps over them. "It comes with the territory," I say, cocking my head toward Damien.

"Well, it'll be my first time in the tabloids," she says. "Guess that means I've finally made it despite the stupid commercial."

"What are you talking about?"

"Damien Stark in a threesome, of course. It'll be all over the Internet by morning, don't you think?"

I do a face-palm. "Jesus, Jamie, do you think you could say that a little louder? Or better yet, not at all?"

"I'm joking," she says, and I know her well enough to know that it's true. I catch Damien's eye and see the tiniest shake of his head. I get the message—he's telling me to keep my mouth shut. Jamie may think that she's joking, but she hasn't lived with the paparazzi like Damien has. Or, for that matter, like I have. Depending on who has seen the three of us together, the bullshit story that she just suggested isn't outside the realm of possibility.

Well, great. I take a deep breath and tell myself not to worry about it.

"I want another coffee," I say, both because it's true and because I want to change the subject. "And then I think it's time to shop."

13

"I like the cyan one," I tell Jamie, who is debating between a traditional tan leather backpack and one dyed the color of the sky.

"Not too loud?"

"For you? Nothing's too loud."

She smirks, but puts back the tan one. "Okay. I shouldn't, but I'm going for it. I mean, I did just get paid. And I ought to get at least one nice thing out of that damn commercial."

Since I agree, I don't try to talk her out of it. I've known Jamie a long time, and with her, retail therapy goes a long way.

We're inside a specialty leather goods store, and although Damien started out by teasing me about all the sensual possibilities inherent in the collection of belts hanging on the men's side of the store, he has since stepped outside to take a call. I head out to find him, signaling to Jamie who is at the counter waiting her turn to pay.

It takes a minute to spot him, but I finally see him on a bench near a grassy area where some weary parents have settled on the lawn with their kids. He holds up a finger when he sees me, then points to his earpiece. I nod, then sit quietly beside him, enjoying the late summer afternoon.

"No," Damien's saying, "you need to understand me. This is my top priority. I want the entire thing gone over with a microscope. Whatever there is to learn, you learn it. You follow every thread, you go down every rabbit hole. Are we clear? Good. Call me in a few hours with an update. Yes, a few hours. Fine. That's one thing settled, then. What about the gate? Can we speed up the timetable on that? Well, that's good news at least. Get that wrapped up today and make sure everyone has access. All right. Yes. I'll speak to you later."

He ends the call and looks at me, his mouth curving into an automatic smile. If I didn't know him so well, I'd believe that everything was business as usual. But I do know him well, and I can see the hint of worry in his eyes.

"Something wrong?" I ask.

He shakes his head. "Just the ins and outs of running the universe. I've been somewhat absent for the last few weeks. A few things have slipped through the cracks."

"I don't see how," I quip. "You had Stark Central set up in the hotel."

"It's nothing," he repeats, but I know better.

"You're worried," I say.

I can almost see the denial rise on his lips, and I wonder if I need to remind him of the talk we had on the jet. But then he seems to think better of it. "I am."

"Then I know it's not business. You don't worry about business," I add in response to his querying look. "You just take charge."

"I didn't realize I was so transparent."

"Only to me," I say. "So what is it, Damien? Is it Sofia? Is it that motion to release the photos? Has something happened?"

He leans back against the bench and tilts his face up to the sky. After a moment, he plucks his sunglasses from where they are hooked on the collar of his T-shirt and puts them on. "There are just a few things I need to follow up on," he says, turning his head so that he is facing me. "Business about which I'm not worried, but which does require my attention."

"I see," I say, though what I should do is call him out for bullshit.

"And, yes," he adds gently. "I'm still worried about Sofia."

This time, I know that it is the truth. I also know that it's an apology.

"You'll find her. Will you tell me as soon as you learn something new?"

His answer comes immediately. "Of course."

My chest feels tight and I am suddenly aware that I've been holding my breath. It's only then I realize how much had been riding on that one simple question.

Can't you tell me what's going on? I'd begged him in Germany. *Can't you talk to me? No,* he'd answered.

Today, he'd said yes.

Relieved, I lean against him, sighing gently as his arm goes around me and basking in the relief and the knowledge that at least for now, I feel safe and connected.

Soon, Jamie joins us, a shopping bag dangling from her arm. "Y'all worn out already?"

"I'm afraid I need to head back to the house," Damien says. "But you two can continue shopping."

"Not me. Not unless you want to." Jamie looks at me, but I shake my head. I'm pretty much over the shopping, too. "I want the hot tub," she says.

"I think we can go one better," Damien says, then hits a button on his phone. "Sylvia, can you contact Adriana? See if she can get someone to the Arrowhead house this afternoon for Ms. Fairchild and Ms. Archer. Yes, that's right. An hour. Call or text the details once you have them. Fine. I'll be in on Friday."

Jamie aims a very clear *what the fuck* look at me, which I in turn voice to Damien. "What's going on?"

"I thought you two might like massages on the patio," he says, and Jamie immediately high-fives me.

"You know you're amazing," she tells him.

He meets my eyes. "So I've been told."

When we get back to the house, Damien tells us that we'll find bathing suits in the trunk in Jamie's guest room and then shows us how to operate the controls on the hot tub. "Help yourself to whatever's in the fridge," he adds, "including the champagne."

I reach out and take his hand, twining his fingers in mine. I want to keep him at my side, but I also know that he's giving me and Jamie the chance to hang out on our own, something we haven't done in what feels like a very long time.

"Don't work too hard," I say.

"Don't play too hard," he counters.

"Wouldn't dream of it."

In fact, we don't play hard at all. Just the opposite. I'm pretty sure that I have never been quite so lazy in all of my life. For that matter, I am pretty sure that popular mythology has it backward. It's not hell that's hot, it's heaven. Hot and wet with jets that pound away your tension.

Jamie's arms are spread out and she has her head tilted back. "I can't even tell you how much I need this. And a massage, too? I mean, seriously. There is a god, and his name is Damien." She lifts her head long enough to flash me a wicked grin. "Seriously, Nik. I am totally in love with your boyfriend."

"Yeah," I say. "Me, too."

Hours later we are hot tubbed and massaged to within an inch of our lives. I'm as limp as a noodle and splayed out on the huge daybed by Jamie. I want to read, but it's too much work, and I close my eyes and settle into the bliss of total relaxation.

That's where Damien finds me when he finally emerges from his work cave.

"Hey," he whispers, brushing his fingers over my shoulder. "How was your day?"

I blink up at the incredible man smiling down at me. "What time is it?"

"Just past six," he says, which has my eyes opening even wider. I reach for my phone and realize he's right—and that I've been napping for over an hour.

"Never mind," he says. "I can tell how your day was. And I'm envious."

"You could have joined us," I say, giving Jamie a nudge. Like me, she's dozed off. Unlike me, she's rolled over onto her stomach and is now snoring softly into a pillow.

Damien, it turns out, has ordered dinner from a local restaurant, and we have a variety of sandwiches, soups, and salads to munch on during the movie he's planned for us to watch. "I figured I earned some downtime, too," he says. "Assuming you don't mind me joining the party?"

"I think we can suffer through it," I say, brushing a light kiss over his lips. "Thanks," I add. "Jamie needed this. And so did I."

Thursday arrives in much the same manner as Wednesday, although this go-round Jamie actually manages to make pancakes that resemble pancakes. We eat them on the patio with freshly squeezed orange juice, and as I look out over the sun-dappled lake, I can't help but feel like I could stay here forever.

"I'm half-tempted to call Lisa and reschedule for Monday."

"Oh, yes, please," Jamie says.

I look at Damien, but his expression remains calmly bland, offering me no help one way or the other.

"No," I finally say. "I need to see this space, and I want to talk with Lisa, too."

"You're meeting her at ten?" Damien asks, then continues when I nod. "We'll leave tomorrow morning. Edward can meet you at the tower and take you to the property in the limo."

"Um, I don't think so. Let's just leave early enough that you can drop me at home."

"I have early meetings."

"Then we'll have Edward drop me at home."

"That's a waste of time," Damien says. "You can dress here, then go straight to your meeting. I'll meet you afterward and you can give me the rundown."

"No," I say.

"Dammit, Nikki—"

"*No.*" I hold up a hand. "I don't know what's going on, but I know something is. And you can just spill it right now."

Beside me, Jamie stands. "You know, I have a sudden urge to go reorganize my suitcase."

I don't even bother to nod; I'm too focused on Damien, who continues to remain stonily silent.

"Don't do this, Damien. This time whatever secret you're keeping is about me. And we both damn well know it."

He pinches the bridge of his nose, and I see the signs of weariness in his face. "Your car was trashed," he finally says, his voice flat and even. Not with the tone of defeat, but with the level control of someone trying to keep a tight rein on fury.

"Say again," I say stupidly.

"Someone threw paint all over your car," he says. "That's an irritation, but not irreversible. But they also jimmied a lock and filled it with raw fish. I sincerely doubt the smell will ever go away."

"I—" I close my mouth, giving up. I have absolutely no idea what to say. "How do you know?"

He sighs heavily. "I've been concerned about the security at your condo for a while."

"But you already installed an alarm system," I say. After the first anonymous note, he'd asked Jamie if she minded. Because Jamie is not an idiot, she agreed, and Damien's security dudes tricked out the condo's security while he and I were in Germany.

"That's clearly not enough. I arranged with the property management to install a security gate for the parking area and to enclose the entry foyer. Two days ago, my crew found your car. Needless to say, I stepped up the schedule to get that work completed."

I remember him referencing a gate during the call he took while we were shopping. "You told me that call had to do with Sofia," I say.

"No. I said there were things I had to take care of. And that I was worried about Sofia."

"Dammit, Damien, don't split hairs with me. You deliberately obfuscated the truth. Why?"

"Because I didn't want that bubble of yours to pop yet. Not when I'd brought you here to escape reality for a few more days."

"I—" I want to cry out to him that he can't hide shit like that from me, and he can't plunk me in the back of a limo and expect that will keep me safe.

I don't, though. Because I get it. He would have told me eventually—hell, the conversation would be hard to avoid. But he wanted to give me the gift of peace for just a few more days.

"Fine," I finally say. "You're off the hook about not telling me. But I'm not carpooling with Edward."

"You are," Damien says firmly. "I can't protect you from everything, but I'm damn well protecting you from what I can."

"Forget it. I'll have the car detailed. I'll make it work."

"The hell you will. That car's too old for a decent security system, the smell isn't going to disappear, and it's been on its last

legs for a while. You told me so yourself. Besides," he adds more
calmly, "I already had my men arrange to donate her for parts."

I gape at him. "Are you kidding me? No." I shake my head.
"Absolutely not. That car has too much sentimental value. I'm
not stripping her for parts. And who the hell do you think you are
anyway?" I mean honestly, what the fuck?

"I'm the man who would die if something happened to you,"
he says. He's as calm as the lake beyond us, and his level-
headedness in the face of my fury only pisses me off more.

"That doesn't mean you get to micromanage my life. Or dis-
sect my car."

"You want to keep the car, fine. Keep the car. We'll park it at
Stark Tower. You can keep it forever for all I care. But I'm buying
you a new one with a perimeter-based security system, a GPS, an
anti-theft tracking device, and whatever else goddamned security
devices my tech team can come up with." He's not shouting, but
he's coming pretty damn close.

"*You're* buying?"

"Absolutely."

"The hell you are."

"Don't fight me on this, Nikki. Not on an issue of your safety.
You want to keep the Honda, then keep it. I'll bronze the goddamn thing if you want me to and we can mount it in the entry-
way. But you're getting a new car to drive."

"Fine," I say. I know he's right. The Honda's been crapping
out on me at intersections for too long now. And, yes, there's
sentiment, but no, I don't need to keep my fishy car. Damien can
donate it—not that I'm going to tell him that. Not yet, anyway.

But there is no way in hell he's buying me a car, and *that* I do
tell him. "I'll get one myself," I say. "You want to shop with me
and give your opinion, then fine. But I'm writing the check."

"Fair enough," he says. "Until you get it, Edward can drive
you."

"Oh, no," I say. "If we're doing this, we're doing it today."

"Today?"

"There are dealerships all up and down the 10, right? So let's just go home tonight instead of tomorrow morning. I'll get a car on the way."

He's staring at me with an odd expression, as if he's searching for another argument but can't find one. The thought sends a little trill of victory coursing through me. Most people do not win arguments with Damien Stark.

"Fine," he finally says. "Get packed. We can leave whenever you want."

I nod, then stand to go pull my things together. I hesitate for a moment just to look at him.

"Something else?" His expression is unreadable.

"Just thanks," I say, and watch as his features shift to something I think is relief.

"Does this mean you're not mad?"

"Oh, I'm pissed as hell. But I get where you're coming from." I cross my arms over my chest. "But, Damien? Don't do it again."

His mouth curves up into a lazy smile. "No promises. Where your safety is concerned, there's not much room for compromise."

I just shake my head. This is not a battle I will ever win, but all things considered, I suppose that's okay.

"Sucks for Jamie," I say, pausing once more before heading out of the room. "I think she was looking forward to another night."

"She can have the entire weekend if she wants," Damien says. "We'll take the Jeep, but I've got a car in the garage. I'll leave her the keys. Does she know how to drive a stick?"

"Yeah," I say. "She does. What kind of car is it?"

"A Ferrari," he says.

I burst out laughing.

"What?"

"Nothing," I say. "Except that you're one hell of a nice man, Damien Stark."

By dinnertime on Thursday, I have a new love in my life. And although nothing and no one could ever replace Damien Stark, by the time we get back to LA in my brand-new, shiny red convertible Mini Cooper, I am completely and totally in love.

"I hope you're not the jealous type," I tell Damien as I lovingly stroke the leather-wrapped steering wheel. "Because I think Cooper and I are about to become inseparable."

"Interesting," he says, with a wry twist to his mouth. "Perhaps I shouldn't have left the Jeep for one of my assistants to pick up. I mean, if you two want some alone time."

"I know I must seem terribly fickle," I say airily. "But when true love strikes . . . well, you simply have to go with it."

"Yes," he says, looking at me with unwavering heat. "You do."

I take my eyes off the road long enough to grin at him. We're almost to my condo, cruising along Ventura Boulevard. I turn on Laurel Canyon, but then drive right past the intersecting street that leads to the place I share with Jamie.

"Joyriding, Ms. Fairchild?"

I run my hand lightly over Cooper's dash. "A little respect, please, Mr. Stark. We're bonding."

"I may have to call Coop out for a duel at dawn," Damien says. "Because I'm not interested in sharing you. I want you all alone and to myself."

"Do you? I have to admit, I like the sound of that."

"I'm very relieved to hear it."

"Remember what I said about a Lamborghini being almost like foreplay?"

"It will be a very long time before I forget that, Ms. Fairchild."

"A Mini is, too."

"Is that so?" Damien says. "I confess I've never thought of the Mini as sexy. Cute, absolutely. Eye-catching, most definitely. Sexy, I'm not so sure."

"Don't wound Cooper's ego," I say. "Besides, it's not a question of appearance. It's a question of power."

"Is that so?"

"Feel that?" I ask, as I shift gears. Cooper does me proud, cruising up the hill toward Mulholland Drive without even the slightest hint of hesitation. "Power," I repeat. "And endurance. Very important qualities. In a car."

"I couldn't agree more," he says. "Responsiveness. Handling."

"Like I said, all things that turn you on. Ergo, foreplay."

I turn right and pick up speed as Coop takes control of the famous curves along Mulholland Drive.

"And what turns *you* on?"

Since I don't want to go careening off a mountaintop, I don't look at him. "You do," I say.

For a moment he says nothing, but I feel the weight of his gaze upon me. Then his voice, rough and demanding. "Pull over."

"What?" We've rounded a curve, and are back on a straightaway, so now I shoot him a quick glance.

"There," he says, pointing to a dirt-covered area overlooking the valley. It's the kind of place where tourists snap pictures and teenagers come to park. "Pull over, stop the car."

I do as he asks. "What on earth—" I begin, as soon as I've killed the engine.

I can't finish the question, however, because his lips are upon mine, his hand on the back of my neck urging me forward. His mouth open. Hot. Demanding. Taking. I moan and lean forward, craving the feel of his body pressed to mine—then howl in pain when the gearshift stabs me in the gut.

"I think it's Cooper who's the jealous one," Damien says with a wry twist to his mouth. "Are you okay?"

In my head, I'm running a monologue of very colorful curses. To Damien, I just nod.

"Stay put," he says, then opens his door and gets out. He walks to my side of the car and opens the door for me, then holds out his hand. I take it and let him pull me to my feet.

"I think I destroyed the mood," I say.

He turns so that we are both facing the valley and the panorama of lights stretched out against a blanket of night. "No," he says. "Just changed it a little. But how can there be anything but romance when we're floating above a blanket of stars?"

"Romance, Mr. Stark?" I tease. "Not hot and sweaty sex in the back of a tiny car?"

"Romance," he says, with such passion that I have to lean against the side of the car to remain upright.

"Damien . . ." My voice is soft, choked with emotion.

"I know." Gently, he strokes his fingertips over my cheek. "Close your eyes."

I do, my lips slightly parted. He touches my hair, strokes my back. And then I feel the butterfly soft brush of his lips at my temple, then the corner of my eye. I grin, not only from the sweetness of it, but because he is touching me so delicately that it almost tickles. And then his lips are upon mine, so achingly tender that tears well in my eyes.

"Hey," he says when he breaks the kiss and cups my chin. Gently, he runs the edge of his thumb under my eye, wiping away an errant tear. "None of that." His eyes are so full of love I could get lost in them.

I wrap my arms around him, then sigh when he folds me into him. "I love you," I say, but my voice is so low that I doubt that he hears me. It doesn't matter though. Right then, the words aren't necessary. Right then, all we need is each other.

14

As Damien said, my building has essentially been turned into a fortress. The parking area is now gated and monitored full-time by security cameras. I pause at the security box, flash the card that Damien hands me, and watch while the electronic elves slide the massive thing open. The action is smooth, and we're past the gate in no time.

"It looks nice," I say, because despite feeling a bit coddled, I do appreciate all he's doing to protect me. More, I understand that it's not enough. That he's going to worry. And the fact that I won the Edward-as-driver argument remains a sore spot with Damien.

"It does," he says. "But I'm more interested in efficacy than in curb appeal." He shifts in the car to look back at the gate. "Someone could climb that pretty easily."

I glance at the gate in the rearview mirror. "Spider-Man maybe, but not normal people."

"That grid pattern could be a ladder." He types something into his phone. "It's the typical design for a property gate, but most gates only serve the purpose of keeping non-residents from parking in the spaces. They're a deterrent. I want more."

I hear the *ping* of his phone and realize he's sent a text.

"Who are you—"

"Ryan. My security chief. I want him on this first thing."

I roll my eyes, then slide into my parking space. I feel a twinge of regret at the absence of my Honda, but it passes quickly. She's not gone, after all. Just relocated to the garage beneath Stark Tower until I decide what to do with her.

Since the mailbox is probably overstuffed, we exit the parking area through the pedestrian gate and walk up the sidewalk to the front entrance, with Damien rolling my suitcase and me schlepping my carry-on. When I'd left for Germany, the foyer was a somewhat shabby alcove with the mailboxes off to one side and a staircase on the other. Now, that alcove is protected by a massive—but tasteful—iron gate. More than that, the space has been given a face-lift. New paint, large pots with flowering plants. Even a water feature.

"Your doing?" I ask Damien.

He says nothing, just holds out his hand for my key, then gathers my mail.

I follow him up the stairs, a little amused, a little exasperated.

The front door is more or less the same, the "more" being the addition of yet another deadbolt to the two locks that were already there. I glance at Damien in question.

"Better," he says, but he's tapping out another text, and I know that "better" doesn't mean "good enough." Apparently Ryan can look forward to a busy Friday.

Inside, my apartment looks exactly the same, right down to the huge iron bed that dominates the living room and the white cat that blends in with the pile of pillows on the couch. Lady Meow-Meow lifts her head as we enter, then stands, stretches, and leaps daintily to the floor. I expect her to come over for a scratch and cuddle, but instead she just blinks her huge, accusing eyes at me, then turns around and strolls to the back of the apartment, tail lifted high, butt in the air. She pads up the stairs, turns into Jamie's room, and disappears.

"I guess she told you," Damien says, amusement lacing his voice.

"At least she looks well fed." Jamie told me she left Kevin, our cute but spacey neighbor, in charge of feeding the cat. Considering I sometimes wonder how Kevin makes it through the day, I can't say that I fully endorsed her choice of pet sitter.

I drop my bag on the floor and toss the mail onto the bed. "I can't believe she left it here," I say, though of course I can. If left up to Jamie, the bed will become a permanent fixture, much like the pile of clothes at the bottom of her closet or the science project that is undoubtedly growing in the fridge since I wasn't around to detox the condo every few days.

Damien has left the suitcase by my bag, and now I unzip it, then rock back on my heels with a frown. This is the part about traveling I really don't like. It's crammed full, and I am not looking forward to sorting through everything—to wash, to hang, to iron. I fall back on the time-honored ploy of procrastination, ignoring my luggage while I sort through the mail. Bills, bills, junk, magazines. While I'm doing that, Damien stalks my apartment, checking out the newly installed motion sensors and other gizmos that his team has hooked up throughout the place.

As he returns from my bedroom, I notice one letter that stands out from the pile. Its return address catches my attention—*Stark International*. I smile and glance up at Damien, expecting a knowing grin. He is focused on his phone, however, tapping out a response to yet another text message that has recently pinged.

Since I'm not inclined to wait, I slide my finger under the flap, unsealing the envelope. As I do, I notice that Damien is returning his phone to his pocket, which I take as a sign that he's finally done. Ryan, I think, must be relieved.

I tug the single sheet of paper from the envelope and unfold it.

I expect sensual words and decadent language. What I find makes my blood run cold.

HIS PAST WILL ALWAYS HURT YOU

I gasp and drop the paper to the floor.

"Nikki?" Damien is at my side immediately, but he has approached from the opposite side of the bed, climbing on and clutching my shoulders. "What is it?"

I take a deep breath and force myself to get my shit together. Someone is playing with me—the text, my car, now this. But it's only a piece of paper. Just a goddamn piece of paper. A frisson of fear snakes through me, but I force it under. I can deal with this. I can handle it.

"Nikki."

"There." I point to the floor, then slide off the bed to retrieve it, but Damien is too fast, and he snatches it up before I am able.

He holds the paper between two fingers, his fingertips and nails turning white from the pressure of his grip. I look more closely at the message, maybe expecting some sort of clue to leap out at me. But there is nothing on the sheet but those words, which look like they were actually typed by an old-fashioned manual machine.

"Where did you get this?" His voice is calm and even. I point to the envelope that is still on the bed, and Damien uses a nearby catalog to flip it over. I see his expression and know he's seen the return address. *"Son of a bitch,"* he snarls, then lashes out against the bedpost so hard the whole thing shakes.

I wait a moment, then keep my voice even as I ask, "Someone got hold of your stationery?"

"No," he says. "The motherfucker just wanted you to think it was from me. Look closely—don't touch," he adds as I lean in.

"It's printed with a regular laser printer. Our envelopes are professionally embossed. *Shit*." He runs his fingers through his hair and takes a breath, then he focuses his attention on me. "Are you okay?"

"I'm fine," I say truthfully. "I was freaked at first, but that was just shock. Really," I say, because he is still looking hard at me, and I can see the concern in his eyes. "I'm okay now. Honest. I'm more pissed than scared."

He nods slowly, as if weighing the veracity of my words. "All right," he says. "Get me a freezer bag. I'll get this to Ryan in the morning."

I hurry to the kitchen, a bit surprised he isn't summoning Ryan right then. But considering the note came through the mail, I suppose time isn't of the essence.

When I return with the bag, I find him pacing the room. He comes to meet me, takes the bag, and then uses his shirttail to slide the note and the envelope inside. He drops it on the bed, and then turns to pull me into his arms. "I'm sorry," he says after a moment.

I pull back enough to face him. "What the hell for? You're not the one sending me nasty notes or dumping fish in my car."

"I'm not," he says. "But it would appear that I'm the reason."

"That's hardly breaking news." We both know that without Damien, I'm not interesting enough to attract the attention of either the media or a stalker. But if that's the price of being with Damien, then I'm willing to pay it.

"No. I suppose it's not." He is silent for a moment, then says, "I want you to move in with me."

Oh. I take a step backward and sit on the edge of the bed again. I can't deny that I've wanted to hear those words for a while. Yes, I know that there are still shadows clinging to this man—that there are secrets that he may never reveal. But we have overcome so much already, and being with him feels so right. Already I wake up in his arms most mornings, and on the days when we sleep apart, I feel bereft.

There have been hints before that he wants me to move in, but this is the first time he has spoken it outright. Under different circumstances, my heart would be fluttering with glee. But as I glance at the plastic bag with that vile letter, all I feel is a chill.

Slowly, I lift my head and look at Damien. His expression is firm and businesslike. This is the face of an executive, not a lover, and my answer comes quickly to my tongue. "No."

"What?"

I stand. It's hard enough to win a battle of wills with Damien Stark; I sure as hell can't do it on my ass. "I said no."

"No?" His voice is very low and as sharp as a knife. "God-dammit, Nikki, why the hell not?"

I force myself to remain resolute. Because the truth is that I *do* want to live with him. Hell, I never want to leave his side. But not like this. "Do you want me to live with you because you love me or because you want to protect me?"

He studies me for a moment, then shakes his head as if in exasperation, which, frankly, pisses me off. "I want you with me, Nikki. And dammit, you want it, too."

Since I can't deny that, I stay quiet. Sometimes silence is the best policy.

"Shit," he says, more to himself than to me.

I point to the letter. "As much as I hate that, the bottom line is that mail can't hurt me, Damien, and the condo is safe. Your own team scoped it out. Or should I assume that the security team at Stark International does subpar work?"

"I have certain expectations regarding everything I own." He's striding toward me as he speaks, the power seeming to come off him in waves. I swear if I look closely, I could see the electrons shimmer in response to his passing.

I cock my head. "Am I one of your possessions, Mr. Stark?"

He stops right in front of me, and even though I am determined to hold my ground, I find that I am having a hard time breathing. "I believe we had an arrangement," he says as he traces a fingertip lightly along my collarbone. My lips part and my legs feel weak. He knows the effect he has on me, damn him, and I close my eyes and succumb to the sensation. The trill of tiny sparks that seem to radiate through my body. That heavy, demanding longing between my thighs. I draw in a breath, and murmur a single word: "Damien."

"There are rules, remember?" I think I hear a smile in his voice. The confidence of a man who thinks that he has won. "You're mine, Nikki. Whenever and however I want. And *wherever,*" he adds, cupping my breast in his hand and squeezing my nipple between his thumb and forefinger so hard that it makes me gasp as pain mixes with pleasure and rockets through me all the way to my sex. "And where I want you is with me."

"I am always with you," I say, though I have to fight to form words. I open my eyes, my body on fire and desperate for his touch. I want his hands on me. I want his cock inside me. I *am* his and I want to surrender to him right there, to let him have me however he wants.

I want all that—but I also want to win this battle. And so I draw in a breath and say, slowly and firmly, "But I'm not moving in with you."

He grabs my arms and pulls me to him. "Dammit, Nikki, this isn't a game."

I raise a brow. "Isn't it, *sir?*"

I see him flinch, then the jerk of his arms as he releases me, pushing back so that he can stalk away from me.

I exhale, regretting my moment of bitchiness. "Damien, I'm fine." My voice is gentle but firm. "That letter gives me jitters, too, but it's just mail and bullshit. No one's in the condo. I mean,

Jesus, you've turned this place into a fortress. Just give it a rest, okay?"

"The hell I will," he snaps. "I want you safe. Nothing is going to happen to you. I'm not losing you the way—" He cuts himself off and I'm left gaping at him.

"What? Dammit, Damien, is this about Sofia? You think her having gone missing has something to do with you?"

"I don't have a clue why she's gone missing," he says.

"And it's driving you crazy. And you aren't telling me a goddamn thing." I want to be understanding, really I do. I get that the situation is eating at him. His friend has disappeared. Some asshole is stalking me. And some potentially malevolent benefactor arranged for the dismissal of the charges against him in the worst way possible. He's trying to grab control of all that, and it's just slipping through his fingers. I get it; I do.

But at the end of the day that doesn't change a thing.

"Do not fight me on this, Nikki."

"Hell yes, I'm fighting. Why bother to put the gate around my apartment if you're not going to trust that it will do its job? I mean, I don't like getting nasty mail any more than you do, but for all we know it was mailed from Antarctica."

He strides to me, all power and control and cool masculinity. He reaches out and his finger brushes my cheek, the shock of his touch sending sparks through me. "I don't like being defied," he says.

I suck in air, determined not to melt or back down. "I don't like being bossed around." I shift my feet, mentally planting my stance along with my posture. "You're not winning this one, Damien. Deal with it."

His finger trails down my neck to the collar of my T-shirt. "Do you have any idea how frustrated I am right now?"

I shudder, the light pressure of his touch sending all sorts of decadent promises swirling through me. "I know what you're doing." My words tremble. "It won't work."

"Won't it?"

I close my eyes, shivering as his fingertip follows the curve of my breast. "I'm not giving in."

He fists his hand around the collar of my shirt and tugs me close. "I'll have you safe," he murmurs. As he holds me in place with one hand, with the other he captures my waist.

He eases me backward, and I feel the bed press against the back of my thighs. My body tingles with awareness, but also with something new. This is the Damien I know so well, but there's a quality to his touch I haven't felt before. A take-no-prisoners attitude that excites me, making my inner thighs tingle and my cunt throb for his touch.

"I want to cup my hand around you," he murmurs, sliding his hand over my sex as if in illustration, and then making me gasp when he uses that grip to lift me up onto the bed, the pressure from his thumb on my pubis and his palm over my sex so intense it sends tremors though me, like portents of an explosion to come.

He lays me out on the bed, one hand stroking circles on my sex and the other cupping my breast. I moan, my hips gyrating to meet him, my back arching up to increase the pressure of his hand against my painfully sensitive nipple. "That protective bubble you mentioned? I want to keep you locked inside. Whatever it takes," he says. "You can't possibly know how much I need you."

"I do." I am not entirely sure how I manage to form words. Whatever game we are playing, I have conceded long ago. Whatever he wants from me, he can take. All I want right now is his touch.

Despite the heat in his eyes, the small shake of his head is almost playful. "It's too big, too powerful. There is no start and no end, nothing with which I can measure the length and breadth of what I feel for you. I look at you and wonder how I can possibly survive the riot of emotions within me."

"You make it sound almost painful." My words are soft, gently teasing.

"You and I know better than anyone how pain and pleasure walk hand in hand. Passion, Nikki, remember? And with you, it fills me."

I swallow, undone by both his words and by the intensity with which he is speaking them.

"I want to hold you close. To cherish and protect you. To draw you in until we are so close that I am lost within you. I want to take you to bed, to watch the way your skin tightens beneath my fingers, the way your body awakens under my touch. I want to trail kisses over you until you are lost in so much pleasure that you don't know where you end and I begin. I want to tie you up and fuck you until there is no doubt that you are mine. I want to dress you up and take you out, and show you off, this beautiful, vibrant, brilliant woman. Everything I've built? All my companies? All my billions? They have no value compared to you."

I open my mouth to speak, but he hushes me with a gentle finger to my lips. "So no, Nikki. I will not take chances with your safety. I will not fight. I will not be defied. You don't want to move in with me. That's fine. I'll move in with you."

"Wait." I shift, trying to prop myself up on my elbows. I'm still floating in a sensual haze and not at all sure I heard him right. "What?"

"You heard me. End of subject."

"Damien, I—"

His hand is still on my cunt, and he slides a finger under my thong and inside me. I throw my head back and moan, only to be silenced by his firm, hard kiss. "I'm going to tie you up now, Nikki, and there will be no argument, no retraction. Are we clear?"

I nod helplessly. Liquid desire pools between my legs, making me hot and needy. My nipples tighten and my skin seems to vibrate simply from the pressure of the air against it.

"But first, I need you naked." He slides his hand out from between my legs, and I mourn the loss of contact. Then he takes the hem of my T-shirt in his hands and skims it off me. He runs his finger over my bra, and I sigh from the delicious sensation of his fingertip gliding under the edge where my breast is bursting against the cup. "I like this," he says, his voice soft. "I think we'll keep this on. Now turn over," he adds, making a circle with his fingers. "On your hands and knees."

I lift an eyebrow, and he swats my ass.

"Over," he repeats.

I'm tempted to defy him again, just for the pleasure of another swat, but I'm afraid that he might see through that ruse and shift the nature of the punishment to something less physical. Like not touching me. And that isn't something I think I can stand. So I comply, and then he unzips my skirt and skims it over my hips, taking the wisp of a thong with him.

"Beautiful," he says, rubbing his palm over my rear. "Now put your head on the mattress, but keep your ass up." He brushes my thighs, urging my legs apart as my arms rest against my inner thighs. "Oh, yes, baby." I hear the heat of desire in his voice and it makes me even more wet.

"I want your ass in the air and your cunt open to me. I'm going to fuck you, Nikki. I'm going to fuck you until we lose ourselves in each other. Until the universe swallows us whole. I'm going to make you come harder and longer than you ever have before, baby, and I'm going to feel every shudder, every ripple of that orgasm as it rips through you because I am going to be right here holding tight to you, buried deep inside you. And, Nikki, I'm not ever letting go."

His jeans brush my bare ass, and I can feel his erection straining against the denim. He leans over me, his hands stroking my back, then his lips brush the curve of my ear. "You can either be quiet, or you can say 'Yes, sir.' There aren't any other choices."

My body is on fire, my cunt throbbing, muscles clenching in anticipation of being filled. I know he needs this. Needs to feel me beneath him, warm and solid and safe. And, yes, submitting. Giving myself to him. Completely. Willingly. Hell, even desperately.

"Yes, sir," I say. It is all that I can manage.

I can't see his face, but I hear the smugness in his voice when he says simply. "Good."

I expect his touch, but he leaves me on the bed with an order not to move, then slides off and kneels down by my suitcase. My face is turned in that direction, but from this angle, I cannot see what he is doing. I consider moving, but once again I don't want to risk punishment. Or, rather, I don't want to risk the wrong kind of punishment.

He stands soon enough, and when he does I see that he has pulled out two of the new thigh-high stockings that we bought from Marilyn's Lounge.

"What are you doing with those?" I ask, but he doesn't answer, just slides one under my leg and arm, then binds my forearm to my calf. He circles the bed and repeats the process on the other side of me as I protest that he's ruining a perfectly good pair of stockings.

He chuckles. "For a good cause," he says. "Trust me. This view is amazing."

I can only imagine what he sees. I am on the bed with my shoulders and cheek pressed to the soft bedding. My arms are splayed back and bound to my calves. My rear end is high in the air and my legs are spread, undoubtedly giving Damien quite the view of my very wet, very needy sex.

"I want to see you," I beg. "Please, Damien. I want you naked, too."

"Do you?" He moves to stand in my field of vision, then tortures me a little by removing his clothing so painfully slowly. His chest is well-muscled and dusted by a sexy smattering of chest hair that I like to tease with my fingers. My fingers twitch now, thinking about the feel of him against my hand, the hot skin and hard muscle of his abdomen. He may not have played tennis professionally in years, but there is nothing soft about Damien, and whether he's in a thousand-dollar suit or a fifty-dollar pair of jeans, he is sex and power and sensuality personified.

As if he realizes that he's driving me crazy, he hooks his thumb into the band of his jeans. I can see his erection bulging against the denim, and my body throbs simply from the knowledge that he is as turned on as I am. My nipples are hard and erect, rubbing almost painfully against the rough lace of my bra. My sex is drenched. And when I breathe in deep, I catch the scent of my own arousal.

I whimper a bit, and keep my eyes on Damien.

Slowly, he peels the jeans off. They're slung low on his narrow hips, and as I follow that disappearing trail of hair down to where it nestles against the base of his cock, I have to silently curse Damien. I want to touch him. Hell, I want to suck him. But I am trapped. Trapped and turned on and so goddamned needy.

He is naked now and fully erect, hot and huge, and my sex clenches in anticipation. He moves back to the bed, and I feel the mattress shift as he gets on behind me. His hands are warm upon my hips, and when he strokes the tip of his cock down the crack of my rear, I have to bite the comforter in order to anchor myself as bone deep shudders rake through me. Not an orgasm—but close enough that I am teetering on the very edge of desperation.

"That's it, baby," he says as his hands stroke my back, and the hard length of his cock continues to tease my ass.

My skin is hot and blood pounds through me. I can feel my pulse in my throat, in my temples, in my heavy, swollen breasts. Most of all, I can feel the blood surging in my sex. Pounding me, teasing me. Making me want so much more that I wiggle my ass shamelessly and beg Damien to please take me now.

"Not just yet," he whispers, and it is all I can do not to scream with frustration. He leans closer, his voice a low, sensual tease. "Do you remember what you told me once? About how you own a very nice vibrator?"

All the blood that was pounding in my cunt now seems to rush to my cheeks.

Considering everything I've done with Damien—not to mention everything he's done to me—I don't know why the fact that I own a vibrator should raise modesty flags, but it does.

"Nikki?" He rubs his palms over my rear, then slides his hand down to stroke my sex. Slowly, he slips one finger inside me, then another. My body responds greedily, the muscles of my vagina tightening around him, my hips thrusting, my breathing coming fast and shallow. And then, suddenly, his hand is gone, and there is nothing. Just that electrical charge that I always feel when Damien is near. But there is no touch, and I close my eyes and whimper in frustration.

His low chuckle rises from behind me, and I do not doubt that he understands the extent of my discomfiture. "Do you want me to touch you, Nikki? My palm stroking you? My fingers filling your cunt? Do you want me to spread you wide and thrust inside you, our bodies moving together, my hand on your clit stroking and teasing until we both explode?"

I bite my lower lip, determined not to answer aloud. He already damn well knows what I want.

"Then tell me where, baby. Just tell me where."

"Drawer," I manage. "Bedside drawer."

He is back quickly, and he has the small pink vibrator in his hand. He turns it on, and I hear the familiar buzz, then feel the decadent vibration as he trails it over my ass cheeks, along my spine, down the back of my thigh. Slowly he slides the vibrator over my sex, and I close my eyes, letting the pleasure roll through me. "Is this how you use it?" he asks. "Stroking your clit? Making it hard and hot and ready? Or like this?" he asks, slipping it easily into my so-soaked sex. "Or maybe both?" He moves the toy in a slow in-and-out motion, but angles the device so that with each thrust, the shaft brushes my clit, the vibrations enough to send tremors through me, but the sensation not lasting long enough to let me come.

"I—yes," I say, because I'm having a hard time remembering the question.

He slides the vibrator deep inside me, then holds it there. I bite my lower lip as pleasure builds at my core, then starts to roll out in slow, languid waves. "I don't like you saying no to me," he says.

"If this is my punishment, I think I may have to say it more often."

"Mmm." It's not even a word, but it holds all sorts of promises—and punishments—and when I feel his other hand, slippery with lube, slide up between the cheeks of my rear, I can't help the frisson of desire and trepidation that shoots through me.

"Damien," I say. "What are you doing?"

"Fucking you," he says, as he teases the pucker of my ass with his well-lubed thumb. He stretches me even as he keeps up the erotic rhythm of the vibrator inside my sex. I feel the head of his cock pressing against me, then the pressure and bite of exquisite pain as he thrusts inside. He waits, letting my body acclimate to his thickness, to the way he's filling me so deliciously and completely. I am completely exposed to him, completely used by him—and so desperately excited by him.

Slowly, he begins to thrust, matching the strokes of his cock with the motion of the vibe. Deeper and deeper, each stroke filling me, teasing me. His hand brushes my clit as he moves, his other anchoring me with a firm hand on my hip. "You're so hot," he says. "So wet, so goddamned tight around me."

"Harder," I say, wanting him to take me even further—all the way to the edge. "More."

I can tell by his low, animal groan that my words have excited him even more.

And then the power of reason leaves me. He is pounding into me, and my shoulders shift almost painfully on the bedclothes. I can't hold on—can't anchor myself, can't adjust to accommodate my own pleasure. I am Damien's, to use as he wants, and it is that single thought that fills my head when Damien's hand closes tight upon my hip and he slams hard against me, coming so powerfully inside me.

The shudders of his body crash through me and that spins me over the edge. Pleasure and pain and need and hunger slam together at my core, sending me shooting off into space, with Damien's name upon my lips.

When the tremors stop, he gently unties me, then strokes my body, easing tight muscles and setting my skin afire again. Somehow, I end up on my back with Damien hovering over me, his fingers playing upon my skin, his expression one of exquisite tenderness.

I can almost taste his strength and control, and I feel safe and warm and loved, as if there is nothing in the world that can touch us. Nothing that can harm us.

But even as that thought seems to hang in the air, the shrill crash of glass shatters the night—followed by the irate howl of one very pissed-off cat.

15

The rock that smashed through the curtained window near the front door is painted black with the exception of four white letters that have been stenciled in block letters on the smooth surface:

SLUT

I stand about two feet from the thing, my feet in flip-flops, my entire body trembling. *This* is not just a piece of paper. This is more. This has crossed a line and as I dig my fingernails into my palms, I am suddenly, acutely aware of just how fragile my grip on control has been.

The rock on the floor seems to goad me, but I am not touching it. Not because I know that the police will want to check it for fingerprints, but because of the vaguely superstitious feeling that if I do, something horrible will be transferred from it to me. As if it is some sort of contaminant that has managed to enter my world, and the best thing I can do is run from it.

That's not what I need to do, of course. What I need to do is fight.

But how the hell do you fight what you can't see?

As if in answer, Damien eases my clenched fist open and twines his fingers with mine. I hold tight, letting his touch calm me. Sticks, stones, gossip—I will weather it all if he is at my side.

Right now, he is on the phone with the head of his security team. The police have already been called, but there's no way that Damien will leave this to them. He finishes the call, hangs up, and turns that laser-like focus on me.

He lifts our joined hands. "Are you okay?"

"Yes," I say, then repeat the word for emphasis. "Yes, I'm fine. Now, I'm fine."

His eyes search mine, as if he's looking for the message under my words. For a moment, I don't understand what it is that's bothering him. Then I realize I am standing in a spread of shattered glass. I close my eyes. I'd been too focused on the rock earlier. And then Damien had taken my hand. But if he hadn't, I know I would have felt that familiar compulsion, and those shards would have been nothing more than glittering temptation.

"I'm fine," I repeat firmly, and squeeze his fingers. "I have you."

"You do," he says, and though his eyes are soft, his tone is businesslike. "I'll give you the choice of Malibu or downtown, but until we catch whoever is doing this, you *are* staying with me. And that is not a subject that is open to debate any longer."

Since I'm not an idiot, I nod agreement. I meant what I said earlier, but this has crossed the line into actual danger. And I'm not risking my safety on a point of honor.

"I'd rather stay in Malibu," I admit. "But there's no furniture." The house was barely finished before we left for Germany, and I assume the pieces he'd rented for the party honoring Blaine and the reveal of my portrait have already been returned to whatever warehouse they came from.

He nods toward the bed. "I'll have it brought back," he says. "And I'll have Sylvia arrange to rent enough furniture to make the rest of the house livable." He pulls me close for a soft kiss. "We can decorate slowly, and as we find pieces we like, we'll kick the rented pieces out on their asses."

I roll my eyes, but I can't help but smile. I had almost come undone when Damien had told me that he wanted us to furnish the Malibu house together. I don't want to lose that because some asshole is throwing rocks at me. Damien, of course, understands that without me having to tell him.

"What about Jamie?" he asks. "Is she staying with us, or are we getting her a hotel?"

I slide into his arms, suddenly overwhelmed and grateful and so full of love for this man I'm not sure that I can stand on my own. "Thank you," I whisper. "Knowing Jamie, she'd love to stay at the Malibu house."

"I'll have Sylvia get a key and the security code to her in Arrowhead, and send someone over here to pack some of Jamie's things. She can go straight to Malibu when she returns."

"Thank you," I say again.

"What else do you need?"

I move out of his arms and go sit on my sofa. "Can you arrange to just have all this be over?"

"I wish I could," he says, dropping down beside me.

The truth is, I am scared. But I don't want to show it. I know Damien will feel responsible. He's not, of course. That honor belongs to whatever psychopathic bitch—because I am just certain it's a woman—has decided to paint a bull's-eye on my size-eight ass.

"Maybe it's Carmela," I say.

"Not her style," Damien says, then adds, "but I have my people looking anyway."

"You've been keeping me out of the loop." I'm not accusing, simply stating a fact. And to be honest, I haven't really wanted to think about it. But I no longer have the cushion of the Atlantic Ocean and all of Western Europe and the entire staff at the Kempinski to separate me from reality. Now I know that whoever is harassing me is here to stay, and if I don't focus on it—if I don't wonder and think and watch my own back—then I'm no better than those idiot girls in movies who go up the stairs in scary houses, even though they know damn well the killer is waiting for them.

This is reality, I think. And whether I like it or not, it's forcing its way into our lives.

"I didn't see the point of burying you in this crap if we didn't know anything."

I cock my head. "You're protecting me again."

"I am," he says. "And as I believe I already explained in rather intimate detail, I don't intend to stop. Do you have a problem with that, Ms. Fairchild?"

"Only if you're keeping me out of the loop to do it," I say. "So what haven't you told me?"

"Not much," he says, and I can hear the frustration in his voice that stems from that simple fact.

"Start with the painting. Have you learned anything about who leaked the story that I'm the model? Or that you paid me so much? Because that first letter came about that time, so I don't think it's a stretch to assume it's the same person."

"I happen to agree with you," he says. "And the short answer is no, we haven't found anyone."

"And the longer answer?"

"Will have to wait." He points to the broken window and the two men who are passing in front of it. "My team."

We meet them at the door, but they choose not to come in until after the police arrive. Instead, they go back outside to canvass the area, pull the feed from the newly installed camera, and do whatever it is security guys do when they're on the case.

"The longer answer?" I press as soon as they're gone.

"We have a few leads. Arnold—he's the investigator I keep on retainer—recently got copies of some security footage from an ATM on Fairfax."

I shake my head, clueless.

"That ATM happens to be across the street from a coffee bar where our intrepid reporter has a habit of meeting with his sources."

"Wow," I say, impressed. Damien had identified the original reporter who broadcast the story awhile back, but the reporter had refused to reveal his source.

"It's going to take a while. The camera's focus is concentrated on a certain perimeter. But Arnold thinks he has a way to pop the focus on the background activity."

"That will take time," I agree. "Especially since we don't know what day he might have met with the source."

"Unfortunately, you're right," Damien says. "But we have a rough time frame, and at the very least he can start pulling prints and getting them to me. With luck, there will be someone I recognize."

"Shouldn't I look, too?"

"You should," he says. "But the odds are good that whoever is doing this is trying to get to me. I have Ryan's team investigating the players in a few particularly contentious deals I have brewing," he adds, referring to his security guys.

"Distract you by harassing your girlfriend, and maybe you won't be such a hard-ass in negotiations?"

"Something like that."

"It might not be business," I say. "You've slept with a lot of women, Damien. Even if you weren't serious about them, that doesn't mean they weren't serious about you. And one of them might be the jealous type."

"Agreed. And we're pursuing that avenue, as well."

"What about the anonymous letter that came to Stark Tower? Or the text I got in Munich?"

"Nothing yet," Damien says. "But we haven't given up." He glances at his watch, then he pulls out his phone and makes a call. "Anything?" he says, then frowns as the person on the other end speaks. "Good thinking," he finally says. "That just might work out well for us."

"That was Ryan," he says to me after he ends the call. "The cameras at the entrance and the parking garage caught our culprit. Tall, wiry. Completely covered in a black hoodie and sunglasses. Kept his or her head down, but Ethan says the gait looks to be male, and quite possibly a teenager."

"A teenager? But—"

"I'm guessing someone hired him. Our perp loiters around the convenience store, asks a kid if they'd like to earn a few extra bucks."

"Oh." It makes sense.

"Fortunately, there are cameras in strip malls. We might get lucky."

I nod. It's a solid plan, but I'm not holding my breath.

"I'm going to assign someone from my security team to you."

My head snaps up. "The hell you are. I'm not living my life under surveillance."

"It's necessary."

"You don't have the Secret Service following you around." It's one thing to stay with Damien, to take reasonable precautions with my life. It's something else entirely to suddenly live in a glass jar like a politician or a celebrity.

"I have a team available when I need them. But there's no indication I'm in danger."

I start to say that I'm not in danger, either. But considering I'd just agreed to move into Damien's house because of flying rocks, I can't really backtrack now. As much as I don't want some dude in a black suit with an earpiece monitoring my every move, I also don't want to be stupid about this.

"Nikki," he says gently. "Do you think I could survive if something happened to you?"

I draw in a breath because I know how he feels. If something happened to Damien, I am certain that I would shrivel up and die.

"All right," I say. "But not someone who flanks me, and not an obvious tail. But if you want to have someone hang out at the office if I end up renting it, I won't object. And I'm guessing you already have access to that tracking device we had installed in the car."

"I could access it," he says. "But not without some trouble. I'd rather install something I can monitor openly."

"Done," I say.

"And your phone," he says.

I frown. "What about my phone?"

"I want to be able to track you with it. There are apps that will allow me to do that. I'm going to install one."

"Just like that? No 'Mother May I'?"

"No," he says and holds his hand out for my phone.

I hand it over.

He downloads the app, fiddles with the settings, then gives it back to me.

Then he takes his own phone out of his back pocket and repeats the process. A moment later, my phone buzzes. I glance at it, open the new app, and see a red dot indicating that Damien is right there in my apartment. "So you'll never lose me, either," he says.

"Oh." I hold tight to my phone, still warm from his hand, and suddenly I'm speechless. Maybe it's the stress of the evening, maybe it's hormonal, but for some reason, adding that tracker to my phone is about the most romantic thing I can think of. "Thank you," I whisper.

"I'm never letting you go, Nikki," he says, taking my hand and pulling me close.

"I'd never forgive you if you did."

The next morning I stand transfixed as Lisa spreads her arms wide to indicate the modest office space. "So?" she asks. She's petite, but so poised that she seems to fill the room anyway. "What do you think?"

"I love it," I say. The space comes furnished, and apparently the owner of Granite Investment Strategies has excellent taste. Not only is the desk large enough to spread out half a dozen projects, but it's also sleek and modern with enough whimsy to be fun, but not so much that it lacks professionalism. The walls are bare, but that should be easy enough to fix.

The love seat is a bonus. The space is small enough that it would have made sense to only have the two molded plastic guest chairs. But the original tenant had managed to work the space well, and the small sofa that sits against the far wall seems to pull the room together instead of overwhelming the space.

"It's available immediately," Lisa says. "My client's very eager."

I run my fingertip over the desktop, tempted. I've been on the fence about leasing office space, but now that I'm actually standing in an office that could have my name on the door, I have to admit that it's pretty heady stuff.

I slide my hand into my pocket and run my fingertip over the edge of one of the business cards that Damien presented to me this morning. *Nikki L. Fairchild, CEO, Fairchild Development.* I'd laughed when I opened the box, but there had been tears, too. Not just because I'm finally, really doing this, but because of the pride I saw in Damien's eyes.

It occurs to me that he must have started much the same way; after all, he hardly sprang fully born from Zeus's head with a tennis racquet in one hand and Stark Tower in the other. No, he started small and worked his way up to gazillionaire status. I smile, oddly comforted by the thought.

"It's a great opportunity," Lisa prompts.

"I know," I say honestly. Because of the circumstances, the terms of the sublease are exceptional. Not only that, but the building has great security—as Damien discovered last night when he made a few calls after the police left. Tenants need a card key to enter the building and clients must be buzzed in by the receptionist, who serves as the gatekeeper between the outside world and the building's twelve tenants.

Even better, it's walking distance to the Sherman Oaks Galleria. If I have a bad day at work, I can console myself by going shopping. And if I have a good day at work, I can celebrate by going shopping.

I sway a bit on my heels, trying to decide. No, that's not true. I want this. But it's scary—like jumping out of a plane without a parachute. Except that I have a parachute. His name is Damien, and I know that he will always catch me.

"I can just work from home," I say lamely.

"No question," Lisa says. "I have lots of clients who do that. Most start-ups begin in the home."

I eye her with surprise; I wasn't expecting solidarity.

"But what about your roommate?" she asks. "Jamie, right? You said she's an actress? Does she have a steady job? I mean, is she a regular on a show?"

"No, but what does that—oh. Right." Jamie is supportive as hell, but she's also my best friend and a talker. If I'm trying to code and she wants to dish about men or her wardrobe or whether or not to get a tattoo on her ass, then it's going to be hard to focus on work. And the rent on this place really is low.

"I put together a plan for you," Lisa says, pulling a leather folio out of her briefcase. It's monogramed with my initials—*NLF*—and she moves to stand by my side as I flip it open, a little bit awed by everything she's done for me.

Inside, I find a plan for networking that focuses on women in tech and entertainment. "There are at least two dozen organizations in town focusing on women in tech-related fields," she explains. "You can't ask for a better way to meet potential business partners or clients. As for the entertainment contacts, it's a bit of a stretch, but you're on the radar now, like it or not. Might as well use it."

I'm not sure I want to trade on my rather unwelcome celebrity status, but I can't help but agree with her assessment.

She flips a few pages in the portfolio and shows me a rough profit and loss statement that factors in the cost of the office space along with income projections based on her research into the app market. I'm happy to see that the few apps I already have on the market are beating the averages.

"That's conservative," she says. "But as you can see, I expect you to be very solidly in the black within six months, and any start-up capital that you pull from your savings will be fully recouped."

I continue to flip pages, a little in awe. "Lisa, this is great. But it must have taken you forever to pull together, and I—"

I hesitate. I want to say that I'm not a client, but it sounds a little harsh.

Lisa must understand what I'm getting at, because she laughs.

"I'm happy to help a friend," she says. "Even one I barely know because we got off to such a crazy start."

I can't help but grin. She's right. Objectively, we hardly know each other. But she's one of those people that seems to fit, and I'm grateful that she started chatting me up back when I worked for Bruce, and that she didn't get scared away when he fired me and the paparazzi shit hit the fan.

"Not that I'm totally altruistic," she adds, with a gleam in her eye. "I expect some awesome referrals." Her phone rings, and she holds up a finger as she looks at the display. "I need to take this," she says. "Take a look at the rest of that and give me a sec."

I nod, then take the portfolio over to the single window at the side of the room. It's large and lets in enough light that the room feels airy and pleasant. I glance down and realize that it overlooks Ventura Boulevard. I lean forward so that my head is almost touching the glass, but from this angle, I can't see the Galleria. What I do see, however, is the black sedan parked on the street across from the building. It's familiar, and it only takes me a second to remember where I saw it before—on the street in front of my condo just this morning.

Security guys.

I think about the protective bubble that I so desperately crave, but I know that it has already cracked. Or maybe it was only an illusion to begin with. Either way, Damien and I are living in the real world now. And, honestly, I can't deny that after last night, I'm happy to have someone watching my back.

The shrill ring of my phone interrupts my melancholy thoughts. I grab it out of my purse, then freeze when I see the caller ID—Giselle Reynard. Oh, joy.

I consider letting it roll to voice mail. Giselle is not on my favorite people list. Not only did I recently discover that she and Damien dated years ago, but I also learned that she told her husband, Bruce—who happened to be my boss—that I was the girl in the erotic portrait that now dominates one wall of Damien's Malibu house. Still, I can't help but feel sorry for her. I know she and Bruce are in the throes of a contentious divorce. And I know she feels guilty for revealing my secret. As a gallery owner who deals with nude portraits all the time, it simply didn't occur to her that the secret was important to me.

Besides, Damien is one of her best clients. I'm undoubtedly going to continue to see her socially.

So, yeah, I answer the call. "Giselle," I say lightly. "What can I do for you?"

"I was actually hoping I could do something for you." Her voice is light and airy, as if we are chatting over cocktails.

"Oh. Um, okay?"

She laughs. "Sorry. That was rather vague, wasn't it? But Evelyn was just at the gallery, and she mentioned that you're considering getting office space. I thought perhaps I could come take a look. Give you some ideas for sprucing it up. Maybe lend you a few canvases to add color."

I frown, because I'm really not sure why she'd want to do that. "That's incredibly nice of you, but I'll probably just cover the walls with white boards."

"Oh. I see."

Across the room, Lisa has finished her call. *It's okay,* she mouths. *You can redecorate.*

"I just wanted to make the offer." Giselle pauses for a moment. "The truth is I know I can never make it up to you for what happened, but I thought this might be a start."

Well, shit.

"Listen," she says, and the airy quality is gone from her voice, replaced by something much more genuine. "I know we got off on the wrong foot. Blaine is a good friend and a client, and he absolutely adores you. It goes without saying that Damien adores you. I feel terrible that my stupidity hurt you."

"I appreciate that," I say. And then, because I really should have one wall that isn't entirely covered with notes and code, "How about this afternoon? Maybe around four?"

She agrees eagerly, and when I hang up, I see Lisa looking at me, her expression somewhere between smug and amused.

"Ah," I say with a grimace. "It is available right now, isn't it?"

She laughs. "We never did get that coffee. Come on. There's a Starbucks on the corner. We can go over paperwork and do the ceremonial latte-based key transfer."

And just like that, I have an office. I'm not Damien Stark yet, but I'm on my way.

16

To the CEO of Stark International—

The CEO of Fairchild Development seeks an appointment this evening to discuss a possible merging of our interests.

As Lisa gets our coffees, I reread my text and press send. Almost instantaneously, I get a reply.

To the CEO of Fairchild Development—

I look forward to whatever merger you have in mind.

P.S. Congratulations on the office space.

I grin, and am about to ask him how he knows that I got it when the door to the Starbucks opens and a skinny guy wearing earbuds bounces in carrying a vase full of daisies and other wildflowers. My heart flutters because I am absolutely, positively certain those are for me. I don't know how Damien knew that I took the property any more than how he knew where to find me. But this is Damien, and as far as I can tell, he has eyes everywhere.

The delivery guy scans the room, his gaze stopping on me. For that matter, everyone's eyes are now on me. The delivery guy glances down at a piece of paper, then boogies over. "Nikki Fairchild?" he asks, a little too loudly, presumably so he can hear his own voice over whatever he's jamming to.

"Thank you," I say as he puts the flowers down and strolls out, shimmying in time to whatever tunes are blaring through his earbuds. Around me, the other customers flash quick smiles, then return to whatever they were doing. One girl, a few years older than me with a pixie face and fabulous auburn curls, mouths *nice* before turning back to the screenplay that is open on the table in front of her. I totally agree.

"Wow," Lisa says, sliding back into her seat.

"Damien is all about the wow-factor," I say with a grin. I pull out the card, then smile even broader when I read it.

Tonight I'll show you just how much a woman with her own business turns me on. Until then, imagine me, touching you. —D

"So now that I've told half the world I have an office," I say, "I guess we ought to do the paperwork." She and I spend the next hour going over the lease and also over some basic business information that Lisa shares with her clients. She gives me a few recommendations for attorneys who can advise me about incorporation, but also concedes that I might just want to ask Damien.

"Not to be crude," she says. "But you're sleeping with the best business resource around. Take advantage of it."

"Oh, I fully intend to," I say, with just enough of a leer that we both start laughing. *Yeah,* I think, *Lisa and I are going to be friends.*

As if to illustrate the point, she tells me that the restaurant two doors down has an amazing happy hour. "Want to check it out next week? You can tell me all about your first few days among the self-employed. Or, hell, drag along your roommate and we'll talk about men. I'm engaged, but that doesn't mean I can't dish."

I laugh. "It's a date."

"Excellent." She stands and hooks her briefcase over her arm. "I've got to go meet a client. You walking back or hanging out?"

"I'm going to finish my coffee and make some notes while all this is fresh in my mind," I say, indicating the folio. I don't tell her that I'm seriously considering a second coffee before I head back to the office. After last night—both the good and the bad—I'm operating on very little sleep.

As soon as she leaves, I scoot my chair over a bit so that the walkway between my table and the next isn't quite so crowded. As I do, I catch the eye of the auburn-haired woman I noticed earlier. Her finger marks a page in her script, and she is looking my way, her brown eyes fixed unabashedly on me. I shift uncomfortably and turn sideways, trying to focus on the folio that is open in front of me.

A moment later I hear the chair across from me scrape the floor and look up to find the woman taking a seat at my table. "I really don't mean to be a huge pest," she says in a voice that is crisp and precise, making me think of the Northeast and prep schools. "But it's driving me crazy. I know you from somewhere and I can't figure it out."

"I'm sorry," I say. "I don't think so." I don't bother to tell her that I get this a lot. It comes with the whole Golden Girl of the Tabloids thing.

"Are you sure? You look so familiar. I'm Monica, by the way. Monica Karts." She eyes me hopefully, then frowns. "Doesn't ring any bells, huh?"

"Sorry," I say. I start to gather my things, my Polite Nikki smile on my face. My mother may have tormented me through most of my youth, but she also drilled good manners into my head. "I probably just have one of those faces," I say with a smile. "But it was lovely to talk to you."

"Oh, hell," she says. "My agent is always telling me I come on too strong." She pushes the chair back and moves to her table. "Sorry if I bugged you. You don't have to leave. I need to get back to this anyway. Audition's this afternoon."

"You didn't run me off," I lie. "I just need to get back to my office." Just saying that gives me a little trill of pleasure. *My* office. Seriously, how cool is that? "Good luck with your audition," I add as I gather my things, and am surprised to find that I mean it. She has a bubbly personality that reminds me of Jamie. Besides, I'm in a pretty good mood.

Since I'm carting a flower arrangement, I decide to blow off the second coffee. I'm almost to the door when I hear Monica call out, "Jamie Archer."

I turn. "You know Jamie?"

"Weren't you at The Rooftop bar about a month ago with her? One of Garreth Todd's parties?"

"Yeah," I say.

"Well, so was I!" She says it in the kind of excited tone I'd expect if we'd both just pledged the same sorority.

"So you're a friend of Jamie's?"

She waves her hand in dismissal. "I barely know her. But I was at an audition with her once, and I remember seeing her there. And you, too. But I think I'm mostly remembering you from the newspapers."

"Great," I say dryly.

"That stuff they said about you was shit," she says earnestly. "Except the part about a reality show. If that's true you should totally take it and make as much money as you can and tell them all to go to hell."

I laugh, because as much as I do not want a reality show, telling them all to go to hell sounds like a grand plan.

My phone rings, and I balance the flowers on top of the condiment bar so that I can retrieve it from my purse.

Monica taps a fingertip on her screenplay. "I better get back to this. But I'm so glad I figured it out. Maybe I'll see you again. I come here all the time."

"Sure," I say, as I answer the call.

"Well, Texas? Are you a proud new business owner?"

"Evelyn! Hang on a sec." I wave goodbye to Monica, then tuck the phone under my chin and pick the flowers back up. I use a hip to push open the door, then start off down the wide sidewalk back toward my office. "Can you believe it?" I ask. "I feel all grown up."

"I'm proud of you," she says. "And I mean that in a totally non-patronizing way."

"In that case, thank you." I actually preen a bit from her words. I fell in love with Evelyn Dodge the moment I met her. She's tough and no-nonsense and says what she thinks. I've pretty much decided I want to be her when I grow up.

"So tell me about the place."

I describe it to her in detail, then mention that Giselle is going to come by later to talk art.

"I probably owe you an apology for that," she says. "I know she's not high on your list these days, but she seemed pretty intent on making it up to you."

"No, no," I say. "It's fine. I've got my jealousy all reined in, and I know she feels bad about what happened." To be honest, I can't help but wonder if she didn't let the truth about the painting slip to someone else who then shot off their mouth to a reporter. I don't mention my theory to Evelyn, though, because I'm afraid she might float the possibility by Giselle. And if it's true, I don't see the point in making her feel worse than she already does.

"So when can I see it?" Evelyn asks.

"It? You mean the office?"

"You're there now, I assume?"

"On my way back from Starbucks."

"Good. Give me the address. I'm in the area. I'll be right over."

She arrives less than twenty minutes later, bursting into my office after being announced by the building's very efficient receptionist. "Not bad," she says, looking around. "Not bad at all."

"You're completely transparent, you know," I say. "There is no way that you were in the area. Sherman Oaks? You? Sorry. Just not buying it."

"Busted," she says with a grin. "No, the truth is I had a meeting with a director friend, and he's doing reshoots all day at Universal. But I would have come to see you, anyway. We have business to discuss, Texas, and I'm damn sure not letting someone else steal my thunder as your very first client."

"In that case," I say as I ease behind my desk, "pull up a chair and let's talk about it."

We end up going down the street to a deli where we spend a full two hours chatting and eating and—at least on Evelyn's side of the table—drinking our way into the afternoon.

"I talked to Charlie today," she says as she stabs at the piece of cheesecake we've ordered to split for dessert. "Couldn't get him to give me the details of why he's still in Munich, but he did mention that Sofia's on the loose again." She shakes her head in exasperation. "I swear, it's a wonder that girl didn't drive Damien out of his head ages ago."

"So she's always been like this?"

"Oh, yeah. Smart as a whip, that one. Reminds me of you in a lot of ways. But she doesn't have your backbone, she's never learned to cope, and she runs instead of fighting."

I'm shaking my head slowly. *Backbone? Coping?* Who the hell does Evelyn think she's looking at?

"Don't you pull that with me," Evelyn says, eyeing me know-

ingly. "You're a survivor, Texas, and we both know it. I never
played the bullshit card with my clients, and I sure as hell don't
do it with my friends. And it's a damn good thing you're a survivor, too. Because no one else could last a week with our boy."

That makes me grin. And, honestly, so do her words. Because
the more I think about them, the more I realize how true they are.
Yes, I've got some ginormous issues, but I've been tackling them.
And for the most part, I've been beating them.

"I can tell you the exact way it'll play out when she finally
turns up, too. Damien will head over to London to make sure
she's okay and get her admitted to yet another facility. And the
press will start speculating that Damien's tossing Sofia aside in
favor of you. Or vice versa."

"Tossing her aside? But they're not together. Damien told me
they haven't been together since they were kids."

"When has the truth ever bothered the press? Every time
they're photographed together, the London papers practically
have them engaged. It'll be more interesting this time around,
now that you're in the picture."

"Interesting isn't the word I'd choose," I say dryly.

"If you can't make them stop, at least let them entertain you,"
she says. And I have to admit, that's probably good advice.

"Speaking of speculation," she continues, "the rumors are
also flying that I'm returning to agenting."

"Are you?"

"Fuck no," she says, with a sound that is somewhere between
a guffaw and a snort. "But my old firm's been doing the full-court
press, trying to get me back behind a phone and a desk. And you
know what? Who knows. Maybe if they sweeten the pot enough
I'll reconsider. Right now I'm just amusing myself watching them
run around talking up potential projects. Like yours," she adds
with a wicked grin.

"Mine? My what?"

"Take your pick, Texas. There are producers salivating to get you on reality TV. And there are at least half a dozen companies looking to hire you to do product endorsements. Want to be the face of a makeup line? I could arrange it like that," she says with a saucy snap of her fingers.

I just shake my head. "This is the weirdest city."

Evelyn snorts. "Hell, yes it is."

"If they're just looking for a face, tell them to look at Jamie's. I look better in real life than I do on film, but Jamie was made for the camera."

"Good point there, Texas." I'm joking, but I'm not entirely sure Evelyn realizes that.

I'm still buzzing from sugar and conversation when Evelyn heads back to Malibu and I return to my office. I study the portfolio of Blaine's work that she left with me and make a few notes for the app she wants me to design. I want it to stand out—to have more functionality than simply as a portable display case—and I am so engrossed in brainstorming that I don't realize the time until the intercom buzzes and the receptionist tells me that a Ms. Reynard is in the lobby.

"Oh, right. Send her on back." I remain seated when she comes in—I'm the boss, after all—and greet her with my Professional Nikki smile. Another perk of my horrific childhood—I am well-versed at hiding my emotions under a variety of tried-and-true pageant-quality smiles. So I am confident that Giselle has no idea that I'm still wary—or that tiny seeds of jealousy remain buried just below the surface, ready to sprout if she says the wrong thing or looks at Damien with the slightest hint of attraction.

The truth is, I don't want to be wary or jealous. I don't like that girl, and I don't want to be that girl. But I can't flush from my mind the simple truth that she did date Damien—and that where Damien is concerned, "date" most likely means "screwed."

"Nikki!" she chirps as she comes through my door, and I have to force myself to up the wattage on my smile. Giselle reminds me of Audrey Hepburn—her hair, her frame, her poise. I do not usually get intimidated around other women, but around Giselle, I feel off my game, and I can't help but think that this is a huge mistake.

If she notices my hesitation, she's kind enough not to say anything. Instead, she focuses on the space, her eyes roving over the empty walls and the furniture before landing back on me. "It's a great space," she says. "Small, but airy and well laid out. This beige on the walls is hideous, so that's the first thing we'll want to change. Then we'll want to hang some art. Not too much. Probably one large piece to anchor the room, and then a few smaller pieces to provide some balance. I have some artists in mind—I'll bring a portfolio by the next time I come. And some paint chips, too. Something professional, but bright. Maybe a pale yellow," she adds, almost to herself.

I glance around, trying to imagine the walls in yellow. I have to admit, it might look nice.

She seems to realize she's gone into the zone, and aims a ten-thousand-megawatt smile in my direction. "Thanks again for letting me do this."

"Sure," I say. "I have to be honest. The rent on this place isn't bad, but it's more than I planned to spend my first year out of the gate. I don't know that I can justify a decorating expense, too."

She drops gracefully into one of the molded plastic guest chairs. "No, no. You misunderstand me. This is my treat. Well, for the first year. Then if you want to keep the canvases, you can either buy them or we can discuss a lease. As for the painting, this place is a shoebox—no offense—and I'm sure I already have the perfect color in storage."

I tilt my head, trying to process this. "Giselle, I know that you didn't mean to upset me when you told Bruce about the portrait.

If you owe me anything, it's an apology, and you've already done that." I don't mention Damien or my little stabs of jealousy. Other than having a history with him, she's done nothing to incite the little green monster.

"I appreciate that, I really do. But I want to do this. I know how much all the press bothered you, and I can't help but think that maybe that's my doing, too."

I sit up straighter. "What do you mean?"

"Well, I obviously wasn't thinking. What if Bruce said something? What if I told someone else and just don't remember? What if someone overheard us talking?"

Her words echo my earlier thoughts. "Even if that's what happened, it's blown over. And, honestly, Giselle, I don't want to stick my nose into your business, but can you really afford to work for free?"

For the first time her expression loses some of the long-lost-girlfriend cheerfulness, and I know that I have hit a nerve. What I'm not sure of is if I've crossed a line. I'm about to apologize and tell her that it's none of my business and if she wants to work for free, then more power to her, but she continues before I have the chance to speak.

"The truth is that I can't afford to make ends meet with just the gallery. I know that Damien and Evelyn aren't gossiping about me, but at the same time, people talk, so I'm sure you've heard that my divorce is not, well, pleasant."

She pauses, and I smile and murmur the appropriate condolences.

"Be careful of men," she says darkly. "Fuck them, but don't trust them. Not any of them." She looks hard at me. "That's a lesson I should have learned before I married Bruce. It sure as hell applied to the men in my life back then. All of them," she adds.

"I couldn't live like that," I say coldly. I'm not sure if she's trying to be a bitch or do the girl-bonding thing, but I don't care.

I don't want to think about the fact that she dated Damien, much less discuss it. And I sure as hell don't want to hear about why I shouldn't trust him.

She exhales and slouches a bit so that she no longer looks like one of LA's beautiful people but like a harried commuter. "Sorry. I'm too bitter by half. The point is that I need to increase my cash flow, and so I'm ramping up my design work again. And I could use this—doing your office, I mean. I don't want to be crude, but having Damien Stark's girlfriend on my client list isn't going to hurt my business."

Strangely, that makes me feel better. I don't particularly want to be friends with Giselle, and I'm relieved to realize that she isn't looking to be besties with me, either. Business is different, though, and if she wants to bling out my office so she can promote her talent, then as far as I'm concerned that's a win-win. Especially if she can do most of the work when I'm not actually in the office.

"All right," I say. "I guess we have a deal."

"Fabulous." Her bright smile has returned, banishing the look of defeat. "I'll pull some material together and give you a call. In the meantime," she adds as she rises to her feet, "be sure and give Damien a kiss for me."

She sweeps out of my office, and I watch her go, bemused. After a moment, I shrug it off. If she's playing games, I'm not going to get drawn in. And if I'm imagining things—well, then I really need to get over it.

I spend another hour making notes for Blaine's app, but then I can't take it anymore. The sun is setting outside my window, and I still haven't heard from Damien. I try his office, but Sylvia tells me that he's still in meetings. "It's been a crazy day," she says. "Since he just got back, everyone wanted a piece of his time."

I can't help but smile. I understand the feeling.

"He should be done soon, though," she says. "Shall I have him call you?"

I tell her not to bother, and then switch over to my messaging app to send him a text. To the CEO of Stark International from the CEO of Fairchild Development: Regarding my previous request for an appointment, does this evening fit on your calendar?

I don't expect a quick reply and am surprised when my phone *pings* almost immediately. I think I can squeeze you in.

I practically trip over my fingers typing the reply. I'll be right over.

No. I will. I have plans for your new office. . . .

I smile in anticipation and wonder how I'll survive the time between now and when he arrives.

Since I can't concentrate on work with the prospect of Damien's pending arrival hanging over my head, I abandon Evelyn's art app in favor of going through my emails and clearing them out. I make the mistake of opening the one my mother sent while I was in Munich. The one that tells me that I really should work on my personal skills, because ignoring her calls and emails is simply rude and not the way she raised me. I see that your current fling got away with murder, **she writes**. Hopefully that means you'll quit playing Florence Nightingale to his troubles. It's simply a waste of time, and there are any number of men who are equally as eligible. Honestly, Nichole, once you pass the ten-million-dollar mark, one man is essentially the same as any other. Think about what I've said. And call me. Kisses, Mother

I want to delete it. Right at that moment, actually, I want to delete it even more than I want to breathe. I don't want that woman in my head. She may not have ever taken a knife to my flesh, but I know without any doubt that she bears as much responsibility for the scars on my hips and thighs as I do. I want to delete that email and prove to myself that I've moved on.

I want to . . . but somehow I can't quite manage.

Fuck.

I slam the top down on my laptop, not bothering to close any of my programs.

"Bad first day?"

I look up to find Damien leaning against the door frame. He's dressed for the office in a tailored gray suit, white shirt, and a burgundy tie, and he looks for all the world like a long, tall drink of sin. "Not anymore," I say. "How did you get in?"

"Apparently your receptionist reads the papers. She knows we're together."

I lean back in my desk chair and eye him. "Are we?"

He steps inside my office, then pulls my door shut behind him. He pauses, then very deliberately locks the door. "We are."

"Well," I say as I feel the temperature rise between us. "That's very good to know."

"You look very authoritative behind that desk, Ms. Fairchild," he says, then glances around the small office. "So this is where the magic happens?"

I'm grinning. Whatever remnants of gloom remain from my mother's email have been firmly swept away. "It's pretty cool, isn't it?"

"It's wonderful," he says. "I'm so proud of you. Tell me all about your first day."

I give him the rundown on the lease and on Giselle. I can hear the lilt in my voice, the excitement from setting off on this new adventure. And I see my own happiness reflected in Damien's smile. "I even have my first client," I add, then tell him about Evelyn's app for Blaine.

"You're amazing," he says.

"It feels good. You were right," I add. "I took the plunge and it feels great."

"I knew it would," he says, then lowers his voice to add, "I thought of you today." He strides toward me as he speaks. The room is small, and it doesn't take him long to cross to my desk. "I pictured you the way you were last night."

"Oh." I swallow as the temperature in the room rises.

"Then I pictured you like that here. Naked and bound and ready for me. Wanting me." He comes around the desk, his eyes never leaving my face. I feel my pulse beat in my neck, and I'm having a little trouble breathing.

"I—oh. Yes."

"It's intoxicating, you know."

I squirm a bit in the desk chair. As far as I'm concerned, it's his voice that's intoxicating. "Um, what is?"

His eyes dance with heat and humor as he leans forward and puts both his palms on my desktop. "Knowing that I can bring a powerful woman like you to her knees. A woman with her own company, her own empire. Knowing that I can make her wet with my words. That my voice can make her nipples peak and her clit tingle. That I can shove her skirt up and turn her over her very own desk and spank that perfect white ass until it glows and then, when the scent of her arousal covers the desk and fills the room, I can fuck her until she comes so hard she screams for mercy."

"Oh, God, Damien . . ." My blood is pulsing, my body quivering.

"Stand up, Nikki. Go over toward the window."

Though I'm not entirely sure my legs will hold me up, I comply. He looks me up and down. The high-heeled red pumps, the tailored skirt, the silk shell under a light summer jacket.

His eyes never leave mine as he sits in one of the guest chairs. "Take off the jacket."

I do, tossing it over the arm of my chair behind the desk.

"Now the skirt."

There is a challenge in his voice, and I know that he expects me to protest. To tell him this is my office and that I have a receptionist just a few feet outside that door. I don't. This is exactly what I want, too, so I reach behind me, tug down the zipper, and let the skirt fall to the floor, revealing the red thong panties.

He says nothing, but I can see the heat building in his eyes, and my body responds immediately, my sex quickening, my nipples getting tight and hard beneath the lace of my bra. "Well, Mr. Stark," I say as I slowly walk toward him. "What do you want from me now?"

His answering smile is like a slow caress, and ripples of desire break through me like foam upon a sandy shore. "Stop," he says, when I am about five feet from him.

I do, my heart pounding with anticipation.

He lifts a finger and makes a spinning motion. I roll my eyes, but take a step forward, do a runway-style turn, and then repeat the process, effectively rotating a full three-hundred-sixty degrees for him. I put my hand on a cocked hip and tilt my head. "Like what you see?"

"Oh, yes," he says. He leans back in the chair, his casual posture belied by the tension I see in his face and shoulders, and by the firm slant of his mouth. His gaze flicks over me, and I swallow, hyperaware of my body's reaction. Of how I react whenever I'm around this man. No wonder he always says that I glow. Damien is like a switch, and it is he who turns me on.

The thong is wet against my sex, and the pressure makes me even more needy. It's not the thong I want touching me—it's Damien. He, however, remains resolutely still, his hands resting on the arms of that uncomfortable chair as he examines every inch of me, his gaze lingering at that tiny triangle of material.

"Spread your legs—that's my girl. Now stay still for just a moment."

My skin prickles, as if my body is anticipating his touch and is protesting that his hands aren't upon me and his cock isn't deep inside me. Then his eyes drift lower still. I don't move, even though I know what he is seeing. The scars. Not too long ago, I would have curled up on the floor and cried if someone looked at me so intently. Hell, that is exactly what I did when Damien did that very thing. Sometimes it amazes me how fast my world has changed with Damien in it. And not just my world, but me. He's my anchor. Something to hold on to as I dig deep inside myself to find a strength I never even knew existed.

Somehow, though, Damien always knew that it was there. More, he trusted that I would find it, too.

He has always seen so much. Not just the beauty queen. Not just the scars. He's seen all of me, and no matter whether I'm in panties and high heels or the most couture of evening gowns, I am always standing naked before him.

Once upon a time, I would have found that thought terrifying. Now, I take comfort in it.

But this is not a moment for deep reflection, nor do I want to think about scars or strength or the battles that we have fought. All I want is Damien. And I want him right now.

Boldly, I take a step toward him.

"No," he says. "Stop."

"Stop?"

He arches a brow.

I cock my head a bit to indicate I understand, then raise a brow. "Yes, sir."

"Good girl. Now spread your legs, just a little. That's right," he says when I comply. "Stay like that."

I am about two feet from him, and breathing hard. He is sitting in the chair, which puts him about eye level with the red swath of material that barely covers my sex.

Slowly, he lifts his eyes. "There's something I want," he says.

Shock waves cut through my body, because I want it, too. I want Damien inside me. I want his cock in my mouth, in my cunt.

I want him to whisper to me, to make love with words in that extraordinary way that he has. I want him to fuck me so hard and so deep that I cry out from that singularly exquisite pleasure that is wrapped up in pain.

Most of all, I want him to touch me.

I start to take a step toward him, but he stops me with a single shake of his head. It is a miracle that I don't weep with frustration.

"Not that," he says.

I swallow, suddenly uncertain. "Then what?"

"I want to watch."

"Damien . . ." I have touched myself for him before, but not like this. Not like a show. I swallow, a little bit embarrassed, but undeniably excited, too.

"Close your eyes," he orders.

"Why?"

"Because I said to."

I close my eyes.

"Good girl. Now take off your top. Do it slowly. Take the hem, and hold it as you trail your fingers up. That's it, just like that."

I do as he says, trying to breathe steadily as I slowly peel the silk blouse off. It's not easy, and I feel my stomach twitch with my breath, with the intimate touch of my own fingers.

"Imagine it's me," he says. "My hands easing your shirt off. My hands cupping your breasts, pulling the cup of your bra down so that you spill out over the top. That's it," he says, as I follow his lead and adjust the cups to expose my breasts and nipples. "Do you feel my touch? The way I'm tugging your nipples? The way I'm stroking my fingertip over your areolae?"

My breasts are full and heavy, my nipples puckered with desire. I pull gently on my nipples and the corresponding tug in my sex makes me gasp.

"Damien—"

"I know, baby. You can feel it, can't you? The way your sex throbs. How hard your clit is."

"Yes."

"We've done this before, remember? Our first night. You in the back of my limo, and I was miles away on my phone and so hard I thought I'd explode."

I nod. It's one of my most vivid memories. I was drunk and heady with lust, but I was alone and I could fool myself into believing that the extent of my arousal was my own secret.

Now, there is no hiding how turned on I am. And even though this is Damien, who has seen me at my most wanton, my most needy, it has always been for him that I have opened myself. Now, it is my own touch that I am craving. My touch, and his words. I feel naughty. Reckless. And, so help me, I want him to take me all the way. I want to finger myself until I come in front of him—and when I do, I want to open my eyes and see my own passion reflected right there on his face.

"I didn't have the pleasure of watching then. I intend to enjoy it now."

"Yes. Yes." It's the only word I can manage. It's the only word that fills my head.

"Slide your right hand down. Take your time, baby. You have such soft skin, I want you to feel it. To touch it."

Once again, I comply. I keep my left hand on my breast, almost like an anchor, then spread my right so that my palm grazes my belly, my pelvis, and then my fingers dip under the band of my thong. I bite my lower lip as my hand slides over, then moan as my fingertip brushes my clit before easing farther down to soft, slippery flesh.

"Open your eyes," Damien orders. "Look at me and touch yourself."

"I—" But my words die on my lips when I open my eyes and

see his face—the bold heat in his eyes, the flush of his skin. His hands are on the armrests of the chair, and he is gripping it so tightly I can see the whites of his knuckles. And his cock is so hard beneath his tailored trousers that I am afraid it will split a seam.

"Fuck me," I whisper. "We both know you want to."

"More than anything," he says as our eyes meet and lock. Sparks burst through me merely from the connection of our gazes, and the heat grows in anticipation of his touch. "But no," he says, making me want to weep. "This is about you. I want you to feel it, too."

"Feel what?"

"The pleasure I take from your body," he says simply. "I want to watch. I want to lose myself in the vision of you." As if in illustration of his words, his eyes drag slowly over me. "Don't stop, baby. Slide your fingers inside. Tease your clit. Let me see it. Let me watch the way your skin moves when you're about to come. Each tiny gasp, each shudder. The way you drag your teeth over your lower lip. The flush that colors your skin before orgasm, and the just-fucked look in your eyes after you come."

I am so hot, so wet, and I do as he says, fingerfucking myself hard and then lightly teasing my clit. I am dizzy with lust, and I reach out with my other hand, taking it off my breast so that I can clutch the side of my desk to steady myself.

"Oh, God, Nikki. Do you know how much watching you turns me on? How hot you make me? I have only begun to memorize the bits and pieces that make up you. You are my obsession."

"Yes," I whisper. "Oh, yes."

The sharp shrill of my phone fills the room, and I jump. "Don't stop," he orders. "Just ignore it."

I do, too lost in this sensual haze to care about something as foolish as a phone. I grind my hips in time with the rings, then keep going even after it stops. I hear the *ping* that indicates a voice mail, followed by the buzz of a text message.

I manage to stifle the urge to throw my phone out the window.

"Don't even think about it, baby. Just this. Just us. You're so close, Nikki. God, I can see it on your face, in the way your lips are parted. Imagine it's my mouth on your cunt, my tongue stroking you, tasting you. Baby, you taste so good."

I whimper, so close, but not quite there, and my hips grind against my own hand. Soon, soon, so very soo—

"Ms. Fairchild?"

The receptionist's voice bursts through the speaker, and I jump, feeling guilty and exposed, even as Damien bites out a curse.

"Ignore it," he growls, but the voice continues, unable to hear our side of the conversation.

"Mr. Stark's assistant is on the phone," she says, as cold fingers of dread trail up my spine. "Apparently a Ms. Archer has been trying to reach you. I'm afraid there's been an accident."

17

I release Damien's hand and burst through the door to Jamie's tiny room on the third floor of the San Bernardino hospital, then sag with relief when I see her sitting up in bed watching *SpongeBob*. There's a nasty bruise rising on her left cheek, and a white bandage taped across her forehead. Other than that, though, she looks intact, and for the first time since Sylvia called, I breathe easily.

"I'm sorry!" she says the second she sees us. "I'm so, so sorry."

"But are you okay?" Thanks to Damien's helicopter, it didn't take us that long to get here, but I still spent the entire flight imagining the worst. Now I rush to her side and wince at the bruise that covers one arm, then disappears under her hospital gown.

"I'm banged up, but I'll be fine. Really. But—I mean—oh, shit." She glances Damien's way. "Oh, God, Damien. The Ferrari's toast. I totally fucked up."

"You're not badly hurt," he says, moving to my side. He twines the fingers of one hand with mine, then takes Jamie's hand in his other. "That's all that matters."

"Is the other driver okay?" I ask.

"It was just me," she says, her voice as anguished as I've ever heard it. "I'm such a fucking loser."

I am fighting hard not to cry. "You're not, and you know it. It was an accident," I say, but Jamie just shakes her head and doesn't meet my eyes.

I frown and glance at Damien, who looks at least as concerned as I feel.

"So tell me what happened," I say gently. I ease up to sit on the edge of the bed and Damien pulls up a chair. I put my foot on the seat cushion beside his leg, and he rests his hand on my ankle, just below the platinum and emerald bracelet. I focus on his touch, grateful for his strength and so desperately relieved that he is here with me.

Jamie sniffles and drags the back of her hand under her nose. "I went down the mountain to go check out some happy hours," she says. "I mean, I had this frigging awesome car, so why not, right? And I met this guy and he was so totally hot." She looks toward Damien and shrugs almost apologetically.

"Would you like me to step out?"

Her eyes widen. "No! I mean, you deserve to know how I totaled your car. And it's not like my reputation doesn't precede me, right?"

Damien, wisely, stays silent.

"Go on," I prompt.

"Well, there were sparks, you know? And I haven't banged anyone since Raine except for that one time with Douglas," she says, referring to our horndog of a neighbor. "Honest," she adds, holding her hand up in a Boy Scout salute. "I was practically a nun while you two were in Germany. Anyway, he needed a ride home, and I was happy to oblige because, well, why wouldn't I be? And that part was great. And the part after was great, too," she adds, cutting her eyes toward Damien.

I get it. For that matter, I'm sure Damien gets it, too. She fucked the guy. A perfect stranger. But this isn't the time for yet another lecture, and I bite back my reprimands and instead say simply, "Go on."

"So I'm lying there, right? And it's nice. I mean *he's* nice. Or at least, I think he is. Until this alarm clock beside the bed goes off. Then he sits up and starts pulling on his clothes."

I catch Damien's eye. I do not like the direction this is heading, and I already know that it ends badly.

"I ask him why he's getting dressed, and he snaps at me to hurry. Because his wife—his fucking *wife*—is going to be home soon and I need to get the hell out of there."

"Oh, Jamie . . ."

"I know, I know. Believe me, I know. But right then I was just pissed. And scared, because he tells me his wife's a cop. I mean, seriously, it's like a goddamned movie of the week or something." She draws in a deep breath. "So I'm hurrying, right? And he's pushing me to move faster, and he's basically turned into this total asshole. And I swear, if she wasn't a woman who carried a gun I would have stayed and told her that her fucktard of a husband screwed around. But I'm not keen on getting shot and he's practically screaming at me by now."

"And somehow the wife caused the accident?"

Jamie shakes her head. "Other than by coming home and scaring the crap out of me? No. But I pull out of his house and I head down the street to get out of the subdivision and back to the main road. I'm distracted, and I know I'm driving faster than I should, and—oh, Damien—I'm so, so sorry. But that was it. Just too fast. I wasn't being reckless, I swear to God. But when I turn the corner, this other car is pulling out. They couldn't have planned the timing better if they tried. I mean, it was like they were just waiting for me to come, which is stupid, right, but that's just the kind of day I was having. So I swerve, and I lose control and I wrap the car around this huge stone fence that marks the edge of the development. The airbags did their thing, but I still managed to bang my head." She presses her fingertips to the bandage on her forehead. "I'm not even sure what I hit it on."

Her shoulders rise and fall as she takes a deep breath. "So that's it. The whole thing was my fault. I was pissed off and driving too fast and the whole goddamn thing is because I spread my legs for some fucking stranger who only wanted a quick lay while his wife was off catching bad guys."

I know she wants me to console her. To tell her it wasn't her fault at all. And sure, that kind of accident can happen to anyone. But Jamie has fucked around for too long, with me and everyone else telling her that it can only end in trouble. I'm not about to say "I told you so," but I'm also not going to tell her it's no big deal and that it could have happened to anyone.

"You scared the shit out of me, James," I finally say, and feel the tears well in my eyes again. "What would I do if something happened to you?"

Jamie got lucky—that's the basic, bottom-line, absolute fact. A few inches in another direction, a few miles per hour faster, a little bit of oil on the road—just one tiny change and things could have been much, much worse.

I shiver, unnerved by the direction of my thoughts. By the knowledge that I could not stand to lose my friend. And by the certainty that if the worst happens, it is the sharp steel of a blade that I will crave—and if Damien is not beside me, then it is a blade that I will turn to.

Unnerved, I squeeze my hands tight, feeling my nails dig into my palms. Damien's hand tightens around my ankle.

I sigh and savor the connection. For right then, it is enough.

When the nurse comes in to take Jamie's vitals, Damien goes out into the hallway to find someone who can bring pillows and extra blankets. There is a hideously uncomfortable chair in the room that pulls out into a hideously uncomfortable bed, and that is where I am sleeping tonight, curled up tight against Damien's side.

Despite the uncomfortable bed and the nurses visits that wake us every three hours or so, I am actually somewhat refreshed when I'm awakened the next morning by the smell of strong, slightly burned coffee.

"Nectar of the gods," Damien says as he presses the Styrofoam cup into my eager hand. I sip it, make a face, and take another long swallow.

"The gods aren't too picky this morning," I say.

He brushes a kiss across my lips. "I'm sure Edward will be happy to stop for a latte."

I frown, confused. "Why is Edward here?"

"I'm sending you and Jamie home in the limo."

"We're not riding back with you?" I hear the near-whine in my voice and immediately wish I could take it back. Yes, it's Saturday, but the man has an empire to run, and he's already been away from it for far too long. "Sorry," I say. "I know you have to work."

"There are things I need to take care of," he says, and something in his tone catches my attention. "I'm going to San Diego," he adds, obviously noticing my frown.

"Oh." His father lives in San Diego, and I realize that he is going to confront the man about the photos sent to the court. I do not envy him the trip. My mother may have failed Parenting 101, but Jeremiah Stark never even took the class. "Hurry back," I say, even though what I want to do is throw my arms around him and keep him safe. I do not want to see his heart wounded any more than it already is. And yet at the same time, I'm silently cheering inside. He could have so easily told me that he had business meetings, but instead he let me in. "I love you," I say.

He cups my chin and tugs me in for a kiss. "Stop worrying. I'll be fine."

I nod, desperately hoping that he is right about that.

Since the cogs of the medical establishment do not turn quickly, it's a full two hours before Jamie and I are finally settled in the limo. "If I have a mimosa, are you going to lecture me?" Jamie asks.

"I haven't lectured you at all," I reply indignantly. "I've been extremely non-lecturey. And it's not like you have a drinking problem, James."

"You're right," she says as she pours two and passes me one. I'm not really in the mood, but I take it anyway. Best friend solidarity and all that. "I don't have a drinking problem; I have a fucking problem."

I happen to agree, but I wisely say nothing and just take a sip from my mimosa. Since Jamie is a reasonably observant person who happens to know me well, my silence isn't lost on her. She shrugs. "I know," she says. "Nothing you haven't been telling me for years."

"I just don't want to see you get hurt," I say. "You were lucky, James. But this could have been bad."

She doesn't meet my eyes. I'm not surprised. Jamie has moments of self-awareness, but long contemplation is not her strong suit. But at least the wheels are turning.

"I called Ollie," she says. I blink, confused by the transition. "I'm elaborating on my fucking problem," she says, by way of explanation. "I called him after Raine got me fired from the commercial."

"Oh, Jamie," I say. "You promised me. For that matter, he promised me. He told me there wasn't anything going on with you two anymore."

"Wait. You talked to him? When?"

"He was in Germany," I say. "The firm sent him over to help with the trial. You didn't know?"

She shakes her head. "I haven't seen him. Not since . . . well, not since he came over that night."

"You called him." It's not just a statement. It's an accusation. Hell, it's a reprobation.

"I needed someone to talk to, and he's the dude who had the golden ticket."

"And you slept with him?" I'm pissed. I'm seriously pissed. As much because they did it as because Ollie lied.

"We didn't! I swear!" She holds up her fingers in a Boy Scout salute. "But there was a tug, you know?"

I'm relieved. But it's a cold kind of comfort. "He's engaged, Jamie. And he's a mess."

"As to the first, I know. As to the second, so am I. Maybe we're soul mates."

"Friends, yes. Lovers, no." Just the idea makes me shudder. I can picture the movie of their relationship in my head, and it is definitely not one of Evelyn's romcoms.

"I know," she says. "I really do. You'd be proud of me. Nothing happened."

"Proud of you?" I repeat, hearing what she's carefully not telling me. That had it just been up to Ollie, something would have happened. *That* part he left out.

"You're missing the point," she says. "I didn't sleep with Ollie. And I really wanted to because of the commercial and I felt lower than dirt, and, well, you know. But I didn't—and I thought maybe that meant I was getting my act together." She sucks in a breath. "And then I go and fuck an asshole and wreck Damien's Ferrari."

I may have used a blade against my own flesh to cope, but Jamie uses men. From a distance, it looks like my method is the more dangerous, but sometimes I'm not so sure. For years, I've seen the way Jamie's casual fucks rip her up. Now, I'm afraid I'm seeing a different kind of danger. "The bottom line is that I worry about you."

"I know you do," she says simply. "I do, too."

For a few moments, we're both silent, and I think that we're done. Then Jamie draws her knees up and hugs herself. "I'm thinking about going back to Texas."

My mouth hangs open and I am literally speechless. Of all the things she might have said to me, this was not even on my radar.

"I can't afford to keep the condo, though. So you'll have to find another roommate. Unless you move in with Damien. If you do that, I might sell. The market's gotten better. I might even make enough to buy a place in Dallas and have some cash left-over to pay Damien for at least part of the mess I made of his car. I figure my condo should cover about a hubcap, don't you think?"

"Wait, back up. What are you talking about? You hate Dallas. You've always hated Dallas."

"Look at me, Nik. I'm a mess. I go from fucking movie stars to screwing strangers. But all I'm really doing is screwing myself."

"I don't disagree," I say baldly. "But moving to Dallas doesn't change anything but geography."

"Maybe that'll be enough. Maybe there's too much noise here. Too much temptation."

I want to tell her she's wrong, but I'm not entirely sure that she is. All I know is that I don't want her to move fifteen hundred miles away. But what I want and what Jamie needs are two entirely different things. "Just think about it before you do anything rash," I finally say.

Her eyes meet mine and we both laugh at the irony of my words. "I wouldn't dream of it," she says, and we laugh even harder.

We leave the serious shit behind and spend the rest of the ride cranking up the tunes, singing along with Taylor Swift, and downing mimosas. Because, after all, you can never have too much vitamin C.

"Did you see that we're finally famous?" Jamie asks, about the time we see the skyline of downtown LA.

"What?"

"Or, I am. Damien's been famous forever, and you've been racking up your share of the press, too. But check it out." She rummages in her purse for her phone and then passes it to me. "I took screenshots of all the stuff I found on the Internet. Just check out my photos."

I do. There, mixed in with pictures of an absolutely gorgeous guy, are candid shots of me and Damien and Jamie at the shops at Lake Arrowhead. Eating, talking, laughing. There's even one with Damien's arms around each of our waists. She peers over my shoulder and taps the screen. "That one's all over Twitter," she says. "I'm not sure if it's because Damien's famous or because he's fuckalicious, but it's totally gone viral."

"Maybe it's because of you," I say. The photographer caught Jamie in a laugh, her eyes bright, her hair shining. It's the vibrant and beautiful girl in the picture that I know so well, but I can't help but fear that the image Jamie has of herself is the one sitting beside me in the limo. Battered and bruised and not quite sure where to go next.

It's not until we reach Malibu that Jamie presses her hands against the window, peers out at the world with her brow creased in confusion, then turns to me. "This is not Studio City," she says, as if I am the one who is confused.

"You're staying at Damien's Malibu house."

Her brows rise and her smile turns devious. "I was kidding about that threesome. But if it's important to Damien . . ."

I put my hands over my ears. "I can't hear you," I say over and over again until she breaks down and starts laughing.

"Seriously," she says, "why am I staying in Malibu? Because if this is my punishment for wrecking his Ferrari, he kind of missed the mark."

"Not punishment," I say. "Pragmatism." I go on to explain about the rock and the stalker-style text.

Her eyes are wide when I finish. "Whoa. At least you don't have to deal with your fruitcake of a mother. You can thank me for taking *that* burden off you, anyway."

"You've been dealing with my mother? How? Why?" I have no idea what she's talking about, but since I wouldn't sic my mother on my worst enemy, I'm already sympathizing with Jamie.

"She called me about a week ago—in a total Elizabeth Fairchild snit, I might add—and told me that since I was your best friend, could I please get you a message. Apparently—her words, not mine—you are emotionally confused, overwhelmed by your rich and bossy new boyfriend, and taking the whole thing out on her by ignoring her calls and emails."

"Shit," I say. "Sorry."

"No, it's okay. When she called, I was pissed off at my mom for some bullshit thing I don't even remember now. After talking with your mother, I was practically giddy about my entire family tree."

"Thanks," I say dryly. "Now I feel better."

She just grins. "Anyway, I guess she's pissed that you sent someone to get all those old pictures of you, but then you ditched her calls. I'd ditch the calls, too, Nik, but why on earth would you tell someone to see your mom for old pictures? Who do you dislike so much you'd send them her way?"

"I didn't," I say as a finger of worry trails down the back of my neck, making me shiver.

"It may not be bad," Jamie says, obviously seeing the concern on my face. "It's probably just a reporter. Someone putting together the definitive article on the girl who got Damien Stark."

Somehow, that doesn't make me feel any better.

She cocks her head and points a finger at me. "As of now, we're entering a worry-free zone. For the rest of the day, nothing but sand and surf and margaritas." She thrusts out her hand. "Deal?"

"Deal," I agree, because that sounds pretty damn good to me.

18

My margarita-inspired dream is wildly erotic. A hot mouth closed tightly over my breast. Strong hands stroking my splayed legs, moving upward with sweet determination until the two thumbs are close enough to brush over my swollen and eager sex. I open my eyes, but I see no one. There is only the touch of his hands and the brush of his lips and—oh, please—the hard length of his cock inside me.

I cry out for Damien—my voice noiseless in the dream—but he does not appear. There is simply that touch. That pressure. That insistent stroking of flesh against flesh, the rise of heat, and the steady, growing scent of arousal. I am lost in it. Lost in this sensual haze that surrounds me. It is Damien—it is always Damien—but though I reach for him, my arms find only air.

And then there are hands upon my breasts and the hot, hard head of a cock between my legs. I cry out as he thrusts into me, his movements rhythmic but frenzied. Over and over he pounds in a violence that seems to carry us up and up, a wild dance, a dangerous coupling. My heart batters my chest, my body aches deliciously—he is using me, pounding me, and the power of his thrusts are such that I wonder I don't pass out from the desperate intensity of his fucking.

My body quakes as the force of an orgasm rips through him, and I reach up to pull his body closer to mine, knowing that in this dreamworld he will remain ephemeral and I will clutch only air.

But I am wrong, and my fingers find heated skin and taut muscles.

Damien.

I open my eyes to find him balanced over me, his cock going soft inside me. His eyes are hard on mine, and we are both breathing hard. I feel gloriously alive. Well-fucked and adored. But I also see the storm in his eyes and something that comes dangerously close to regret.

I want to reach out and slap it off his face.

"I used you," he says, his voice as tight as the muscles of his chest.

"Yes," I say, then hook an arm around his neck. I lever myself up and capture his mouth in a deeply sensual kiss that has his cock twitching inside me. I pull him down, wanting him pressed hard against me, not balancing above me, and hold him tight. "God, yes." I hook my feet around his legs, keeping him there, his skin hot against mine, our bodies still connected.

When I look in his eyes again, I see that the storm has faded. I sigh. I do not know what happened between Damien and his father, but I know enough to understand that it ripped him up and it was to me that he came. That it was my body and my touch that helped him work through his demons.

I hold him close, still astounded that we have such power over each other. That we are the balm to each other's soul. It humbles me. And, yes, it terrifies me. Because how could we ever survive if we lose each other?

I fall asleep in his embrace, but when I awaken, I am alone in

the room. I sit up and glance around. Despite all the time I've
spent in this house, this is the first time I have gone to sleep in the
master bedroom. The iron bed upon which I sit used to be in the
third-floor open area, but Damien had obviously decided on a
more traditional approach when he had the bed moved back to
his house.

Other than the bed, though, there is no furniture in here. And
there is no Damien.

I frown and climb out of bed. It's still dark, and I grapple in
my purse for my phone, then groan when I see that it's not yet five
in the morning.

I consider falling back into bed, but I know that is not possible. I need Damien. And, I think, he needs me, too.

His shirt is on the floor, and I put it on. The house is huge, but
I have a plan of attack, and I go first to the library—a mezzanine
that essentially floats beneath the third floor, visible from the
massive marble staircase, but accessible only by a secret elevator
or a set of stairs hidden behind a door off the utility area. The
lights are low, casting shadows over the cherrywood shelves and
glass cases that display the few things from Damien's childhood
that he values enough to keep. The area is filled with memories,
both delicious and bittersweet. Damien, however, is not here.

I continue down, cutting through the commercial-grade
kitchen to the gym that takes up much of the north section of the
house. I cock my head, listening for the thud of Damien's fists
against the punching bag or the clatter of weights rising and falling on the machines. There is nothing, however. Just a silence that
seems to stretch on forever.

He is not in the pool, either, and as I stand, confused, on the
flagstone decking, I begin to fear that he has actually left the
property, possibly going downtown to his office. It occurs to me
that I didn't go into the master bathroom, and if he was going to
leave me a note, that would have been the most logical place.

I start to turn around to go back to check, figuring that if there is no note at least I can get my phone and text him, but I pause when I see the dim glow of lights off to the right.

I focus on them, trying to picture the layout of the property in my mind. Damien's garage—a massive underground bunker that would make Batman drool—is roughly in that direction, but I'm pretty sure it's more inland. But if the light isn't coming from the garage, then what could it be? There was nothing else dotting the property when we'd walked along the landscaped paths before we'd detoured our lives to Germany. Nothing except the ocean in the distance and a flattened area where Damien told me he was considering building a tennis court.

I freeze.

Surely not . . .

I hurry in that direction, and as I get closer, I hear an odd *chunk-thwap* and realize that I have found him.

I can tell by looking that the court hasn't been finished for long. The net is brand-new and not the least bit weathered. The surface isn't scarred at all. The ball machine that is currently firing at Damien glows bright and shiny under the towers that cast a faintly yellow glow over the whole area.

And there in the middle of it all is Damien.

I draw in a breath, overwhelmed by the sight of him. He wears nothing but gym shorts, and his chest shimmers from the light sheen of sweat. The muscles in his arms and legs are tight, and he moves with the grace and power of a wild animal as he rushes forward, swings, then attacks the ball. He is power and poetry, grace and perfection, and I feel my body tighten in response to the beauty that is Damien.

But he is broken, too, and my heart squeezes as I continue to watch him. Over and over, he moves and hits, his feet moving in a perfect rhythm, his body pushed to the edge. There is no emotion on his face—no smile of self-satisfaction when he nails the ball—just pure concentration, as if this is penance, not pleasure.

There is a chaise in the shadows beside the court and I sit on it automatically, transfixed by the sight of him.

I do not know how long he duels with the machine. I only know that when it stops spitting balls out, he shouts a curse and hurls his racquet. I yelp, surprised, and Damien whirls to face me, his expression a mix of shock and concern.

"I didn't want to interrupt you," I say softly. I ease off the chaise and move onto the court—and into the light. "I'm sorry. I shouldn't have stayed."

"No." The word is rough. "I'm glad you're here." He takes my hand and pulls me close, and sweet relief flows through me.

"You didn't tell me you went ahead with the court."

"How could I not after you teased me with the possibility of you in a tiny tennis dress?" His words are light, but they do not penetrate the shadows in his eyes. "I've had a crew working on it since just before I left for Germany."

"I'm glad." I smile up at him, and I am genuinely happy. Tennis has been a constant in his life, but Richter stole the joy, and Damien hasn't played since he quit the circuit. The knowledge that he is finding his way back to something that he loved bubbles through me.

That happiness, however, is tainted. Because I saw the storm in Damien's eyes when he took me so wildly only a few hours ago. And I saw the fury of that same storm just now as he attacked the stream of balls.

"Was it your father?" I ask gently. "Is he the one who turned the photos over to the court?"

I see the shadows cross his face again, and when he turns and starts to tug me toward the edge of the court, I fear that he isn't going to answer. But we are not returning to the path. Instead, he sits on the lounge where I had been only moments before. He stretches his legs out in front of him, and then pats the space beside him. I lay on my side, propped up on my elbow so that I can watch his expression as he speaks, but it takes so long for him to begin talking that I start to wonder if I'd been wrong about why he has brought me here.

I am about to suggest that if we are going back to sleep, the bed inside would be a much more comfortable choice, when he shifts and looks at me.

"I don't think it was my father," he says. "He seemed genuinely baffled when I confronted him about the pictures."

"Oh." My brow furrows with worry and confusion. "So you don't have any idea who it could be?" That would certainly explain the storm I saw in his eyes.

"I don't," he agrees. There is silence. Then, "I'm worried about Sofia."

I don't understand the transition. "I know you are, but she'll check in. If she's playing roadie to a band in Shanghai, she's probably not—"

"I'm afraid she's running," Damien says simply. "I'm afraid someone's harassing her." He strokes my cheek, his eyes burning into me.

"Oh, God," I say with sudden understanding. "You think someone is trying to get to you through the women you love. Me. Sofia."

"I think it's possible." He scrubs his hands over his face and through his hair. "I think a lot of things are possible. All I know for certain is that those goddamn photos were my salvation whether I like to think about them that way or not."

"They were," I agree.

"And I still don't know who or why, which leads me to think that someone is playing with me. They'll reveal themselves eventually, and when they do, they're going to want something from me. Tit for tat."

I want to argue with him, but what he says makes sense. I sit up and draw my knees to my chest. "But how does that tie in with Sofia being missing?"

Even in the dark, I can see the way his eyes cut away from me.

"Damien?" I press. "What aren't you telling me?"

I hear him draw in a breath. "Richter abused her, too." The words are flat, matter-of-fact, and they chill me to the bone.

"Oh."

He continues without pausing. "If there are photos of me, there are undoubtedly photos of her. Someone delivered a set to me—through the court, but still to me. What if someone did the same to her?"

I tremble. I think of how the photos wrecked Damien, a man with so much strength it awes me. What would they do to this fragile girl? "But wouldn't she call you? Aren't you the one she'd turn to for help?"

"I don't know. Sofia is many things, but predictable isn't one of them. She once disappeared for six months. Turned out she screwed some guy who did time making fake passports, and since I haven't been able to find any evidence that she left the UK under her own name, I can't help but wonder if she's hooked up with him again. She's smart and she's fearless. She's lived on the streets, so if she feels like she needs to hide, she can disappear better than anyone. Most important, she's fucked up enough to happily fall off the grid."

"I get that you love her, and I get that she's not entirely stable, and I get that you're worried. But, Damien," I say gently, "she's an adult. And no matter what your history, she's not your responsibility."

"Maybe not, but it feels like she is."

I can't help but nod in understanding. After all, Jamie's not my responsibility, either. I sigh and stretch out beside Damien. He presses a kiss to my forehead, then links his fingers in mine. A moment later, he presses a button on a remote control.

The lights on the court wink out, and we are thrust into a darkness broken only by the gentle glow of a blanket of stars spread wide across the sky above us.

19

After Saturday's drama, I want to bottle Sunday so that I can keep it close and pull it out whenever I need it. We spend the day doing everything and nothing. Even Damien turns off, abandoning his quest to find Sofia or my stalker or the bastard who leaked those photographs in favor of entering a purely vegetative state with Jamie and me.

Jamie and I rouse ourselves from our prone positions around lunchtime in order to take a walk along the beach. Damien doesn't join us, claiming he's too engrossed in his reread of Asimov's *I, Robot*. Considering Damien's love of science fiction, I do not doubt that the book has captured him, but I also know that the reason he's not coming is because I asked him not to. I want some time to interrogate Jamie about her announcement that she is considering moving back home to Texas.

Once we're actually out with the sun and the surf, though, I can't seem to find the right moment. Instead, we chatter about nothing as we walk all the way through Damien's property to the ocean, then north up the beach to our nearest neighbor. He's tall and muscled and his coffee-colored skin is slick with the sea. He waves at us as he comes out of the water with a surfboard. Jamie, I think, is going to have a heart attack when she sees him.

"Who is he?" I whisper as we turn around and head back toward home.

"That's Eli Jones. He won the Oscar for best supporting actor last year." She shakes her head. "You really are hopeless."

"I am," I say. And, since I doubt I'll find a better transition, I add, "It's going to be hard to focus on your acting career if you move back to Texas."

She lifts one shoulder in a shrug. "Yeah, well, we both know that it's a long-shot career. It's not like I've taken LA by storm."

We're both barefoot, and now she kicks her toes through the water, sending droplets flying. They twinkle for a moment in the sun, then quickly fall, lost once again to the churning water of the ocean. I can't help but think of Jamie; I want more for her than fifteen minutes of fame, and I fear that my lack of enthusiasm for her move is more about me than about what is best for Jamie.

"Whatever you decide," I say firmly. "You know I've got your back."

We've crossed the beach and are trudging back up the path to Damien's house when my phone rings. I pull it out from where I've stashed it in the pocket of my terrycloth cover-up and am surprised to see Courtney's name on the screen.

"Hey, Courtney. What's up?" Courtney is Ollie's fiancée, and we've known each other for years, though not as well as I'd like since she is constantly traveling for her job. Still, she's sweet and genuine and I think she loves Ollie. I love him, too, but I don't love the way he fucks around, and even though Ollie ranks higher than Courtney on the best-friend-o-meter, I can't help but feel that she deserves someone better.

Beside me, Jamie's eyes are wide. *What is it?* she mouths, but I can only shrug.

"Ollie and I want to know if you and Damien are free on Tuesday night. Jamie, too. Is she with you? Ollie said she's staying with you and Damien this week?"

I glance sharply at Jamie. She hadn't told me that she'd told Ollie where she's crashing. I shouldn't feel suspicious—after all, they were friends before they fucked, and I hope they'll be friends after—but I can't help but be nervous.

"Yeah," I say, looking hard at Jamie, whose sheepish expression only makes me more nervous. "She's here. What's up on Tuesday?"

"Nothing specific. But I don't have any trips this week, and we haven't seen y'all in forever. I told Ollie that we should all go to Westerfield's. You know it, right? That place in West Hollywood."

"I know it," I say wryly. Westerfield's is one of Damien's properties.

"So can you come?"

Part of me wants to say no, because I'm terribly afraid that there will be drama. But a bigger part of me still hopes that Jamie and Ollie and I can get back to where we were. "Sure," I finally say. "We'll be there."

By the time evening rolls around, we have lounged by the pool, walked along the beach, played air hockey in a game room that I didn't even know the property boasted, and watched the first two Sean Connery Bond films while stuffing our faces with popcorn.

For dinner, Jamie suggests that we roast hot dogs on sticks over the fire pit, and then make s'mores. It's calorie-laden and gooey and fun, and as I lay beside Damien and lick chocolate off his fingertips, I can't help but wonder if life can go on like this forever.

It can't, of course, but for these few hours I am enjoying the sanctity of life within this bubble.

It ends all too soon, though. At ten, Sylvia calls to patch
Damien in on a conference call with one of his Tokyo suppliers.
He kisses me lightly, then heads inside to take the call. I watch
him go, sipping my whiskey and enjoying the way his ass looks in
his favorite threadbare jeans. Jamie, I see, is also appreciating the
view. She meets my eyes, then grins. "What? Like you don't know
he's hot?"

"Trust me," I say as I lean forward to grab another square of
chocolate. "I am fully aware of his hotness."

"Making another?" Jamie asks, passing me the bag of marsh-
mallows.

"Nope. Just eating the chocolate."

"You okay?"

I glance up at her. "Chocolate isn't always a sign of a deep
emotional crisis."

"Good. Glad to hear it."

I put down the chocolate, suddenly wary. "Why?"

"No reason." She holds up a hand as if warding off my non-
existent protest. "Really. I was just wondering what was going on
with the whole stalker thing. Not that I don't totally love it here,"
she adds quickly. "But, hey, I like being around my stuff."

"I get that," I say. "But I don't think Damien's security folks
or the police have learned anything new."

"Must be driving Damien nuts."

"It is," I say. "That and trying to find Sofia."

"Who?"

I realize that I haven't told Jamie about Sofia, so I give her the
abridged version, mentioning only that she's a friend of Damien's
from his tennis days, that she's a little fucked-up, and that she's
missing. Probably doing the roadie thing with some band, but
until that's confirmed, Damien's worried.

"And you're not jealous?" Jamie says.

I raise my brows. "Are you saying I should be?"

"Ex-girlfriend, and now he's obsessed with finding her again? Shit, I'd be pulling my hair out."

"Thanks," I say dryly. "I appreciate the mental health pep talk."

"Yeah, well, as we've established several times over, I'm not anywhere near as together as you."

"I think you have me confused with someone who doesn't cut," I say.

The look she gives me is as serious as I've ever seen on Jamie. "I think you have you confused with someone who does."

I stay still for a moment, not answering, but looking at myself through Jamie's eyes. Have I really gotten my shit together? Maybe not entirely, but I've been doing pretty damn well. And I owe all that to Damien.

I think about the times when I've started to slide—the times when Damien has caught me—and I wish that Jamie could find someone, too. Someone who gets her and doesn't put up with her shit. Someone who's not just looking for a fuck buddy or a one-night stand.

Someone who'll love her.

"What?" she says, peering at me through narrowed eyes. I just shake my head.

She reaches out for the candy bar, and breaks off two squares. Then she uses the squares to sandwich a marshmallow. She doesn't bother to melt it over the fire; she just bites in, her eyes closed in what looks like near-orgasmic joy. "Damn, but I do love chocolate."

I stand up. "I'm going to bed before I eat any more of that. Do you want me to wake you in the morning? I'm getting up early to go to the office." Those words are at least as delicious as the chocolate. I have an office. My very own office. Seriously, how cool is that?

"I'll disown you if you wake me up," she says. "Now go."

She waves her hand regally. "If I can't have sex, I'm going to at least finish off the last of this chocolate."

I'm asleep by the time Damien comes to bed, and he's gone again when I wake up. I have a vague memory of being wrapped in his warmth at one point during the night, but for the most part, I'm feeling bereft. At least until I find the note in the bathroom promising me something delicious that night—and maybe even dinner, too.

Cooper has magically appeared at the Malibu house, and I can only assume that one of Damien's elves drove him there while Damien and I were at the hospital with Jamie. However it arrived, I'm grateful, and I slide happily behind the wheel and head out for the long trek to Sherman Oaks. I'm starving, and my usual traveler's mug of coffee isn't cutting it this morning. Damien once introduced me to the world's best croissants from a local Malibu bakery, and since I can arrive at my own office at whatever the hell time I want to, I decide to make a detour.

The Upper Crust actually has a drive-through, but I decide to park and go inside. I think I want a plain croissant, but I'm more than willing to be tempted by something truly decadent like *pain au chocolat* or a sticky, gooey cinnamon roll that is positively dripping with icing. As it turns out, it's the apple fritter that seduces me, and as I pay for it and an extra large latte, the little bell on the door jingles and Lisa walks in.

I lift my hand to wave, then immediately drop it. She's hand in hand with a man I know—Preston Rhodes. The head of acquisitions at Stark Applied Technology.

For a second, I think this must be one of those Big, Amusing Coincidences. But then I see Preston's smile of recognition—and Lisa's grimace.

Well, fuck.

"Damien," I say, my temper rising as each piece of the puzzle falls into place. "You didn't talk to me that first day in Burbank because I was the new girl at Innovative," I accuse. "You did it because Damien asked you to." I'm proud of myself for keeping my voice level, but considering the way Preston looks between us and slinks away, I don't think I'm quite as calm as I think I am.

"It wasn't like that," Lisa says.

I cock my head. "He didn't ask you to reach out to me?"

"Well, yes," she admits. "I guess it was like that." Unlike mine, her voice really is calm. Perfectly level and perfectly reasonable. Which, naturally, pisses me off more.

I cross my arms over my chest and stare her down.

"He told me that you were considering going out on your own. That you already had some smartphone apps on the market that were doing well, and that you were working on developing some web-based apps that he thought would make a serious splash in the market."

"And?"

"And he told me that you were unsure of yourself as a business owner."

"So he figured if I wouldn't listen to him, maybe I'd listen to you?" While I've sought out Damien's advice on the financial end, I've hesitated to ask him to step in to help me with the business. At the same time, I've been reluctant to launch until I felt like I knew what I was doing. Lisa is the perfect bridge between my insecurities and my needs, once again proving how well Damien knows me—and that he is still keeping secrets and pulling strings.

I remember how he told me that he'd checked Lisa out. Damn the man! He didn't have to check her out—he knew her. Hell, she's engaged to one of his top employees.

"I'm so sorry," Lisa says. "He asked me not to tell you, but the truth is I didn't even think about it after that first time we met in Burbank."

I exhale. "Honestly, it's not you I'm annoyed with."

She sighs, and the professional veneer slips. I see the core of the woman I've come to know—the woman I thought was becoming my friend. "Come on, Nikki, you know how he feels about you. He wasn't trying to be underhanded—he only wanted to help you."

"Help drive me crazy," I say, and Lisa laughs.

"I really am sorry." Her expression is genuinely contrite. "So are we still on for happy hour sometime?"

"Sure," I say, because no matter how mad I might be at Damien—and right now, I am very mad—I'm not going to screw up this nascent friendship with Lisa. "Actually, I'm meeting some friends at Westerfield's tomorrow. Why don't you guys come, too?"

"Are you sure?"

"Absolutely," I say firmly.

"I'd like that," Lisa says. "Text me the details?"

"Will do," I promise.

"And don't kick Damien too hard," she adds. About *that,* though, I'm making no promises at all.

It takes all my willpower, but I manage not to call Damien from the road. We are definitely talking about the whole Lisa bullshit, but we're going to do it in person once I've cooled down a bit—and have figured out what I want to say and exactly how I want to say it. Damien is far too adept at distracting me, and I have no intention of being distracted.

Giselle calls while I'm in the car, and we make plans to meet at the office to go over a color palette she's picked out. As soon as I hit the freeway, though, I can tell that traffic will be a bitch. I have no idea what time Giselle left Malibu, but it's possible that she's got a thirty-minute head start, so I call my own office and tell the receptionist—whose name I have forgotten—to let Giselle into the space if she gets there first.

As it turns out, traffic isn't just a bitch, it's a raging, angry bitch from hell, and it takes me well over an hour to get from the Upper Crust in Malibu to my office in Sherman Oaks. I've finished both the coffee and the fritter by the time I arrive, and so I park Coop and walk down to Starbucks to get a refill on caffeine. Monica is at the same table, and she looks up and waves when I come in.

"How'd the audition go?" I ask.

She frowns and makes a thumbs-down motion. I make the appropriate sympathetic noises and get in line for coffee. I get a fresh latte for me and then, because I'm in a bit of a mood, I add an extra black coffee, and have the barista put a container of cream and some sweetener in a bag. Then I deliver the coffee to the security guy who tailed me from Malibu and now sits in his car in the office's covered parking area. "You must be bored out of your mind," I say. "But I really do appreciate it."

He thanks me, tells me his name is Tony, and assures me that it's not boring at all. I don't believe him, but I appreciate the lie.

I'm not surprised to find Giselle in my office when I get there, but I am surprised by the wide swaths of color she has painted on my walls. She must see the surprise on my face, because her eyes go wide, and she immediately starts apologizing. "It's so much easier to pick a color if you have an actual patch on the wall. Those cardboard paint chips will only get you so far."

"No, it's okay, really. I like the blue," I add, pointing to a patch of sky blue she's painted by the window.

"One of my favorites as well," she says. She glances at her watch. "I know you have work, so let me finish putting some of these colors up, and then I'll come back tomorrow with a few canvases for you to choose from, and you can tell me which colors sing to you."

I agree readily, though I don't know how much singing the colors will do. As far as I'm concerned, the blue is just fine. But Giselle seems determined to make this a process, and since it's important to her—and I'm going to get a freshly painted office out of the deal—I am happy to go with the flow.

My cell phone rings right as I'm firing up my laptop. It's Jamie, who is calling to gloat about the fact that she going to spend the day luxuriating on the beach while I slave over a hot keyboard.

"Not that I wouldn't rather be shooting a commercial," she adds. "But I'm all about the glass being half full."

I laugh. "Glad to hear it. And, James," I say, "just because the beach is private doesn't mean it's private, you know?"

"No naked body surfing?"

"Not even topless," I say, smiling.

"Tell your man that I'll fix dinner tonight. We can call it rent. What do you want?"

"I'm good with anything," I say. "And if you need to go to the store, just get Edward to drive you." I frown, realizing how easily the instructions have come from my lips. Edward doesn't work for me, after all. And yet here I am sliding into the mistress-of-the-house role.

I have to admit I like it—even if I am still irritated with Damien.

"My friend Jamie," I say to Giselle after I hang up, even though she hasn't asked. "She's vegging at the Malibu house today."

"Sounds nice."

I glance around my office feeling a bit smug and very happy. "Maybe," I say. "But this is good, too."

"I'm excited for you," Giselle says. "And impressed by how quickly you're working to get your name out there."

I frown, confused.

"The article in today's *Business Journal*," she says, as if that will make it all crystal-clear for me. "About the app you're de-signing for Blaine. I think it's great that you're turning all that nasty press about the portrait around and using it to promote your new business."

"I didn't contact the *Journal*," I say.

"Oh." She frowns. "I guess Evelyn or Blaine must have. Either way, it's great publicity."

Great, maybe. But also odd. And as soon as Giselle leaves, I pick up my phone to call Evelyn and ask if she sent out a press release. I don't mind if she did, but I would have liked advance notice. If for no other reason than I'd like a copy of the article for my scrapbook.

Before I get a chance to dial, however, the receptionist tells me that I have a delivery. I open my office door to find a messenger with a huge box of chocolates. I take it, bemused, and read the card. *Forgiveness and chocolate go together.*

A wry smile twists my lips. Apparently Damien spoke with Preston Rhodes.

I consider calling him, but decide to wait. It will serve him right to squirm.

Promptly ten minutes later, there is another delivery. A gift basket filled with fancy liqueurs surrounding a huge bottle of Macallan whiskey. The man knows me well. I check the card and laugh out loud. *Forgiveness goes even better with alcohol.*

Funny, maybe. But I'm still clinging to my irritation.

Still, I can't deny that the edge on my anger has dulled a bit.

When the next delivery is announced, I'm already waiting by the door. I tug it open and gasp to see Damien himself standing there. He's holding a shopping bag and carrying a single red rose. There is both amusement and apology in his eyes, and I have to fight the familiar tug that urges me to take the packages from him and wrap myself in his arms.

I realize we've been standing like that for too long when he clears his throat. "Can I come in?"

If I'd heard even the slightest hint of laughter in his voice, I would have slammed the door in his face. But his voice was flat and respectful and despite the whimsical nature of his gifts, it is clear that he knows my frustration with him is genuine.

"For a bit," I say. "I have work to do."

I step aside, and he eases in, his arm brushing mine as he does so. I feel that frisson of awareness that I associate with Damien and draw in a tiny little breath. If he hears me, he doesn't show it. He just strides into my office, puts down the bag, then hands me the rose. "I'm sorry," he says.

I shake my head and face him, legs parted, my hands on my hips, totally exasperated. "You are a brilliant man, Damien Stark. Which is why I don't understand why you can't get it through your head that this kind of thing pisses me off. It's one thing— one very annoying thing—to ask Lisa to seek me out and help me. It's another thing to lie to me about checking her credentials."

"I have checked her credentials," he says. "It's just been a while."

"You know what I mean."

"I do," he admits. He steps toward me and the air between us thickens.

I step back. "Dammit, Damien. You can't just pull shit like that."

"Are you going to ignore her advice? Cut her off?"

"No. She's my friend. *Despite* you," I add. "Not because of you. And don't you dare argue that what you did makes no difference because we ended up genuinely liking each other."

"I know the difference," he says seriously. "But I have a blind spot where you're concerned, Nikki."

"Aw, really? That's so romantic." I cross my arms over my chest. "Get over it."

He chuckles, then crosses the space between us before I can back away again. His arm is around my waist and he pulls me close so that my pelvis is hard against him. I feel the length of his erection, and I want to be annoyed that he's hard despite the fact that I'm mad at him. I can't, though. Because I'm turned on, too, my body tingling and already melting against him. Hell, I'd gone damp the moment he stepped into my office. "You can fuck me," I say breathily. "But I'll still be mad at you."

He closes his mouth over mine for the kind of kiss that positively melts a girl. "Tempting," he says. Then he releases me, takes two steps back, and returns to me with the shopping bag. "For you."

I take it warily, then peek inside. It's full of tissue paper, which I pull out to reveal a box shaped like a doghouse. I glance at him, confused, then pull the box out of the bag and open it. Inside are a dozen sugar cookies baked in the shape of dog bones. Each has *I'm sorry* lettered upon it in silver icing.

"Okay," I say with a grin. "You're officially out of the doghouse. Thank you for the cookies," I add. "And don't do it again."

"I'll do my best," he says. "But it's safer not to make promises."

I can't help but laugh. This is one of the foibles of being in a relationship with a man like Damien Stark. But the more important fact is that as much as he drives me nuts, we are talking about this stuff. It's light in the shadows. It's glue on the bubble. Because the more solid we are, the longer we can hold back the world.

"Thanks for coming," I say. "You could have waited and talked to me tonight."

"No," he says simply. "I couldn't have."

"Lunch?"

"Unfortunately, that I do have to pass on."

"Too bad, though I suppose it's just as well. I've accomplished absolutely zip today. I take it your day is busier what with a universe to run."

"My universe today extends only to the two of us."

At first, I think he's being romantic. Then I see the hard lines of his face. I push the box aside and perch on the edge of my desk. "You've learned something. Is it good or bad?"

"A bit of both, actually."

"All right. Tell me the good first."

"The court ruled against the motion to unseal the photos."

"Damien," I say. "That's huge."

"It is," he agrees. "But the press isn't stupid. The odds are they'll try the back-door route and do the same thing I'm doing— try to figure out who sent the evidence in the first place."

"Have you learned anything new?"

He hesitates, then nods. "About the photos, no. About our leak regarding your portrait, yes. Turns out the ATM camera was very effective."

"Seriously? That's wonderful. Who is it?"

"I still need confirmation," he says. "Let me see where it goes, and then I'll lay the whole thing out for you."

"Okay," I say, though I'm disappointed he won't tell me right then, even if he is still investigating. I consider pressing the point, but decide not to. I don't think that his closed-mouthedness stems from the desire to keep secrets but simply from Damien's innate need to keep control. Of his business. Of information. And, I think, glancing at the doghouse-shaped box, of me.

The intercom buzzes. "Ms. Fairchild, you have another delivery. May I send them back?"

"Sure." I glance at Damien, but he holds up his hands. "This one's not from me. I swear."

I don't believe him, of course. At least not until I take the envelope from the courier and see Damien's face. "Let me open it," he says sternly.

My chest goes cold. The negligible weight of the plain manila envelope turns heavy in my hand. "You don't think . . ."

"I don't know." He reaches for it. "But I'm going to find out."

I pass him the envelope, irritated with myself for not having the guts to rip it open, and at the same time desperately grateful that he's there beside me. He holds the envelope in a handkerchief, then uses a small pocketknife from his keychain to open it. He pushes the envelope at opposite corners so that the slit gapes open, then starts to peer inside.

"No," I say firmly. "I want to see when you do."

His expression is tight, and I expect him to say no. But then he nods. I move to stand beside him, and then he upturns the envelope over the desk, spilling the contents onto the polished surface.

Six photographs. Me in kindergarten. Me in a tiara at my very first pageant, my hair in ringlets. Me, me, me, me.

In every photograph, my face has been crossed out with a red pen pushed so hard into the photographic paper that the emulsion has been scraped off, leaving a series of ragged red X's where my face should be. There is one piece of paper mixed in with the photos. Block letters cut like a cliché from newspapers and pasted on the sheet: *YOU DON'T EVEN EXIST*

I stare at it all, surprised that the room is silent. Surprised that I'm not screaming, because this is so very wrong. But the world is as silent as death. Hell, the world looks like death. No noise. No color. No light.

It's all gray. Even those red X's have faded to gray. And the gray room is actually shifting to black. A cloudy, inky black that surrounds me, blanketing me, drawing me down, down, down . . .

Nikki!

Nikki!

I feel a sharp sting across my cheek. "Nikki!"

"Damien." It's my voice, but it sounds horribly far away. I lift my hand and touch my cheek.

"Sorry," he says, though he sounds more worried than sorry. "You fainted."

"I—what?" I sit up, groggy, and realize that somehow I've ended up on the love seat. I focus on Damien. "Fainted?"

I haven't fainted in years. Not since I was accidentally locked in a storage closet during college. Dark enclosed spaces have always freaked me out, and I'd passed out. But never have I simply slipped into a faint like this.

"You had reason," Damien says, correctly reading my face.

Those photos. *My* photos.

I shiver. Whoever did this is in my life. This isn't just nasty texts. This is flat-out targeting me. And if I don't exist, then what the hell does that say about their endgame?

I draw in a breath and try to calm the machine-gun beat of my heart. I sit up straight, my hands on my thighs. My skirt is hitched up a bit, and I clutch tight to the bare skin above my knees, digging my nails in tighter and tighter, using the pain to help pull me out of this fog.

I breathe deep. "My mother," I say. "Whoever is doing this got these from my mother."

Beside me, Damien gently plucks one hand off my thigh and holds it tight. Guiltily, I relax my other hand.

"Your mother?" he says. "What are you talking about?"

I relay Jamie's conversation with my mother.

"This is good," Damien says, releasing me long enough to type out a text on his phone. "It's solid information," he adds, since I must look confused. "A definitive connection. I'm going to have Ryan speak with your mother. I think he'll have better luck getting her to cooperate than I will."

I nod, then arch my neck as I look toward the desk. There is nothing there. "Where—"

"I put them away." His voice is as gentle as the hand that

eases my fingers once again off my thigh. I jump a bit; I hadn't realized I'd started again, but I can see the small red crescents where my nails cut into my skin.

"I—" I look away. I'm too transparent, my wounds far too visible. I desperately wish that I didn't need the pain, but I do. I *do* exist, goddammit, and if I'm going to have any chance of pulling myself back together, I need it desperately.

"Tell me," he says softly. "Tell me what you need."

I look down at the fading crescents. "You know," I say, my voice low.

"I do, baby." He slides off the love seat to kneel on the floor. His hands are on my knees and he gently spreads my legs. "You want me to touch you." His voice is as gentle as the pressure of his thumb upon my inner thigh. "You want me to fuck you. You want to feel the sting of my hand against your ass or the burn of a rope around your wrist."

His words mesmerize me. They slide over me like warm water, seductive yet dangerous. So deep I could drown in them.

"You want to draw in the pain—to turn it around inside you." His hands slide roughly over my thighs, pushing the skirt up around my hips to expose the white lace triangle over my sex.

My breath comes faster now and I am hyperaware of my body. Of the way the nubby upholstery presses into my thighs. Of the heat coursing through me, running in vibrant currents from Damien's hand to my cunt, to my breasts, to my nipples. I arch my back and slide forward a bit with my hips. I want to feel his hands upon me. Hell, I just want to *feel*. I want the explosion, and yet at the same time, I want *this*. His touch. His words. His slow build to passion and that sharp sting of pain mingled with pleasure that I know is coming.

He grabs the hem of my shirt and pulls it over my head in one swift, violent motion. I hear myself moan and feel my breasts tighten with need as the muscles of my sex clench with longing. Damien tosses the shirt aside and grabs my hip with one hand, shoving the skirt up around my waist. With the other hand, he fingers me over the lace panties, rubbing and teasing me through the delicate material as I spread my legs wider in shameless, wanton greed.

I want it hard and fast. I want to latch on to the pain—to use it as a rope to find my way back. I want it—and I am certain that Damien understands it.

His fingers glide over bare skin on either side of the thong, so close to my sex and my clit—but without actually touching—that my frustration is almost as keen as the pain he knows I am craving. He slides the hand on my hip up to my breast, then pinches my nipple through my bra as he yanks the thong to one side and slides three fingers deep inside me.

My breath comes in shudders and I squirm against him. I'm no longer sure what I need anymore except him. And now. Oh, please, now.

"You want the pain because it's what gives you the power to beat it—to haul yourself back and say fuck you to the world. It's a gift, Nikki—that red-hot sting. And I will be the one to give it to you."

He tugs his fingers out of me, then flips me over as if I weigh nothing and carries me toward my desk. He puts me on my feet in front of it and orders me to bend over. I do, the bulk of my skirt between my hips and the edge of the desktop providing some padding.

He stands off to one side, and as I watch, he tugs his belt free. I bite my lower lip, imagining the feel of leather against my rear. I wanted his hand, but this—oh, yes, I can imagine it. The shock, the sting. The building sensation as I close my eyes and grab hold, letting the pain focus at my core.

"Is this what you want?" he asks, and from his tone I realize he had not intended that. But Damien is nothing if not adaptable, and I see the tip of his head and the rise of his brow. Then the slow smile when he nods. He moves behind me, one hand stroking circles on my bare back. "You'll have my hand, too, because I can't bear not to touch you. But if this is what you need—"

He punctuates the word with a lash to my ass and I cry out from surprise and pleasure. The sting is exquisite, and I bite my lower lip, then moan in delight as he rubs his palm over the tender flesh. There is another sting, then another, and with each I feel myself getting wetter. I imagine my rear turning red, and Damien's large hand cupping me tenderly, stroking away any lingering pain that I have not claimed and drawn inside.

"Is that what you needed?" he says after four strokes. He is behind me, his trousers and briefs gone. His palms are on my rear, and his cock is hard between my legs, the length of it stroking me and teasing my clit. "Do you need more? Tell me, Nikki. I want to hear what you need." His voice is raw with excitement, and I know that he needs this as much as I do. And that knowledge turns me on even more.

"You," I say, lifting my ass and spreading my legs wider. I grip the sides of the desk and sigh from the sweet sensation of my breasts hard against the desktop. "Inside me now. Like this. Right here on my desk. And hard. Please, Damien, fuck me hard."

"Oh, baby." He thrusts inside me, using his hands on my hips to piston us together as he pounds and pounds, using me, taking me. I feel the stirrings of my climax inside me, and squeeze my eyes shut, wanting to draw it out. He is so thick, and he's going so deep, and all I want is for this to last. The sensation of him filling me. Of every thrust causing the bunched-up material to rub against my clit. I am lost in a sensual web, and it isn't until I feel the tremors run through Damien and know that he is close, that

I start to let myself go so that—oh, God, yes—I can explode when he does, my body squeezing tight around him, drawing every last bit of pleasure out of him.

And then, sated and breathing deep, I sink my head down onto the desk with a moan of deep satisfaction.

He molds his body over mine, and I do not know how long we stay like that. Then he scoops me up and carries me back to the love seat, curling me up on his lap and covering me with his suit jacket.

I snuggle close, then lift my head to look at him. I cleave now to Damien instead of the pain, and the beautiful, wondrous thing is that he understands. Hell, he understands better than I do.

A single tear escapes and he brushes it away with his thumb, his eyes like a question mark.

"I need you, Damien—God, I need you in ways that you understand better than I do. But I feel so selfish. So—"

He lifts a brow, but his smile is gentle. "Are you under the impression that I don't need you, Nikki?"

"I—no. But I—" I stop, confused. Because the truth is, that has been my fear, but now that he has spoken it aloud, I feel foolish. I think of the way he claimed me the night he lost himself in a flurry of tennis balls. And all the times that he has bound me, controlled me, as a counterpoint to a world spinning away from him. We soothe each other, and I know that. I *see* that. And yet I still cannot quell the fear that while Damien wants me desperately, he doesn't need me the way I need him. That he doesn't love me as desperately as I love him.

He runs his fingers through my hair. "Do you remember what I told you in Munich? About not wanting to touch you with those images in my head."

Remember? How could I forget? But all I say is, "Of course."

"I wasn't entirely accurate."

"Oh." Since I don't know what else to say, I simply wait.

"Pictures or not—those memories are always there. I can't shake them. I've never shaken them. But you make them tolerable." He is looking hard at me now, the emotion so raw it seems to cut right through me. "You're what gives me strength. If I am what centers you, Nikki, then you are what anchors me. Every time I touch you, every time I bury myself deep inside you—Nikki, don't you see? You are the talisman of my life, and if I lose my grip on you, then I have lost myself."

"Damien," I say, because I need to hear his name. His words swell inside me, as if they will make me burst at the seams. But I hold tight to them, for they are too precious to lose.

But though I believe his words, I cannot help but realize that however much he might think I anchor him, when the abyss loomed in Germany, I had no power to pull him back.

The thought makes me shudder, and I cling to him harder.

Because those photos are still out in the world. And they have the power to destroy the man that I love.

20

By Tuesday morning, I once again feel like I have a grip on my life.

Damien and I did not stay at my office on Monday. He held me, fucked me, helped make me whole again. But that was not a place I wanted to be, and he took me to the Tower apartment, his penthouse at the top of Stark Tower. During the drive, he called Ryan, instructing him to go out to the Malibu house to check on both the security there and on Jamie.

In the penthouse, he settled me in a bath with a glass of wine. He pampered me with wine and cheese in bed. He coddled me with old movies, and he made love to me so sweetly my body sang, and when morning came I was willing to give the world another chance.

I am also acutely aware of reality, and that is why I am being driven to work by Edward, who I have learned is not only Damien's driver, but part of the security team. And he has assured Damien that he will walk me into the office himself.

Which is why he balks when I tell him I want to stop first at Starbucks.

"Ms. Fairchild, this one doesn't have a drive-through."

"Just park in front. I won't be five minutes."

The privacy screen is down, and I can see his scowl when he looks at me in the rearview mirror.

I tilt my head and scowl back at him. "Do you really think someone is lying in wait in the coffee shop for me?"

"I think that anyone willing to call your mother for photographs is willing to study you, learn your habits, and be very, very patient."

Since I can't argue with that, I invite him to come in with me, sweetening the pot by offering to buy his coffee.

We're standing in line, chatting about *The Fountainhead*—the audiobook he's currently engrossed in—when the door opens and Monica comes in. She waves and hurries over. "I was hoping I'd see you today. I wanted to tell you to ignore them. They're just money-grubbing pricks."

I glance at Edward. I have no idea what she's talking about. From the expression on Edward's face, though, I think that he does.

"What?" I say, first to Monica and then to Edward.

"You haven't seen? It was on one of those gossip sites this morning," Monica says. "It's probably been tweeted all over creation."

"What has?" I repeat, speaking slowly and clearly.

Edward reaches into his messenger bag and pulls out an iPad. He taps it a few times, then hands it to me. "Mr. Stark thought it would be better not to bother you with this today."

"Oh, really?" I glance at the screen and my stomach curls. *Yeah,* I think. *I could have lived without this.*

The article is topped by a picture of Jamie in a teeny-tiny bikini walking on the beach. That picture features an inset of Damien's Malibu house, along with helpful text to inform the average reader that Jamie is in Malibu, strutting her stuff at the home of billionaire Damien Stark.

266 J. Kenner

HAS STARK BEEN NICKED FROM NIKKI?

According to sources in the know, billionaire Damien Stark—who some believe recently bought his way out of a murder conviction—has cooled his red-hot romance with pageant pretty Nikki Fairchild in favor of Nikki's roommate, Jamie Archer, an up-and-coming actress more recently seen on the arm (and who knows what else) of heartthrob Bryan Raine. According to sources in the Inland Empire, Archer was recently hospitalized following an accident which landed Archer in the ER and one of Stark's prize Ferraris in the junkyard. And yet she's still residing at Chez Stark? What do you think, kiddies? Surely it must be love.

But has Stark really ditched the Fair Child? Or is the king of excess looking for excess in his women, as well? According to insiders, Archer and Fairchild have been on-again-off-again lovers for years. True? We don't know, but photographs circling on Twitter show the threesome looking all too cozy recently in Lake Arrowhead where Stark keeps a mountaintop love nest.

"That," I say as I pass the iPad back to Edward, "is a load of crap. But Jamie's going to be pleased. They said she was up-and-coming, after all."

"So you're not pissed?" Monica asks.

I shake my head. "Irritated. I'm sick to death of my personal life being twisted around in the press. But the story itself? It's such bullshit it's funny."

"Well, I'm totally relieved," Monica says. "I mean, I figured it was all crap, but it got to me anyway. I had a bad breakup," she adds.

"I'm sorry."

"We were hot and heavy for a long time, and then he decided he was in love with someone else. Men," she adds, glancing at Edward with a tight little smile.

"That must have hurt." I try to imagine Damien tossing me aside for somebody else, but the image just won't play in my brain.

"Oh, yeah," she says. "It was like someone took a knife and sliced my heart to bits. But I'm okay," she says with a sigh. "What we had was really special. And that girl? She's just a fling. Temporary. He's going to come back to me. I know it."

I want to tell her to move on. Instead, I just smile and say, "I really hope you're right."

I treat Edward to a latte, and he walks me to the office. "I'll bring the limo around as soon as we have you inside," he says, then goes with me into the building and past reception. Once I'm settled in, he disappears, presumably to park the limo in the lot and listen to his audiobook until I'm ready to go.

Despite the fact that the last time I was in this office I was treated to images of myself with my face scratched off, I actually manage to get some work done, and I'm feeling rather smug about my productivity when Giselle calls to tell me that she won't be coming by to show me any samples today.

"No problem. I'm going to skip out in a few hours anyway." Tonight I'm cutting loose at Westerfield's, and Jamie and I have already planned to spend hours obsessing about our wardrobe before we decide on the perfect outfits. Coupled with the flavored vodka we'll undoubtedly be sipping, the whole process should be fun. "Is everything okay?" I ask Giselle.

"Couldn't be better," she trills. "A client coming in. One of my best ones."

"Better be careful who you say that to. Damien won't be keen on getting knocked from the top slot."

There's a pause, and then she lowers her voice. "To be honest, Damien is the client. But promise me you won't say a word. I have a feeling he wants to buy a canvas for your office."

I laugh, delighted. "Really? I promise to be surprised."

I'm still smiling when Damien calls. "Hey," I say. "I was just about to head back to Malibu to get ready for tonight. Are we going to grab something out for dinner, or do you want me to bribe Jamie to cook?"

"Why don't you two pick your favorite restaurant—my treat—and I'll meet you at the club later."

"Work?"

"A meeting. I have a feeling it'll run long."

"Oh? Where will you be? We could have Edward swing by and pick you up when you're done."

I'm baiting him, of course, but he gives nothing away.

"You girls have fun," he says firmly. "But not too much fun. Not until I get there, anyway. And, Nikki," he adds, "I've already spoken to my manager about security at the club, so they're stepping it up a notch. You'll be watched."

"All right," I say. I'd expected as much.

"And I'm sending Ryan to the club. I want him with you until I get there."

Now I do feel guilty. "Poor guy. He probably used to have a life before he had to start chasing my monsters."

"There's nothing he likes better than taking down a monster," Damien says. "And the fact that I pay him so well makes it even more fun. Trust me, you don't have to feel sorry for Ryan."

I laugh. "Okay, then. But, Damien? Please hurry."

Westerfield's is loud and fun, with some of the best bartenders and DJs in the city. Ollie and Jamie and I discovered it even before Damien was on my radar, but we've been by a few times since, and the bouncer who mans the VIP entrance gives me a little salute as Jamie and I approach. Edward escorts us to the door, but he doesn't follow us in, returning instead to the limo.

I'm wearing a slinky silver skirt and matching tank top with three-inch silver shoes. Jamie is my opposite in all black, the color unusually sophisticated for her. The style, however, adds the kick that Jamie usually finds in color. It is essentially backless, all the way down to the dimples just above her ass. The bodice is held in place by a series of loose black cords that crisscross over her shoulder blades. If someone with a pair of scissors took a snip, the dress would come tumbling down. We both look hot, if I do say so myself.

"Looking good, Ms. Fairchild," the bouncer says as we strut past him. "Knock 'em dead, Ms. Archer."

"This is why I love Damien," Jamie says as we move down the exclusive hallway. "He hires staff that know how to properly suck up."

I laugh as we reach the door that opens onto the public area of the club. Ryan emerges from the shadows to join us. He nods politely, but I see just the hint of a smile when he nods at Jamie. And, unless the light is playing tricks, I see an answering smile touch her lips.

Worry starts to buzz around me like a persistent gnat, and I tug on one of the black cords crisscrossing Jamie's back to slow her down.

"What?" she says.

"That's what I wanted to ask." I cut a glance toward Ryan, and even in the dim light I see the way her cheeks flush.

I remember that Ryan went out to the house last night to check on security, and have to clamp my mouth shut so that I won't scream. "Tell me you didn't sleep with him," I ask when I'm sure I won't explode.

"Swear to God," she says. "We talked. And he's a total gentleman. I made him eggs."

"You what?"

She lifts a shoulder. "He came out in a hurry because of that shit with you and the photos. And he hadn't eaten. So I made him eggs. And he said he really liked them. Next time, I might try to make him a waffle. What?" she demands after a moment, peering hard at my face.

I realize I've been staring at her, a little pleased, a little baffled. "Nothing," I say. "Just—I'm glad he likes your eggs."

"Hey. What's not to like?"

She doesn't wait for an answer, just tosses a grin over her shoulder and hurries to catch up to him. I follow, then slow to a stop when I realize my phone is buzzing. I tug it out of my tiny purse and see the text from Giselle. I open it eagerly, hoping for gossip about the canvas Damien has bought for me. Instead, I stare at her words as if she'd written them in hieroglyphics.

I'm so sorry. I truly wanted to make amends. Things got out of hand.

I read it again, but it doesn't make any more sense the second time than it did the first. I hit the button to call her back, but the call just rolls to voice mail.

"What is it?" Jamie asks when I catch up to her.

I shake my head. "I'm not sure. I'll tell you later." The club is too loud for conversation, and I don't know enough, anyway.

We're in the main area now, just a few yards away from the dance floor. I glance around and finally see Ollie and Courtney waving from across the room. I already know that Lisa's not coming, after all; she left me a voice mail earlier telling me she had to go to Sacramento on business, but promising she'd take a rain check.

Jamie and Ryan make it to Courtney and Ollie before I do. I take my time approaching, my eyes searching the area for Damien, but I see no sign of him.

"Hey, Courtney!" I'm genuinely happy to see her and pull her into an enthusiastic hug. My greeting to Ollie feels more forced, but we loosen up on the dance floor. Whatever issues we have between us, a danceable beat is sufficient to take the edge off.

"Listen, Nik," Ollie says a half hour later as we are catching our breath to a somewhat slower song. "Can we talk?"

I stiffen, because I thought we'd tabled our shit for the night.

He doesn't seem to notice my reaction, though. He leans in so that I am sure to hear him. "I just wanted to say I'm sorry. About the grief I've given you about Stark, I mean."

I pull back so that I can see his face—and so that he can see my surprise.

He draws in a deep breath. "I know about the photos, Nik. Nobody should have that in his past."

It's warm in the club, but I feel suddenly cold. "He doesn't want your pity."

"And he doesn't have it. I'm just—I don't know. I guess I'm just saying that I know what kind of shit you went through as a kid, and now I know what he has to live with."

I tense, but I say nothing. I can tell he's not finished.

"Stark's not ever going to be on my favorite-people list, but I've seen the way you two are together, and I really got to see it in Germany. I think you're good for each other."

I swallow, the ice in my veins melting into a lump of tears in my throat. "We are."

His smile is tentative. "So that's it. That's my apology. I won't say that I'll be asking the guy out for drinks and male bonding, but, well—"

A bubble of relieved laughter bursts from me. "Thanks," I whisper.

"Wanna go get a drink?"

"No," I say. "Stay and dance with me some more."

He grins, and we slide back into the music. I can't say that we're completely healed, but we're better, and I feel lighter around Ollie than I have in a very long time.

After four straight songs, I am ready for a drink, so when Courtney comes by and suggests it, we go eagerly with her. Ollie gets waylaid by someone he knows from work, and it ends up being just Courtney and me who ease up to the bar. I tell the bartender to put our drinks on Damien's tab, and he agrees so easily that I know that not only has Damien already instructed the staff to cater to us, but they have all visually identified me. I'm being watched. Protected. And although it feels a bit strange to be caught in the spotlight like that, I can't deny it makes me feel safer.

But I won't feel truly safe until Damien shows up and I can slide into his arms.

"What happened to the destination bridal shower?" I ask Courtney as we wait for the drinks. I have to practically shout to be heard, and I just know I'll have no voice at all tomorrow.

"I think it's off the agenda," she says.

"Why?" I expect the answer to have something to do with her nightmare of a travel schedule. Instead, she nods toward the dance floor where Jamie has her arms up in the air and her hips gyrating between Ryan and Ollie.

"I should hate her, you know," Courtney says without malice, and that chill rushes over me once again.

"What are you saying, Courtney?" I ask, praying that I'm wrong.

I see the rise and fall of her chest. "I'm not going to marry him," she says. "I don't want to be that woman whose husband cheats on her, and I don't want to get married because I'm a good choice. I can't do that to myself. Hell, I can't do that to him. We'd be miserable in a year and divorced in two."

"Oh." I try to swallow, but my mouth is too dry. I'm shocked by her words, and I feel bad for Ollie, who is going to know he fucked up, and that will make it all the worse. But at the same time, I'm glad. As pleased as I am that Ollie and I are on the mend, he did fuck this up with Courtney, and everything she's said so far is dead on the money. "When are you telling him?"

"Soon. Maybe tonight. I just need to get up the courage." She shrugs. "It's not that I don't love him. It's just . . ." She trails off, as if she doesn't quite know how to say it.

"Don't worry," I say, clutching her hand. "Believe me, I know."

I have had too many drinks and danced too many dances by the time Damien finally arrives at the club. Heads turn, as always, and the crowd parts. He strides straight toward me, and I watch, transfixed, as he moves across the dance floor, not quite able to believe that all of that power and grace belongs to me. That out of everyone in that club, I am the one who will see him naked. Who will feel the heat of his mouth upon my skin. Who will cry out when he thrusts himself deep inside me.

He hooks an arm around me and kisses me hard. I cling to him. I am somewhere in that place between buzzed and wasted, and I feel every beat of the loud music reverberating through me. I am sweaty with exertion, my skin slick, my clothes clinging to me. I lift myself up on tiptoes and press my lips to his ear. "I want you. Now."

I am not exaggerating; I am desperate for him. But considering we're on a dance floor, I hardly expect my wish to come true. So I am surprised when he grips my arm and steers me toward the back of the club, then tugs me into a small elevator that he calls with a card key.

Despite the fact that I'm in a haze, I can't help but notice the tension in his face. The hardness of his eyes. Not to mention the fact that he has yet to speak one word to me.

"Damien? What is it?"

The elevator opens and we are in an office. One wall is entirely glass, and I remember seeing it from below. It is made of reflective glass and surrounded by lights so that anyone who looks up sees only the distorted reflection of dancers surrounded by the glare of colored lights.

But from up here, we have a perfectly clear view of the club.

It is to that wall that Damien pushes me, until my back is to the glass and the dancers writhe beneath us and there is nowhere else for us to go.

The heat in his eyes is unmistakable, and I feel the corresponding pull inside of me. I don't know what has happened or why he needs this, but right now it doesn't matter. I am his, and he can take me however he needs.

How he needs, is rough.

He shoves my skirt up and rips off my panties, making me gasp. He lifts my leg and hooks it around him, so that I am completely exposed. The air against my hot sex makes me tremble, but it is the rub of his jeans against me as he tugs me toward him that sends tremors running through me.

His erection strains under the denim, and I gyrate my hips, stroking myself along his denim-clad cock, wanting to feel it inside me, needing him to fill me.

I meet his eyes, and he stays silent, but the need I see on his face is as potent as my own.

I practically dive for the buttons of his fly, then watch enraptured as he springs free. I want to touch him, to stroke him, but I have no time. He holds me by the hips, shifts my weight, and impales me on him so hard and fast that I swallow my scream.

He thrusts us both backward, slamming me against the glass, and for a moment, I imagine us tumbling over, falling to the dance floor, still connected, still fucking, while the whole world looks on. The fantasy only makes me more wet.

His gaze locks on mine as the intensity of his thrusts builds. I see his release growing in his eyes, and tighten my leg around him to pull him closer at the moment he goes over.

He shudders, still deep inside me, and I reach between us, my fingers rubbing his cock as I stroke my clit, faster and faster until I come, too, and my muscles tighten around him, pulling from him the last waves of the orgasm that still rocks through both of us.

Finally, we sink to the ground, breathing hard, our clothes and limbs tangled around us.

When the ability to move returns, I prop myself up on my elbow to look at him "Do you want to tell me what that was about?" I ask softly.

He reaches for me, then cups my face, his thumb stroking lightly over my chin. "Nobody fucks with what is mine."

I frown, not understanding. "What's yours? You mean me?"

He doesn't answer, but the darkening intensity of his eyes tells me what I want to know.

"What happened?"

"I paid a visit to Giselle earlier. You won't be working with her again."

His words propel me to a sitting position. "What the fuck?" I think about her text. "Goddammit, Damien, quit talking in riddles and tell me what's going on."

He lifts his hips so he can readjust his clothes. Then he stands. I scramble to do the same, and follow him back to that glass wall. "She was in the ATM footage. I confronted her, and she confessed she leaked the story about the portrait so she could get cash to help keep her business going after she and Bruce split. She also sold the story about Jamie and the Ferrari, not to mention the bullshit about our little love nest in Malibu."

"What? No." But even as I say it, I think about the intensity of her expression when I told her Jamie was staying in Malibu.

And I think about all the financial trouble that she told me she was having as a result of her divorce.

Most of all, I think about that text. It was a confession, I now realize. A confession and an apology.

"But she's the one who told me about the article in the *Business Journal*."

"Camouflage," he says. "She sells the story, then tells you. You're both surprised together, and she looks innocent."

My head is spinning. "Wait a second. *You* fired her? She was doing *my* walls in *my* office. If anyone was going to fire her, it should have been me."

"I told you," he says. "No one fucks with what's mine." There is an edge to his voice that I rarely hear. The edge that reminds me that, yes, Damien has a dangerous side. A ruthlessness that helped him win game after game of tennis in his youth, and then claw his way to the top of the corporate ladder without even breaking a sweat. He is not a man to be fucked with.

But that doesn't change the fact that it wasn't him Giselle was fucking with. Maybe the articles were about the two of us, but she'd slipped her way into my office, into my life.

Damien is studying my face, and he's obviously seeing my temper rising. "It's done," he says. "It's over."

"How is it done?"

"I explained to her that my lawyers were more than capable of dragging out multiple actions for defamation and invasion of privacy. She's a businesswoman at heart, so she understands that I can keep a litigation going forever, but she's going to have trouble finding a lawyer whose hourly rate doesn't break her. We came to terms."

"What kind of terms?"

"She turned over all right, title, and interest in her galleries to me. She's relocating to Florida. And good fucking riddance."

I press my palm against the glass, as if the coolness will ease the bite of my temper. "You don't have to fight my battles, Damien."

"I love you, Nikki. I will always fight for you."

His words are heavy with meaning and ripe with passion. They knock me backward and steal my breath. "You love me," I say stupidly.

The corner of his mouth curves up. "Desperately."

I swallow back the knot of tears that has formed in my throat. "You haven't said it," I say. "Not for weeks now."

He closes his eyes as if my words have hurt him, but when he opens them again, it's not pain that I see, but love. He reaches for me and pulls me close. I lean against him, breathing in the scent of soap mixed with sex. It's heady, and I want to get lost in it. Lost in this moment.

"I love you, Nikki," he repeats. "I say it with every touch, with every look, with every breath that I take. I love you. I love you so much it hurts."

"Me, too." I brush a kiss across his lips, then meet his smile. "But you can't protect me from everything, Damien. And you sure as hell can't protect me by keeping things from me. You should have told me about Giselle. Hell, who knows what else is out there you're keeping from me. So just stop it, okay? It doesn't protect me, it just pisses me off."

"All right," he says evenly. I think that's the end of it, but then he continues. "Sofia sent the photos."

I have to rewind his words in my head, because what he is saying makes no sense whatsoever. "The photos in Germany. Sofia is the one who sent them to the court? I don't understand. Why? How do you know? Did you talk to her?"

He moves away from the glass wall to the center of the room. He paces, not like a man trying to solve a problem, but like a man who already knows the answer and doesn't much like it.

"I discovered a discrepancy in one of my father's accounts.

Small amounts siphoned off to an account that I don't have access to. In excess of a hundred thousand dollars, and yesterday I learned that money was filtered to Sofia."

I don't ask him how he knows all of this if he doesn't have access to the account. I do not doubt that Damien Stark has access to pretty much any information that he's willing to pay for. "Why would your father send Sofia that much money?"

"Payment for her testimony," he says. "He wanted her to testify about the abuse—same reason you wanted me to testify. But he didn't know about the photos. She must have found them in Richter's things. She took those, sent them to the court, waited around just long enough to make sure it worked, and then used the money to skip out of Europe."

"How do you know all of this?"

"After I learned about the skimmed money, I had another talk with dear old Dad. He told me."

"And you believe him?"

"I do."

I nod slowly, trying to process all of this. "Does he know where she is now?"

"He says no, and before you ask, I believe him about that, too. Sofia was never fond of my father. I can see her taking his money. I can't see her staying in touch."

"All right," I say slowly. "I understand that you're still worried about her, but this means that you can stop worrying that the pictures will turn up in the tabloids. Sofia won't release them, right?"

"No," he says with more intensity than I would expect. "I'm certain that she won't ever let anyone get their hands on those images."

"So this is good news," I say. "You'll find her eventually—doesn't she always show up?"

"She does, and I may have a lead on her already. I tracked

down David and his band. They just arrived in Chicago from Shanghai. I spoke to David on the phone. He tells me he hasn't seen Sofia, but I don't believe him. I think a face-to-face conference might help jog his memory."

"When are you leaving?"

"Tomorrow morning," he says.

He has stopped pacing, and I go to him, then take his hands in mine. "How long will you be gone?"

"If I'm lucky? I'll be back by dinner."

"And if you're not lucky?"

"Let's hope I am."

21

Since Jamie wants to grab some things from our condo, she rides in with Edward and me. The plan is to drop me by my office, then swing Jamie by the condo. Then Edward will take her back to Malibu before returning to Sherman Oaks to wait for me. While he's gone, I promise to stay inside my office, safe behind the protection of the building's efficient receptionist.

Cumbersome, yes, but since we still don't know who has been sending the stalker-like messages, Damien insisted I keep the security guys, and I agreed. Still, I'm so ready for this to be over that I think if Damien suggested we go live in Antarctica for a year, I would jump all over that plan.

We pop into Starbucks on the way, mostly to get coffee, but also because I want to introduce Jamie to Monica. She's not there, however, and so we take our lattes and head to my office. I give Jamie the grand tour, which takes about twelve seconds, and then soak up her effusive hugs and cries of "I'm so proud of you!"

"If Damien's not back from Chicago by tonight, do you want to rent a movie?" I ask as she's about to head out.

"Sure," she says. "And if he is back?"

I grin wickedly. "In that case, I have other plans."

I settle behind my desk as Jamie rolls her eyes and leaves. It takes me about ten minutes to go through my emails and handle a bunch of administrative crap. I finish tweaking the code on one of my entertainment apps, then push the update through. Then I pull out the web-based app that I've been working on. A cross-platform, multi-user note-taking system that Damien has already told me he'll license for Stark International once I'm out of beta testing.

First, I have to finish coding the damn thing and actually get it *into* beta testing.

I'm so lost in concentration that I jump when the intercom beeps. "Yes?" I snap.

"There's a Monica Karts here to see you."

"Oh." I'm actually a bit irritated by the interruption. I've never seen Monica outside of the coffee shop, and it seems a little odd that she's come unannounced. At the same time, I don't know that many people here yet, and I do like her. And since Damien is out of town, I can always work late and make up for lost time. "Tell her to come on back."

"I love it!" she says as she bursts through the door. "Your own office. That's so cool."

"What's going on? Is everything okay?"

"Oh, man. I don't mean to just barge in like you've got nothing better to do. Honest. But I got these head shots and I didn't see you at Starbucks this morning, and I really wanted to show you today. Is that okay?"

I can't help my smile. Her enthusiasm is effusive. "Of course."

She plunks herself in the chair opposite my desk, then passes me the envelope. "Go ahead. Take a peek."

I frown, because her voice sounds different. What I'd thought was a Northeastern prep school lilt now has much more of a British quality to it.

My thoughts about her voice, however, disappear entirely when I pull out the first photo. It is not a head shot, and as I hold it between two fingers, my body turns to ice and I have to stifle the urge to throw up.

"Gorgeous, isn't he? But I suppose you know that. Go on, then. Pull them all out."

My hands are shaking, and I realize I'm still holding the envelope and the photo. I flinch, then drop them as quickly as if they had burned me.

The picture falls image-side up, and though I try not to look, there is no erasing from my mind what I have already seen. *Damien*. Maybe eleven or twelve. And a girl, her face hidden, who I am guessing is younger. There is more, but I don't want to think of it. It is bad enough to have the image of these children in my head, their bodies joined in some perversion of an adult act. I do not want to think of the other things I saw in the bed with them. Toys and leather and gadgets that no child needs to know exists, much less have experience using.

And I don't want to think about the mirror that hung in place of a headboard, reflecting back the image of the man behind the camera—an adult man, naked and with a hard-on, one hand on his penis and the other holding the camera. *Richter*.

"I said pull them all out." Her voice is cold and seems to come from a very long way away. Somehow, I realize I am in shock. But I don't know what to do about that.

When I don't move, she reaches for the envelope and dumps at least twelve photos out onto my desk. "There's a tape, too. But we won't worry about that now."

I try not to look, but I can't help but see that these photos are more of the same, though each one seems more depraved than the one before.

She leans across the desk and taps the pile of images. "He's mine," she says. "He has always been mine."

"Yours," I repeat stupidly as I fight my way out of the fog. "You're Sofia."

She leans back in her chair and nods approval. "Very good."

"And this is you in these photos?"

She nods.

Everything seems to be happening in slow motion. I am hyperaware of the air, of my breathing. Of every tiny movement and every small sound. It is all deafening and foreign and I want out of this nightmare.

Damien said he never wanted me to see these, and though my heart breaks for the boy he was and the childhood that was stolen, I cannot help but agree. I do not want these images in my office, much less in my head. "Why are you showing me these?" I demand.

"Because you need to understand that he's mine. You don't exist to him at all. Not really. He sacrificed for *me*. He killed for *me*."

I stare at her, confused. "Killed for you?"

She blinks her huge brown eyes. "My father," she says evenly. "Damien killed him to protect me. Ask him if you don't believe me. That's not something you walk away from, Nikki. You're smart. You should know that."

"How did you get the first note to me? The one before the trial with the Los Angeles postmark?"

Her smile starts slow, but grows wide. "See? I knew you were smart. I have friends all over the world. I sent something. Asked them to drop it in a mailbox. Easy."

"That spiel you made about Jamie and The Rooftop bar. Was it true?"

"Other than that I'm one hell of an actress? No. You learn to be patient in the kind of places I've lived. I wait and I watch and I plan." And then, in what seems like a total shift, she blurts out, "He told me about you, you know."

I just sit, watching her, trying to think. Trying to figure out how to get out of here before the fuse that has been burning down on this girl reaches the end, and we both get hurt in the explosion.

"Oh, yes he did," she says without missing a beat. "He came to see me not long ago. All the way to London. He told me he met someone who got through the pain. Who cut and who battled it back. He didn't tell me he was fucking her or that it was you, but it wasn't hard to figure out."

My mind is moving too slowly. *There must be a way out of this,* I think, but it's as if the answer is hidden by some dark, impenetrable mist.

She picks at a hangnail, her mouth turned down into a frown. "I'd already seen you in the tabloids by then, of course, and I was so pissed at him. Another girl in his bed, I'd thought. Another girl, but the one he really wanted was me. Then he told me about the cutting, and that's when I realized the truth. This time he had a reason for fucking some woman." She looks straight at me, her eyes bright. "He was holding you up as an example for me. He thinks I'm all scarred because of what my daddy did, but he's wrong. I know how to turn it around." She shrugs. "But that's all you are to him, you know. Just a stone on the path of my journey. An object lesson for me to follow so that I can get my shit together and be with him. He loves me. He has always loved me. And I was there first. So now you need to move out of the way."

Move? Her words throw me, and I realize with a start that she isn't here to hurt me. No, she's playing a much different game.

"You want me to break up with Damien." I say the words levelly, but inside I'm cheering. I can work with that. I can pretend to agree. I can get out of here. Away from her and to Stark Tower. He'll be back from Chicago soon, and he'll know what to do. How to handle her.

"No," she says. "*You* want to break up with Damien. Because you know that if you don't, what I'll release to the press will destroy him. And isn't that what love is all about, Nikki? Isn't it about protecting the ones you love? Just like the way Damien protected me from my father."

The cold that had begun to recede presses against me again. "You wouldn't release those photos."

She shrugs. "Why not? It's not like anyone can tell it's me. Only Damien is identifiable."

"Why not?" I repeat. "Because you're sitting here telling me you love him. But that would absolutely destroy him."

She shakes her head. "*You're* destroying him. *You're* keeping him from me. If you don't let go, I don't have a choice. How can you not see that?"

She takes a deep breath, then says brightly, "Well, I guess that about wraps things up here." She stands, then nods at the desk and the photos scattered across it. "You can keep those. Like a souvenir. And, oh, I forgot about this." She reaches into her bag and pulls out a small leather case. "I get that this situation is hard on you, I really do. So I thought this might help." She puts the case on the corner of my desk, then hikes the purse back up on her shoulder. "And don't even think about calling your security guy. Those friends I mentioned? I told them to release the photos to the press if I didn't show up or if I got arrested or any silly shit like that." Once again, she flashes that smile. "Nothing personal. I just like to be thorough."

And then she's sweeping out the door, leaving me frozen behind my office desk, staring down at an array of photographs that have the power to destroy the man that I love.

I am frozen, I think. That's why I can't move. Why I am so cold, so goddamn cold.

But I don't want to move. I want to sit here forever. I don't want to see the world outside my office door. It is destroyed. A wasteland. Harsh and desolate.

How could it be anything else now that the bubble has finally shattered and the nightmares have swooped in?

I do not want to see, and yet I cannot help but glance down at the photo on top of the pile. *Damien.* His beautiful face distorted by a grimace that could either be pain or pleasure. The girl, legs wide, head back, back arched in a mockery of passion. She is unidentifiable, but I do not doubt that she is Sofia.

He's mine. He killed for me. He's mine.

With a violence that surprises me, I lurch to my feet, at the same time sweeping my arm out wide, sending the photos, the papers, the pens on the desk flying across the room. All that remains is the small case in the corner, the leather gleaming in the rays of afternoon light seeping in from the window. Reflections from passing cars make the light shimmer so that it blinks out a pattern on the innocuous case. I stare, mesmerized, as if those flashes of light are a message. As if they are calling me, urging me close, trying to lock me inside this new hell into which I have tumbled.

I hear a strange noise as I snatch the case, then realize it is my own whimper. Part of me doesn't want to know, but the other part is too curious to be contained. I unzip it—then stare in horror at the gleaming set of antique scalpels.

A wave of thankfulness so potent that it almost knocks me over sweeps over me. *Yes,* I think. *Thank God, yes.*

But then sanity returns and I back away as if in horror. Only when I reach the wall, do I realize that the case is still in my hand.

Do it.

I tighten my grip and stare down at the blades.

I need to do this. I need it.

Slowly, as if sleepwalking, I return to my chair. I sit. I spread my legs. I yank up my skirt.

And then I press the tip of one shining, beautiful blade to my thigh. Immediately, I draw in a sharp thread of air as a bead of blood oozes from beneath the point of the blade. I shiver, mesmerized. I had not yet meant to cut, but the blade is so sharp, so perfect, that just that simple contact was enough to draw blood. And what now? A quick flick of my wrist? A slow, deliberate cut? Both are so sweetly tempting. Both would ease the maelstrom of ice and fear burning inside me.

Do it.

Do it, do it, do it.

I press down harder, feel the sting of cold steel against warm flesh. I moan from the ecstasy—and then I hurl the scalpel across the room, my cry of "No" echoing in the small space. The scalpel slams against the far wall, then drops to the floor with an unsatisfying metallic *ping*. I snatch up the case and hurl it, too, then leap to my feet and kick the chair, rip out a drawer, and slam my fist into the wall. I want to destroy this place, me, everything. I want to get lost in chaos.

I want the pain.

I want a way out.

I want Damien. Oh, dear God, *I want Damien.*

And then I collapse onto the floor, curl up in a ball, and cry.

Because Edward is not back from Malibu when I emerge from my office, I call a taxi, then step out into the bright sunshine, surprised to find that the earth is still rotating and that people are still going about their daily lives. Don't they understand that the wheels have stopped turning?

I feel as though I am sleepwalking, and when I arrive at Stark Tower, I come in through the street level doors and move in a haze through the ornate lobby toward the security desk. I drift past the guards, and hear Joe call after me, "Ms. Fairchild, are you okay? You look a little under the weather."

I am very under the weather, but I don't bother stopping to tell that to Joe.

I have my own card key now, and I use it to call Damien's private elevator. I ride up with no plan other than crawling into Damien's bed and going to sleep until he returns from Chicago. I want to feel close to him for just a little longer. To breathe in the scent of him.

I want to make a memory of him, because I am about to sacrifice him in order to save him.

I have spent the last few hours thinking this through, and I see no other way. I can't tell him about Sofia's threat. If I do, he might let her go through with it. Might actually let her release those photos thinking somehow that he is protecting me. But I was in Germany with him, and I watched him break. And now that I've seen the photos myself, I am even more certain that those pictures plastered across the tabloids would destroy him. And every time he looked at me, he would see the reason for that intrusion into his life. Even if he could dig himself out of the inevitable hole, it would become a wedge between us. And I would rather walk away now than see our relationship shatter under the weight of something as vile as those photos.

I could go to the police, but how would that help? Then there would be more people aware of the photos and more risk that they are made public.

Even if I could tell him, so what? Could he convince Sofia not to release the photos? Maybe. But then he would live with that threat hanging over him for the rest of his life, and I do not want that for him or for us.

And would he even try to convince her? Or would he simply

take control, doing whatever he had to in order to eliminate a
threat? If what Sofia says is true, he killed Richter to protect her.
Would he eliminate Sofia in order to protect himself? Me? Our
relationship?

I honestly don't know. And, frankly, that scares me, too.

So I will do what I must. I will end it. And then, somehow, I
will try to survive.

The elevator glides to a stop and I quickly wipe away the tears
that have spilled, just in case one of the staff is in the apartment.
The doors open and I enter. I drop my purse on the bench that
surrounds the floral arrangement, then move on through to the
living room.

I stop short the moment I enter the room. Damien is sitting on
the floor carefully lifting a frame from a reinforced shipping box.
"Well, hello," he says with a wide, welcoming grin. "Apparently
I'm getting two presents today."

I suck in air, recognizing the image from just the tiniest corner
that is peeking out. It is the black-and-white photograph of the
mountains at sunset, and I watch, frozen, as he pulls it out, gazes
approvingly at it, and then reads the inscription on the back,
neatly printed above the artist's signature: *To Damien, the sun
will never set on our love. Yours always, Nikki.*

I have to fight not to burst into tears.

"It's beautiful," he says to me. He rests it against the back of
the couch and comes to me, his forehead creased. "Is something
wrong?"

"How was Chicago?" I ask, postponing the inevitable.

"Productive." He takes my hand and leads me around to the
couch. "I was able to convince David to talk to me—he agrees
that Sofia doesn't need to be out on her own. She has too many
issues, and without her meds . . ." He trails off. I don't bother
telling him that I know. And that I agree one hundred percent.

"David let her crash at his apartment here in LA. She's not there now—I checked—but I know what name she's using, so it's just a matter of time."

"What's the name?" I ask.

"Monica Karts. The last name is an anagram," he says.

"I know. It took me a moment, but I figured that out."

"A moment? I just told you."

"No," I say. "She told me. I've known her for a while now. Just casually. Someone to chat with at the Starbucks near my office."

He bursts to his feet, but I take his hand and tug him back down. "Wait. I need to say something, and I need to do it fast. It's why I came by, so please—please just let me get this out, okay?"

I can see the concern in his eyes, and it breaks my heart. But I tell myself there's no other choice. I've been over all my options, and I simply don't see a way clear that doesn't lead straight to Damien being destroyed.

For so long, he's been the one protecting me. This time, I'm doing whatever I can to protect him.

I draw in a breath, both for courage and to try to quell the way my body is trembling. My stomach twists violently, and I'm certain I am going to be sick. I shove it all down. I have to do this. *I have to.* I imagine that scalpel tight between my fingers and then, in what I have to acknowledge as bitter irony, I cling even tighter to Damien's hand, fighting that craving for a blade. For the pain.

"I can't do this anymore," I finally manage to say. "I can't live with the secrets and the half-truths and the obfuscation."

I see shock in his eyes, then pain, and my heart twists.

Very slowly, very carefully, he says, "What are you talking about?"

"Sofia. She was in those photos and you didn't tell me. Richter abused both of you together and you didn't tell me. And you did kill Richter, Damien. You killed him to protect her." I do not look at him. I cannot let him see that I do not blame him.

"Everything I told you about that night was true," he says. I can hear the tight grip he has on control. Any tighter and it will shatter. "All I did was leave out the reason for the fight."

"Sofia."

"He was going to start whoring her out." The words are as rough as sandpaper. "The son of a bitch was going to whore out his own daughter."

"I see." I speak calmly even though my blood runs cold. "But that doesn't—that doesn't change anything." I am wishing for some sort of solution to fly down from the sky. For a magical bubble to swoop in and carry us off. But there is no bubble. There is only cold, hard reality. "I meant what I said. I can't—I can't do this anymore."

I feel the lie pressing against me. I grab it and wrap it tight around me like a cloak. Because I need this lie. This lie has the power to save Damien even as it is ripping me apart. "I can't live knowing that there are more and more secrets underneath," I continue with my rehearsed words. "I can't go on pretending the shadows don't bother me."

"Nikki." His voice is tight and controlled, but I think I hear a hint of panic underneath, and my heart twists. All I want to do is hold him. All I want is to feel his arms around me.

I stand, afraid that if I don't get out of there fast, I will back down. And I can't risk destroying Damien. Not when I'm the one who can save him. "I need to go. I—I'm sorry."

I turn and hurry toward the elevator, but he doesn't let me get away. He grabs my elbow to stop me, and I jerk it back. "Dammit, Damien, let me go."

"We are going to talk about this." The veneer of shock that had been all over him only moments before has changed to something brash and volatile. I see the anger building in his eyes, about to explode out past the pain, the hurt, the confusion.

"There's nothing to talk about. Everything is a secret with you. Everything is a challenge. Everything is a game. This stuff about Sofia. That crap you pulled with Lisa." It is both easy and hard to say these words. Easy, because they are true. Hard, because though his secrets and shadows drive me nuts, I have accepted them as part of the man that I love. And now I am turning that around, bastardizing it in order to create an escape route.

But I have to. I just need to remember that I have to.

"Goddammit, Nikki, do not come in here and dump this on me and expect me to shrug it off and be done with you. I love you. I am not letting you walk out of this room." His wounded eyes are scanning my face, and I know I have to get out. Have to run before he sees the truth under this mountain of lies.

"I love you, too," I say, because it is the only truly honest thing I've said since I walked in this room. "But sometimes love isn't enough."

I see the shock on his face, and I turn and hurry again toward the elevator. This time, he doesn't follow, and I don't know if I'm relieved or brokenhearted.

I step on, keeping my chin high and my eyes wide and dry. Then, as the elevator doors snick shut, I see Damien fall to his knees, his face a mask of pain and horror and loss.

I slide down the polished wall and, finally, lose myself to the violent shaking of my sobs.

22

I keep Sofia's scalpels, and every time Damien calls I squeeze my hand tight around the cylindrical handle of the largest one as I force myself not to answer the call. As I tell myself I cannot call him back no matter how much I crave his voice, his touch. And then, in the silence when the ringing stops, I stare at the gleaming blade and wonder why I don't do it. Why I don't just use this blade and set free all of this shit that's boiling inside me, vile and violent.

I fight it back, though. I force myself not to cut.

But I no longer know what I'm fighting for, and I'm desperately afraid that my strength will give out, and one day I will press that blade against my skin, that I will feel the tug of yielding flesh, and that I will finally succumb. I am afraid that I will have to, because there is no other way to live without Damien.

I have not gone to my office for over two weeks now. At first, Damien called me five times each day. Then he dropped to four daily calls for a few days, then three. Now the calls have stopped altogether and the lure of the blade is even more potent.

I know that Jamie and Ollie are worried about me. That

doesn't take a great intellectual leap to figure out because they have both flat-out said as much.

"You need to get out," Jamie says one afternoon as I am on my bed, staring blankly at all the newspaper clippings and bits of memorabilia I was going to use for Damien's scrapbook. "Just to the corner. Just for a drink."

I shake my head.

"Dammit, Nicholas, I'm worried about you."

I lift my head to look at her, and when I do, I see my reflection. My face is gray and there are circles under my eyes. My unwashed hair hangs limp around my face. I do not recognize myself. "I'm worried about me, too," I say.

"Jesus, Nik." I hear fear in her voice, and she comes to sit on the bed beside me. "You're really scaring me. I don't know what to do here. Tell me what you need."

But I can't. Because what I need I can't have.

What I need is Damien.

"You did the right thing," she says gently. I have told her and Ollie the truth about what I did and why I broke it off. I couldn't keep the secret any longer. I have not told Evelyn that we broke up, but she heard the news anyway. I have not taken her calls; I'm too afraid of what she will say.

"But, Nik," Jamie continues, "now it's time to let yourself heal."

"I just need time," I manage to say. "Time heals, right?"

"I don't know," she whispers. "I thought so, but now I just don't know."

I don't know how many days have passed when Ollie shows up in my bedroom, his expression grim. "Come on," he says, taking my arm and tugging me to my feet.

"What the—"

"We're taking a walk."

"No." I jerk my arm back.

"Goddammit, yes." He grabs a baseball cap from the shelf in my closet, crams it onto my head, then tugs me toward the door. "Corner store. Ice cream. And I'll fucking carry you there if I have to."

I'm standing now, and I nod. I don't want to go out into the world, but I also don't want to fight. And maybe it will help, though I don't really believe it.

"You fucked up, Nikki," he says once we're on the sidewalk.

I don't look at him. I don't want to hear this. I know I did the right thing; that knowledge is as true to me as the sun that now beats down upon us. That truth is the only thing that's helped me survive.

"I've seen him, you know."

That gets my attention.

"I went with Maynard to the apartment yesterday. He's missed too many appointments, and there was stuff that had to be handled. Signed. Life and business moving on. But, Nikki, Damien's not moving on. He's wrecked. Shit, I think he's worse than you."

I keep my head down and keep walking, but every step hurts me. Every second that I am hurting Damien hurts me. "I don't want to hear this," I whisper.

"Just talk to him. Go see him. Jesus, Nikki, fight for it."

That makes me stop. Makes me turn to him. Makes the anger rise enough that it pushes back the pain. "Goddammit, Ollie, don't you get it? I am fighting. I'm fighting every day not to run back to him. I'm fighting because I love him. And because I do, I can't see him ripped to shreds. You saw how he was in Germany, and that was just a few people who saw those pictures. If those photos get out in the world, it will completely destroy him."

"But, Nik," he says gloomily. "He already is."

* * *

The next morning, I pick up the phone. Ollie's words have weighed on me. The dark cloud has pressed against me for too long. The lure of the blade is too sweet.

I can stand it no longer.

"Stark International." It is Sylvia's voice, clear and strong.

"I—oh—I must have hit the wrong button. I thought I dialed Damien's cell."

"Ms. Fairchild." Her voice has lost the businesslike quality. It's gentle now, maybe even a little sad. "He forwarded his cellular calls to the office."

"Oh. Where is he? I'll call the house or the apartment or wherever directly." Now that I have gathered the courage to call, I am determined to do this. I do not know exactly what I intend to say—I haven't thought this out that far—but I know that I need to talk to him. That I need to hear his voice.

"I'm sorry, Ms. Fairchild, I don't know where he is. He left yesterday. No number, no address. He said he was leaving the country. He said he needed time."

I close my eyes and sag down onto the bed. "I see. If he—if he calls, will you ask him to call me?"

"I will," she says. "It will be the first thing I tell him."

In the weeks that follow, I become a gossip hound. I troll websites and Twitter and Facebook and everything else I can think of searching for information about Damien. I find nothing. Nothing except the press speculating about the cause of our breakup.

I've seen nothing about Sofia, either, and so I do not know if Damien located her and got her back to London or if she is still in LA. Because I know Damien, I know they are not together. But I can't help but worry about how Sofia is going to blow when her frustration level from not winning Damien back reaches critical mass.

When yet another Saturday night rolls around, Jamie is determined to drag me out of my funk. "Popcorn and *Arsenic and Old Lace,*" she says, pointing authoritatively to the couch. "I'll make the popcorn while you set up the movie."

I do not argue. I turn on the television, then dig through the basket of DVDs while the local news plays. I'm about to slip the disk in when I freeze.

Damien's face is all over the screen, along with blurred copies of horrific photos that are all too familiar. I realize my hand is over my mouth, and I fear for a moment that I am going to be sick. I stand up, pace, then sit back down again. I need to do something—anything—but I don't know what to do.

"Oh, God." The words are from Jamie, who has come into the living room behind me.

I turn and meet her eyes. "I can't believe she did it. I can't believe that bitch sent those pictures to the press anyway."

"Damien must be a mess."

I nod, then pull out my phone.

"I thought he wasn't there," Jamie says.

I ignore her, keeping my fingers crossed, praying he is no longer forwarding the number.

But it is Ms. Peters, Damien's weekend assistant, who answers the call.

"I'm so sorry, Ms. Fairchild. We haven't heard from him for weeks."

"But the news—he—is he in town?"

I hear the softness in her voice as she says, "I don't know. I wish that I did."

"What else can you do?" Jamie asks, as soon as I've ended the call.

"I don't know, I don't know." I'm pacing the living room, my fingers running through my hair, as I try to think where he could be. I have to find him. I can imagine how wrecked he is, and I can't bear the thought of him suffering through all that alone.

And then, suddenly, I remember. I clutch my phone and turn back to Jamie. "It's okay," I say. "I know how to find him."

The trouble with the phone-tracking app is that it doesn't narrow the area to anything remotely useful. Which is why I'm wandering blind near the Santa Monica Pier. I am thankful—so thankful—that he is back in LA. But I'm beyond frustrated that I cannot find him.

I think that he might be at the Ferris wheel, since he once took me up in it, but when I arrive, there is no Damien. I wander all the way to the end of the pier, check in all the little shops, circle around all the rides.

I cannot find him.

Frustrated, I take off my flip-flops and start schlepping down the beach, but after fifteen minutes of that, I'm no closer to locating him. I cut perpendicular across the beach from the shore to the parking lot and start heading south again, this time through the lot. There aren't many people out, and the lot is thinning, so I have a pretty good view, and I scan the distance looking for Damien's gait, his build, his raven-black hair.

I don't see him.

But I do see his Jeep.

At least, I think I do, and as I say a silent prayer, I take off running across the lot to the black Jeep Grand Cherokee that is parked in a secluded corner. I press my face up to the window so that I can see the interior, and my heart does a twist. It's Damien's, all right; there's his phone sitting right on the console.

Now I just have to sit here and wait.

It is a full hour before he returns. I see him walking up from the beach, looking desperately sexy in faded jeans and a plain white T-shirt. I know the moment he sees me. His perfect gait stumbles, and then he pauses. I cannot see his eyes in the dark and from this distance, but I know that he is looking at me. And then he continues forward again, that same long stride, only this time it's just a little bit faster, as if now he has somewhere that he wants to be.

He passes beneath a circle of light thrown by one of the parking lot towers. I see the weariness on his face along with something else. Something harder.

I stand up straighter. I want to run to him, but I hold back, wanting more to watch him. I have missed seeing him move. Hell, I've missed everything.

And then he is here, right in front of me, his face all hard lines and angles, his black eye dark and accusing, and his amber one flat. I gasp, suddenly afraid. My heart pounds, then I cry out as he roughly grabs my arms, and yanks me to him. His mouth slams against mine, his hands closing painfully around my upper arms. The kiss is violent, harsh. A demand and an accusation all rolled into one. He bruises my lips, our teeth clash, I taste blood. And then he pushes me away so swiftly my back slams against the Jeep. "You left," he says. "Goddammit, Nikki, you left."

Tears stream down my face, and I open my mouth to apologize—to tell him I had to, that I didn't have a choice—but then he's pulling me to him again, only this time his embrace is soft and his mouth is full of need, consuming me, tasting me, as if he can't quite believe that I'm real. "Nikki," he says when he breaks the kiss. "Nikki, oh, God, Nikki."

I cling to him, my hands in his hair, then press my mouth to his again. I cannot get enough of him. His hands slide over my body, his mouth opens to me. My tongue wars with his. I will never have my fill of him, and all I want is this moment, this reunion. I want to drop down to the asphalt and strip him bare right there, and in that singular moment I do not know how I have survived without him.

Then it hits me—I haven't survived. I have been sleepwalking, not living. Because how can I really be alive without Damien?

"I'm sorry," I say when we finally break the kiss. "I'm so sorry she did that. I can't believe she'd do that. She said if I broke up with you—" I cut myself off. I hadn't intended to tell him that.

"I know," he says flatly. "Ollie told me. He told me what you did, and he told me why you did it."

I'm not sure whether I want to slap Ollie or kiss him, but the conundrum soon evaporates under Damien's touch. He strokes a hand along my cheek, his familiar touch firing nerve-endings throughout my body. "You're a goddamn fool, Nikki Fairchild. And I love you desperately."

I swallow tears and cling to him even tighter, savoring our connection and the way he makes me feel.

His hands roam my back, over my ratty Bermuda shorts, up along the backs of my thighs. I moan, craving a more intimate connection.

"I think maybe we should get in the car." He unlocks it and we climb in. The backseats are down and the area has been filled by a mattress. I glance at Damien, amused. "Roughing it?"

"I haven't wanted luxury. I've been living in motels, the backs of cars. I've been all over Europe and I don't think I've really seen one inch of it."

I swallow. Ollie was right. Damien has been just as broken as I have.

"Tonight, I was going to drive to the desert. I thought I'd sleep under the stars. I thought it might help." He points to the roof. I don't know if it's a standard feature or the billionaire add-on, but there is a huge sunroof over the back of the Jeep.

"It wouldn't have," I say. I know, because nothing would have helped me. Nothing except Damien.

"No," he says. "It wouldn't." His eyes roam over me, and he reaches out tentatively to touch me. "Dear God, Nikki. Are you real?"

I can only nod, because if I speak I will surely start crying again.

"Thank God you found me." He pulls me down beside him. I feel like I'm in high school again, and I have to admit I kind of like it.

"I've been looking for you for hours," I finally say. "Ever since I saw the news. Are you okay?" I stroke his face, expecting the same clammy skin from Germany. But the Damien in front of me looks as gorgeous and healthy as always, not to mention exquisitely happy.

"I am now," he says.

"I don't understand why she released the photos."

"She didn't," Damien says. "I did."

I sit up and gape at him. "You? But—but why?"

"Because I didn't have any other choice." He eases me back down, then slides closer. He twines our legs together and his arm goes around my waist. I snuggle in close, and press my cheek against his chest, wanting to be as close to him as possible. "I was dying without you, and once Ollie told me the choice you made, I knew that I had to make one, too."

"But the photos—that's the thing you've been fighting against all along. That abuse is the reason you wouldn't testify. You were willing to go to jail rather than let it go public."

"I was," he says. "But I'm an arrogant son of a bitch, and I don't think I ever really believed that the court would convict me. I don't think I believed that I could lose you." He strokes his thumb along my chin. "But I lost you anyway, Nikki, and I had to make a decision. And the truth is that I'm doing fine. I wouldn't call it an ideal situation having my private life be the topic of editorials and talk shows, but I'm surviving. And it was my choice. Not a decision forced on me because my lawyers said I needed to put up a defense, but a real, honest decision where I weighed what I have and what I fear against what I want."

I shake my head, not following.

"What I mean is that there is only one thing that could rip me apart more than those photos—that *did* rip me apart—and that's losing you. So I balanced the weight of my past against the promise of my future." He brushes a kiss over my lips. "The future won."

My smile is watery. "I'm sorry for what I said to you. About secrets and shadows. I needed you to believe I was really breaking up with you."

"You were right," he says.

"No, not entirely. But we don't have to argue about it. I know damn well your secrets aren't going to start spilling out just because I won that argument."

His smile is soft. "You probably have a point." His eyes soak up my face, and a small smile plays at his mouth.

"What?" I finally say.

"I'm just happy you found me." He frowns. "How did you find me?"

I allow myself the smallest of smug smiles. "Sweetheart, I will always find you."

"I'm very happy to hear that," he says. His fingers trail down my arm, bare in my paint-splattered tank top. I'd been too eager to find Damien to bother changing out of my crappy clothes, though I did manage to take a shower yesterday, so I'm not totally disgusting. The trajectory of his hand shifts, and he cups my breast, his thumb flicking lightly over my nipple, and each tiny tug sends a hot wire of electricity jolting through my belly and down to my sex.

As if he's curious about the effect his touch has on me, Damien trails his hand down, leaving my breast to ease lightly over my tank toward the drawstring waist of my shorts. "I want to know everything you did these weeks we were apart. I don't want to feel like we've missed a moment of our life together. But, Nikki, I don't give a damn about that now. All I want is you naked and wet and open for me."

I meet his eyes, wait a beat, and then peel off my tank top. It has a built-in shelf bra, so I'm now naked from the waist up. "You can take care of the rest of that yourself," I say, putting my hand on his and sliding our joined fingers into the shorts. I'm not wearing underwear, and I buck with pleasure when his fingers stroke my clit, then slide inside me.

"I think you want me, Ms. Fairchild."

"Desperately," I say, then fumble to shove down my shorts.

I lay back, naked, as he leans over me. "Leave your T-shirt on," I say as my fingers work the fly of his jeans. "You look like a sexy rebel."

He laughs. "I am. I thought you knew."

He kicks his jeans off, then brushes a soft kiss over my lips, then nips at my lower lip, catching it in his teeth and tugging lightly before easing his mouth down my neck, over the swell of my breast, to finally suck on my nipple. He draws it in, teases it with his tongue, and slides his hand between my legs to tease my clit in time with the pull of his mouth.

"I've missed your taste," he murmurs. "I've missed feeling you slip beneath my fingers. The way your skin quivers when you're excited. I want to watch you aroused, I want to watch you come. I want to tie you up and spank your ass and make sure you know that you are mine, and that you damn well better not leave me again. But right now, baby, all I want is to be inside you." He straddles me and I feel the head of his cock press against my sex and see the answering rush of pleasure in his eyes. "I'm going to fuck you now, Nikki." His words are low and steady with the quality of a growl. "Hard and deep and very thoroughly."

"Yes," I say. "Oh, please, yes." I spread my legs and I am so wet, so desperately in need of him, that he sinks deep inside me with one long thrust. I am on my back, and I cup my hands on his rear, feeling Damien's tight ass and strong muscles pound into me, harder and harder until all I am is a mass of sensation.

Until all I want to do is spin off into space and take Damien along with me.

My orgasm takes me by surprise, building so fast and so furiously that I cry out when it rips through me. I feel my body clench hungrily around his, and then the sweet tension and pressure of his own release before he collapses, spent, beside me.

"I love you," he whispers.

"I know," I reply. I glance around at the Jeep and can't help but smile. I prop myself up on my elbow and look down at his gorgeous face and sleepy, just-fucked eyes. "How many billions do you have, Mr. Stark? And we're making out in the back of a Jeep? How very gauche."

He flashes the kind of sexy smile designed to make me wet all over again. "Fuck my billions, Ms. Fairchild. All I care about is you."

23

"I want you to know I'm not sad," Jamie says as the moving guys lug my chest of drawers out of the bedroom and toward the front door. As of today, the last of my stuff will be in Malibu and I will have officially moved in with Damien. Despite the fact that I want this more than anything, there are little butterflies dancing in my stomach. But they're soft and the dance is sweet and I'm actually enjoying the sensation.

"I'm completely excited for both of us," she adds. "But you more than me."

Jamie has rented the condo out for the next six months. She decided that Texas made sense—but that she wasn't yet ready to give up on LA entirely. So she's driving back to stay with her parents and, as she says, "think about her shit." Hopefully she'll come back. If not, she'll sell the condo. But at least she doesn't have to decide right now.

I hold tight to Damien's hand. "I'm not going to say that I'll miss you," I say. "Because you'll be back. I'm certain of it."

"If nothing else, I'll be back to bum a week in Malibu."

"Anytime," Damien says.

She glances at her watch. "I gotta go pick up my car," she says. "I left it at the corner for an oil change and all that stuff. I don't really want to get stuck in El Paso."

"Call me tonight," I say as we hug. I blink, not wanting to cry, but afraid I won't be able to help it.

"Hell yeah, I will."

She gives Damien a hug, too, and as soon as she's gone, I turn to Damien, an odd mix of happiness and melancholy rumbling inside me. "We can go, too. I don't need to hang out in my empty room for nostalgia purposes."

"It's not empty," he says, then nods toward my bed.

"I'm leaving it," I remind him. I hardly need a bed at any of Damien's houses, and Jamie rented the place furnished, so I'm sure the tenant won't mind.

"Not the bed," he says. "The package on it."

I look more closely and see the flat white box sitting on the white duvet. I glance between him and the box. "What is it?"

"I'm going to suggest you take a walk on the wild side and open it."

"Funny," I say, but I hurry to the package. I open it and find a fold-up map of Europe with tiny colored stickers already affixed to Munich and London.

"We faced reality and told it to go fuck itself," Damien says. "So now I think we should slide back into that bubble. One month. Europe. A limo. Five-star hotels. And you."

"Doing whatever you want, whenever you want it?" I ask happily.

His smile is slow and decadent. "Ah, baby, you know me so well."

"I can't wait," I say.

"We can go back for round two later," he says. "Right now I can only take a month if I'm going to be back for the gala."

"Of course," I say. The first gala fund-raiser for the Stark

Children's Foundation is only five weeks away. It's Damien's newest charitable organization, the primary mission of which is to help the recovery of abused children through play and sports therapy.

"Just the continent?"

Damien nods. We will not be going to the UK. I'm not surprised. I don't care if I never see Sofia again, and he's not ready to see her, either. For that matter, her shrink probably wouldn't let him.

Sofia had OD'd on the roof of the Richter Tennis Center in West Hollywood about two weeks after Damien went public with the story of his abuse. Because of the timing of the overdose and the certainty that she would be found, the shrink considered it a cry for help, and the courts concurred, both in California and Britain. Now she's in a rehab facility, but this time under court order. I expect that someday Damien will want to see her. In the meantime, he's continuing to support her financially. I don't blame him for that; they have a history, however fucked-up.

"I'd like to spend a few days in Germany, too," Damien says, breezing over the specter of Britain that seems to hang in the room. "We didn't get to explore it before. And speaking of Germany," he adds, pulling a small box out of his pocket. "I bought this for you before the trial got underway. I planned to give it to you after I was acquitted, but I got a little sidetracked."

"Can I open it?"

"Of course," he says, with an odd twinkle in his eye.

I open the box only to find a smaller velvet box inside. My chest starts to feel a bit tight, and my skin feels all tingly. I tell myself not to jump to conclusions as I pull out the velvet box, open the hinged top, and gasp when I see the platinum-set diamond solitaire winking in the lights.

My knees go weak, and I'm glad of the door frame at my back. "Damien," I whisper, terrified of reading more into this than simply a beautiful ring. Another fabulous gift. "You bought this before the trial?"

"I told you," he says gently. "I never truly believed I could lose. Not the trial. Not you. Now I know better than to take anything for granted."

The words are still hanging in the air when he drops down on one knee. He takes my hand, and I get chills. I feel the pull of my facial muscles, but I fight it—I'm simply too scared to smile.

"There's only one woman in the world who can bring me to my knees. So tell me, Ms. Fairchild. Will you do me the greatest honor? Will you be my wife?"

My smile breaks free in a burst of glorious, delighted laughter. I beam at him, this man I love. And as I draw him to his feet and into my embrace, I say the only word I'm capable of speaking, the only word that matters: "Yes."